An Australian Locomotive Guide

Second Edition

Above: Fortescue Metals SD70 ACe, brand new at the Electro-Motive plant in Muncie, Indiana, in June 2012. (Overland Models, Brian Marsh)

Previous page: 3237 and 5917 have just crossed the Great Divide at Cullerin with a heritage train for Cootamundra on 6 October 2014 (Peter Clark)

Next page: Glencore Locomotive XRN 014 leads a loaded coal train through East Maitland on 21 December 2014. (Andrew Leung)

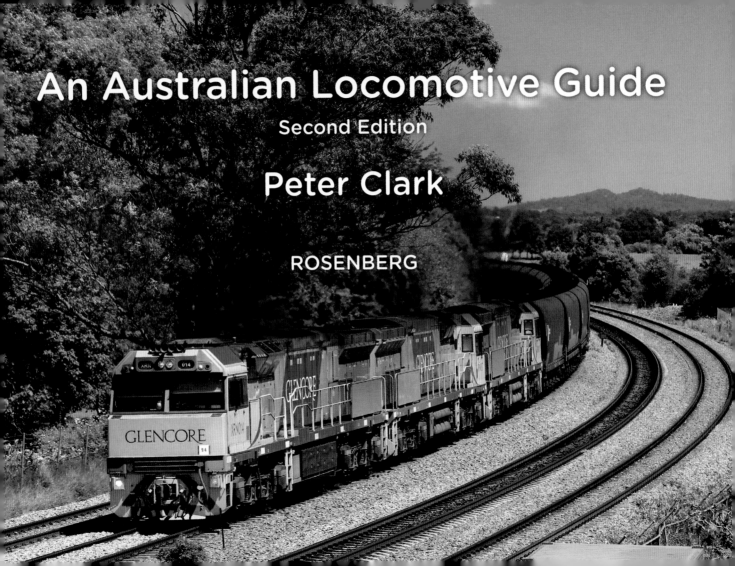

An Australian Locomotive Guide

Second Edition

Peter Clark

ROSENBERG

First published in Australia in 2012
by Rosenberg Publishing Pty Ltd
PO Box 6125, Dural Delivery Centre NSW 2158
Phone: 61 2 9654 1502 Fax: 61 2 9654 1338
Email: rosenbergpub@smartchat.net.au
Web: www.rosenbergpub.com.au
Reprinted 2013
Second Edition 2015
Copyright © Peter Clark 2012, 2015

National Library of Australia Cataloguing-in-Publication entry

Author: Clark, Peter J. (Peter James), 1948-
Title: An Australian locomotive guide / Second edition/Peter Clark.
ISBN: 9781925078640 (Hbk.), 9781925078756 (Epdf)
ISBN: 9781925078831 (Epub)
Notes: Includes index.
Subjects: Locomotives–Australia.
Dewey Number: 625.260994

Cover photographs

Front: Two Aurizon C44ACHi locomotives, 5026 and 5022 climb Whittingham bank with a loaded coal train on 21 December 2012. (Peter Clark)

Back: Genesee and Wyoming locomotive GWA 010 leads two similar units on an empty iron ore train upgrade from Yorkey's Crossing to Wirrida on 25 April 2014. (Peter Clark)

Printed in China by Everbest Printing Co Limited

Contents

Abbreviations

AEI	Associated Electrical Industries
AHRS	Australian Railway Historical Society
AN	Australian National (Railways)
ARG	Australian Railroad Group
CFCLA	Chicago Freight Car Leasing Australia
CR	Commonwealth Railways
CRRlA	Cliffs Robe River Iron Associates
DGG	Deutsche Getriebe GMBH
EBR	Emu Bay Railway
EDI	Evans Deakin Industries
EE	English Electric
EMD	Electro-Motive Division (of GM), later Electro-Motive Diesel
ETSA	Electricity Trust of South Australia
G&W	Genesee and Wyoming
G&WA	Genesee and Wyoming Australia
GE	International General Electric Corporation (USA)
GM	General Motors (Detroit Diesel Division)
HI	Hamersley Iron
IC&E	Iowa, Chicago and Eastern
JRW	Junee Railway Workshops
MN	Mount Newman Mining
MRWA	Midland Railway of Western Australia
MU	Multiple unit
NR	National Rail
NREC	National Railroad Equipment Corporation
NRM	National Railway Museum (Port Adelaide)
NSWGR	New South Wales Government Railways
NSWRTM	New South Wales Rail Transport Museum
PN	Pacific National
PRHS	Pilbara Railway Historical Society
QR	Queensland Government Railways
QUBE	QUBE Logistics, a P&O subsidiary
SAR	South Australian Government Railways
SCT	Specialised Container Transportation
SLM	Swiss Locomotive and Machine Works
TGR	The Tasmanian Transport Government Railways
VR	Victorian Government Railways
WAGR	Western Australian Government Railways

Introduction to the Second Edition

This book describes the diesel and electric locomotives used on the main line and export mineral railways in Australia, and the operating preserved steam locomotives used both on preserved lines and on main lines. This second edition covers many changes and developments since the original edition, including a number of new types from the USA and China as well as new users of existing types.

It covers all the diesel and electric locomotives used by the Australian main line railways whether still in service or not. In the period leading up to this second edition, a number of older types have been sold overseas or scrapped due to changes in ownership of both major and minor operators, although new types are still being purchased. There are two indexes, one listing the locomotives under their current operator, and another listing the locomotives under the name of the operator that introduced the particular class. This allows the examination of a group of locomotives from a particular state railway, for example.

The illustrations have been chosen to show the distinctive features of the locomotives concerned to assist in using the book to identify locomotives in the field, and the book format is intended to allow easy portability. A number of new photographs of existing types illustrate significant changes.

The diesel locomotives are listed according to the type of diesel engine used and are arranged in order of increasing size of engine to show the development of a particular type of locomotive. This layout was selected to show the similarity of types used on different systems, particularly in the era of the state government railways. The diesel locomotives are in alphabetical order of the maker of the prime mover, although for simplicity, exceptions were made for General Electric design industrial locomotives and for Walkers Limited diesel hydraulic locomotives where a standard locomotive design was available with a choice of prime movers. The electric locomotives are grouped by system in chronological order, since there was much less influence in design from the manufacturer than was the case with diesel locomotives, and the design was influenced more by the operator and the operating conditions.

Steam locomotives are organised by wheel arrangement, since this brings together similar locomotives from different systems, much as does the section on diesel locomotives. It also allows comparison of the technical characteristics of steam locomotives intended for similar duties on different systems. In the steam era, it was common to retain older locomotives for service on lighter rural lines, rather than building new locomotives for branch line service. However, modern lightweight locomotives were built in Queensland, Victoria and Western Australia particularly, and these types are well represented in the stock of preserved locomotives.

In Australia, diesel locomotives for main line railways generally fell into two categories – those intended for main line operation, and those intended for use on rural branch lines. In this book, the lighter locomotives are usually found at the beginning of a section, and the heavier locomotives towards the end.

There is a special case regarding diesel locomotives with Electro-Motive engines. The same basic engine was available with either a mechanical blower or a turbocharger which was able to use the blower drive train at lower power settings and run from an exhaust turbine at higher power settings. While this involved mechanical complication, it provided a much better fuel consumption at high power settings. The turbocharged engine was about 50% more powerful than the blower engine with the same number of cylinders. In this book, the Electro-Motive locomotives are grouped by the number of cylinders, with blower engines preceding the turbocharged engines within the group. This is appropriate, since a number of locomotives built with Electro-Motive blower engines were rebuilt with turbochargers later in their careers, and this layout allows the change in characteristics to be clearly seen.

CBH 122 and CBH 120 are seen at the Kwinana grain unloading loop on 17 November 2013. These are standard gauge locomotives, most easily seen by the larger grain wagons which are taller than the locomotives. (Peter Clark)

AN AUSTRALIAN LOCOMOTIVE GUIDE

Seven locomotives at Broadmeadow Locomotive Depot in 1982. The numbering system separated the similar 442 and 80 classes while the larger 81 class was not clearly separated from the lower powered 80 class. (Peter Clark)

Classification

A feature of Australian locomotives is the lack of a consistent classification and numbering system between operators, even those operating in the same area. Around 1900, a popular means of classifying locomotives in Australia was the use of an alphabetical letter with a sequential number starting from 1 for the first locomotive. This system was used in NSW, South Australia, Victoria and Western Australia. The Commonwealth Railways also used this system from the start of operation in 1917. In Tasmania, there was a variation in that each class started from 1. Queensland used the sequential numbers but had abandoned the simple alphabetic system of classification for a system that gave an indication of locomotive power.

New South Wales Government Railways

The NSWGR dated from 1855, with the state government taking over the Sydney Railway Company before it started operation. The title changed to the Public Transport Commission (including other urban transport) in 1972 and to the State Rail Authority in 1980. The operations were corporatised in the early 1990s as CountryLink (long-distance passenger), CityRail (suburban and inter city passenger) and Freight Rail, later FreightCorp for freight traffic. In the early 1990s, interstate freight services were passed to National Rail, a joint operation of the NSW, Victorian and Federal governments. The first two remain under the control of Rail Corp, but FreightCorp was sold, together with National Rail, to form Pacific National.

Locomotives in NSW were numbered from 1 and were identified by the number of the first locomotive of each type until 1889, when William Thow arrived from South Australia and introduced an alphabetic system, initially based on the number of locomotives in the class. Thus classes A and B were the most numerous goods locomotives and classes C and D were the most numerous passenger locomotives.

The steam locomotive numbering immediately preceding the diesel era was introduced by circular 355 in 1924. Locomotives of an older type were given the prefix 'Z' and classes from 11 to 29. Passenger locomotives were given a prefix based on the number of coupled axles. All locomotives of a standard type had three coupled axles and had the prefix 'C'. Classes 30, 32, 34, 35 and 36 were allocated. Similarly, freight locomotives all had four coupled axles and received the prefix 'D'. Classes 50, 53 and 55 were allocated.

There were 191 locomotives of the 32 class, numbered 3201 to 3391. There were 280 locomotives of the 50 class, numbered 5001 to 5280.

Later new classes 38, 57, 58 and 59 were issued. When Beyer Garratt locomotives were introduced, with two sets of four coupled axles, these had the letters AD, 'A' for articulated and 'D' indicating sets of four coupled axles. Class 60 was the only NSW Garratt type, and the number followed in the freight sequence. The prefix letters were rarely used in day-to-day operation.

NSW Diesel Locomotives

The first NSW diesel locomotives were ex US Army switchers and carried US Army numbers 7920 to 7923. These numbers continued to be used, becoming known as the 79 class, and as a result later diesel shunting locomotives also took numbers in the 70 series.

The first main line locomotives were numbered as 40 class above the passenger locomotives but below the freight locomotives. Classes 45 and 46 were reserved for electric locomotives. Main line diesel locomotives were given the classes 41, 42, 43 and 44. Branch line locomotives were given the classes 48 and 49. Later a 47 class was issued, this number having possibly initially been kept for additional electric locomotives. Diesel shunting locomotives were given classes 70, 72 and 73. Class 71 was given to a prototype diesel shunter later sold to Victoria.

Later the single Class 45 electric loco, which was mainly used for shunting by that time, was given the spare class 71. This allowed the Class 45 to be given to a new main line diesel class. About this time more than 100 48 class were delivered, and five-digit numbers were introduced as 4899 was followed by 48100 and so onward.

One hundred 44 class were also built, with 44100 being the highest Classification

A modified version of the 42 class, with EMD power equipment, was numbered 42101 to 42110. A more powerful locomotive type also with EMD equipment was numbered 42201 to 42220. A more powerful version of the 44 class with Alco and GE equipment was numbered 44201 to 44240.

The five-digit numbers were not popular, and often needed to be repeated for train control requirements, so it was decided to use the next free number series from 8001. The next group of locomotives similar to the 442 class were numbered 8001 to 8050. A more powerful type 3000 HP (with EMD equipment) were numbered 8101 to 8180 and later four more units 8181 to 8184 were assembled from spare parts. The next 3000 HP class was the 82 class, and a more powerful 3800 HP type became the 90 class. As had been done before classes above 85 were reserved for electric locomotives, but only classes 85 and 86 were used.

Small diesel shunters were given classes from X 101 and X 201.

There was a proposal to number the 82 and 90 classes after their year of introduction, so they would have been the 94 and 93 classes respectively. Photos exist of both types during construction with those numbers, but common sense prevailed. The 90 class are too heavy for general use, as well as being more powerful, and that is the more likely reason for their number series.

Victoria

The Victorian Railways was formed in 1859 to take over the country rail services to Geelong and Bendigo, being operated or constructed by private companies. An existing private suburban railway was absorbed later. In 1983, the operating title changed to V/Line. The suburban system was separated out as The Met and subsequently privatised, now being operated as Metro. The interstate freight services went to National Rail in the early 1990s. The intrastate freight services, then known as V/Line Freight, were sold to Rail America becoming briefly Freight Victoria, later Freight Australia. Eventually Freight Australia, which had initiated a number of interstate services, was sold to Pacific National.

The Victorian numbering of locomotives is more complicated than almost anyone could believe! The Victorian Railways started off as an amalgamation of railways started as private companies with lines to Geelong and Ballarat. The suburban railway to Port Melbourne remained separate for some years. Early locomotive numbering was duplicated through the merger but a fairly normal system got going in the early 1860s when the decision was taken to number passenger engines with even numbers and freight locomotives with odd numbers. When this actually happened is confused, because locomotives continued to be ordered with conventional sequential numbers. The first locomotive to have only an odd or even number was the 2-4-0 Number 100 in 1872. Odd and even numbers continued until about 1912, when, since only 4-6-0s were being built for both passenger and freight at the time, these began to be given both odd and even numbers.

Class letters were given to locomotives in 1886, by which time the former Hobson's Bay locomotives were included.

Passenger locomotives were given the classes A to N.

Freight locomotives were given the classes O to X.

So, in 1886, the B class was the main passenger engine, an outside framed 2-4-0, slightly smaller than the A class 4-4-0 which was the largest express locomotive. The C class was the suburban 4-4-0 tank used on the former Hobson's Bay lines. The N class was the older 2-4-0T used on these lines. The X class was the largest 0-6-0 main line freight engine, and the Y class 0-6-0 was a slightly smaller main line freight engine. By the time of World War I, the allocation of code letters in separate groups had also been abandoned. Because the numbers were quite confusing because of the previous odd and even system, it was decided to start a new system from 1, and a new C class 2-8-0 with this number was built in 1918. It was also the last new locomotive painted in the red colour favoured by Sir Thomas Tait who had come from the Canadian Pacific. A similar but smaller and lighter 2-8-0 K class was built from 1922 numbered from 100. The numbers of the larger 4-6-0

A^2 class were shuffled to get their numbers between 800 and 999, and the smaller D^D class were shuffled to fit in the 500 to 799 group.

In 1925, the VR agreed to build all future locomotives to be suitable for conversion to standard gauge, and the two types of 2-8-0 were replaced by two types of 2-8-2 for any new construction. This was because the firebox between the frames would not allow conversion to standard gauge. So the C class, then numbered between 1 and 26, was followed by the X class numbered from 27. The K class, numbered from 100 to 109, was followed by the N class, numbered from 110.

The D^D class were split between D^1 (saturated) and D^2 (superheated) locomotives and a new class, D^3, which had a modified K class boiler, was introduced. The D^3 class were numbered backwards from 699, filling a gap in the D^D series. After World War II, the N class were renumbered from 400,

V/Line sold a number of locomotives to independent operators. These continued to operate with their original numbers but in a range of colour schemes, including restored versions of their original VR colours. Great Northern dropped the class letter on their locomotives. (Peter Clark)

and enough new locomotives were ordered to reach 499, but 433 to 449 were never built and 10 locomotives were sold to the SAR as the 750 class. The Y class 0-6-0s swapped numbers with the old K and N series, hence Y 112 today being in the old N number group. The four S class Pacifics were numbered 300 to 303. The first diesel locomotives, the F class shunters, were numbered above these as 310 to 319. The first B class main line diesel used a class and number 60, which had been used by the old 2-4-0 locomotives. The numbers fitted in the gap above the X class 2-8-2s and below the Y class 0-6-0s.

Even more shuffling occurred post World War II in order to fit the new R class 4-6-4s in the 700 series and the new (gauge convertible) J class 2-8-0s in the 500 series. The unreliable S class Pacifics were withdrawn in 1954 and the class and numbers (and names) were given to new diesels which were able to be used for both freight and passenger. These were followed by X class hood units which took the 2-8-2 numbers from 31 to 54. The T class branch line diesels took the class but not the numbers of a very early light 0-6-0. The hump shunting versions of the T class took the class H, of the 4-8-4, but the numbers of the C class 2-8-0.

The first 3000 HP units took the C class of the 1918 2-8-0, but the numbers, from 501, of the light J class 2-8-0. There was talk of swapping the classes H and C to get the 4-8-4 class and numbers on the 3000 HP units, but it never happened. The P class light passenger diesels took the class of an early 0-6-0 and numbers from the C class 2-8-0. The N class main line passenger locomotives took the class and numbers of the post World War II British built 2-8-2s which had been almost exclusively freight locomotives. About this time several B class were rebuilt with N class power as A class, keeping the original numbers. A new G class followed the C class with numbers in the 500 series, with a class used by an early light 4-4-0. The last loco in the VR series so far was 544, numbered after the last G with a class last used by a single small shunter. Rebuilt X class were renumbered to a series from 550, but this occurred under Pacific National ownership, and new units have been built with these numbers, including cabless locomotives, and these received multi-letter codes which had not been used in Victoria since the early twentieth century, XR for 'rebuilt X' and XRB for those without cabs.

South Australia

The South Australian Railways was formed in 1856 and operated trains in South Australia and, until Federation, in the Northern Territory. The SAR used both 1600 mm broad gauge and 1067 mm narrow gauge for its main lines. The Commonwealth Railways took over the Northern Territory lines and in 1917 opened a standard-gauge line linking Port Augusta and Kalgoorlie in Western Australia. In 1975, the Commonwealth Railways became Australian National and by 1978 took over the former South Australian Railways. Australian National was greatly affected by the formation of National Rail, losing most of the profitable long-distance freight services. The remaining intrastate services were sold to Genesee and Wyoming who used the title Australia Southern, and later Australian Railroad Group when they purchased Western Australian operations. This name was retained when the WA operations were sold, and those in SA became Genesee and Wyoming Australia. This operator did retain the former BHP operation based in Whyalla which ARG had absorbed.

Before Webb came from the USA, the SAR used the same type of numbering and letter classification as used in NSW before 1924. This is not surprising since at least one chief mechanical engineer worked for both systems. In South Australia, the broad and narrow-gauge systems had separate number systems starting from 1, but the class letters were in a common list (although there was a single class K used for different sized locomotives of the same wheel arrangement [0-6-4T] on both gauges). There was also a locomotive numbered 'zero' on the narrow gauge.

There were locomotives numbered up to 258 on the narrow gauge and up to 280 on the broad gauge, although the highest numbered locomotives on broad gauge were Tx class 4-8-0s, converted from narrow-gauge T class. These were eventually returned to narrow gauge.

The Webb locomotives were given number blocks well clear of existing locomotives, but no class letters. Initially, only 10 locomotives were built in each class – 2-8-2s in the 700 series, 4-6-2s in the 600 series and 4-8-2s in the 500 series.

In the 2-8-2 and 2-8-4 series, the only gap in numbering was from 736 (the last 2-8-4) to 740 (the first UNRRA locomotive). In the other two groups, lighter versions of the types were built to allow use on track not up to main line standard. The 600 class was followed by the lighter 620 class. The 500 class, by then 4-8-4s, were followed by the 520 class. In each case, 10 numbers were left blank for construction of more of the heavier locomotives when required. This in fact was never needed.

Diesel locomotives were numbered above or below the existing steam locomotive numbers.

The Webb numbers were extended to the narrow gauge post World War II when some Australian Standard Garratts were purchased and numbered in the 300 series and Beyer Garratts in the 400 series. While these were presumably in the narrow-gauge series, there were no broad-gauge locomotives with these numbers.

The first (broad-gauge) diesel locomotives were numbered 350, which matched their nominal horsepower, and fitted between the two Garratt types. The broad-gauge main line locomotives were numbered from 900 and a further group of more powerful shunting and transfer locomotives were numbered 800 (close to their nominal power). Again, only 10 locomotives of each type were obtained, and when later locomotives in these categories were obtained they were numbered with a gap of 20 numbers rather than the 10 left in similar cases in steam days.

The new locomotives were Alco designs built by Goodwin in NSW, the

South Australia used a great variety of colours, and in early AN days the corporate green and yellow just added to the variety. 930, 500 and 830 classes are seen at Mile End in 1982. (Peter Clark)

main line units being numbered from 930 and the branch line units from 830. The 830 class were also used on the narrow gauge, and these were numbered in the same series, but in a separate block numbered from 850 upward. Then for some reason not clear to me, a further batch numbered 871 to 873 were built and sent to work with the 850 series on the narrow gauge. It is possible that these numbers were intended for a more powerful 1200 HP DL-535 type, for which Alco records show a cancelled order from the SAR.

As the steam locomotives were withdrawn, the Webb numbers were reused, 500 on some EE shunting locomotives (with that power rating) and 600 and 700 on main line units.

The final group of new (standard-gauge) 830 class were numbered 847 to 849 and 868 to 870, filling the gap between the former broad- and narrow-gauge numbers and the strange gap in the narrow-gauge numbers. At that time, a number of narrow-gauge 830 class were converted to standard gauge and one unit, 874, was purchased from Silverton.

Later, during AN days, the first locomotive of each class was renumbered to the top of the series, so that no locomotive had the number used to refer to the class as a whole. Thus 830 became 875, and '830' meant only the class and not a particular unit.

Commonwealth Railways

The CR started off in 1917, although the Commonwealth had controlled the North Australia Railway (built by the SAR before Federation) for some time before that. The CR was renamed Australian National in 1975, and later absorbed operations in South Australia and Tasmania. As discussed under South Australia, much of Australian National's main line traffic was lost on the formation of National Rail. National Rail also took most of the later locomotive classes, the BL, DL and AN types. The remaining locomotives went to Genesee and Wyoming who formed the Australia Southern Railroad, later known as Australian Railroad Group. The line to Alice Springs, then owned by ARTC and operated by Pacific National was transferred to FreightLink on the opening of the Darwin line in 2004 and this has since passed to Genesee and Wyoming Australia. The Leigh Creek coal traffic was lost by ARG to Pacific National on a commercial basis.

The CR locomotive numbering started off well, numbering their locomotives from 1 in a single series and giving locomotives a class letter based on wheel arrangement, as follows:

A = 0-4-0	B = 0-6-0	C = 0-8-0
D = 4-4-0	F = 2-6-0	G = 4-6-0
H = 4-6-2	K = 2-8-0	L = 2-8-2
M = 4-8-0		

So far so good!

Modified locomotives or additional types of a given wheel arrangement were indicated by a suffix letter and narrow gauge was indicated by the prefix 'N'. So we had Ga (superheated G), Ka (a copy of the NSW D53, the K being a copy of the D50) and NM (a copy of the QR C17). An anomaly was the steam railcar which had a 2-2-0 power unit, but was classed NB as a second-class passenger vehicle.

Sadly, when the long-awaited fast passenger locomotive arrived (a copy of the NSW C36) it was classified 'C' rather than Gb, and second-hand 4-6-0s ex the USA and Canada became classes Ca and Cn respectively.

When the CR took over two of the US Army GE 44 tonners, (7921 and 7922) they were classed and numbered DE 90 and 91 in the steam series. The first main line diesels were given the class GM and numbered from 1, not taking account of the fact that GM 12 onward had six motors rather than four. These locomotives were sometimes called 'F' for four motor and 'S' for six motor in the period from 1951 to 1970 when they were the only main line units. A few diesel hydraulic locomotives were built, class MDH (for Maybach Diesel Hydraulic) and narrow-gauge main line units were NSU (Narrow Gauge Sulzer) 51 to 64 and NT (Narrow Gauge Tulloch) 65 to 74. Steam loco NB 30 was rebuilt as a diesel hydraulic keeping its steam number, and two second-hand Clyde shunting units were classified NC 1 and 2.

In 1970, the first 3000 HP unit was numbered CL 1. It was similar in equipment to the WAGR 'L', so we assumed that that stood for 'Commonwealth L'. This was at least partly supported by the next purchase, after the Australian National title had been adopted, of AL, which we took to mean 'Australian National L'. The next class was BL, which might have been 'filling the gap' between AL and CL or might have been 'Broad Gauge L', because this was the first in the series that could have broad-gauge wheelsets fitted for running to Melbourne over the former SAR. The next classes were DL and EL, clearly just in alphabetic order. So AN might have been simply the next series, also starting from 1 again, but they could have chosen a letter other than 'N' if they were not trying to use the railway name as initials.

Rebuilt 830 class became class DA, but the similarly powered EMD locomotives became CK, suggesting that consistency was not the strong suit in Adelaide. Both these classes started from 1 again.

AN had a chance to introduce a standard national numbering, but didn't, and ARG later tried to do this, albeit very slowly. AN did not renumber former SAR or TGR locomotives and was not particularly consistent with numbering and classification of new locomotive types.

National Rail

National Rail, having taken over much of AN's main line fleet, managed to get one new class NR and Pacific National later introduced a class PN, so they both acted as if 'AN' meant Australian National. I don't know if any of the personalities were the same in all three operations.

Chicago Freight Car Leasing and the CR Classification System

When Chicago Freight Car Leasing took over the remaining EL class locomotives which apparently NR didn't want and ARG didn't get, it was apparently suggested to them by NSW authorities that they should classify all their locomotives in a similar system to assist in identification of the locomotive owner and train operator. Subsequently, this seems to have been considered confusing by train controllers in particular who were unable to distinguish the renumbered locomotives, and CFCLA have not renumbered more recent units.

The CFCLA system followed a version of the AN system, except that every type had 'L' as the second letter, and it had no significance regarding power.

Following on from EL (earlier letters were all used, of course):
FL 220 was the former CountryLink 42220
GL 101 to 112 were new units rebuilt from 442 class
HL 203 was the former CountryLink 42203
JL 401 to 406 were former 442 class locomotives
KL 80 to 82 were former FreightCorp 49 class
'IL', 'LL', 'ML', 'NL' and 'OL' have not been used
'PL' was already in use for FreightCorp/PN modified 48 class
'QL' has not been used

'RL' was reserved for new units rebuilt from 442 class by MKA and RTS but these were not accepted by CFCLA and ended up with Greentrains and QUBE with the CFCLA classification and number. The United C44aci units were expected to become Class XL but became class CF in line with many other operators using the company name.

CFCLA also obtained ex VR and ex AN units from Great Northern and West Coast, and some C class from Silverton which kept their classes and numbers (or got the letter classes back in the case of former GN units, and the numbers in the case of the C class). The JL and KL classes are getting their original numbers back. Many CFCLA units are painted for Southern Shorthaul in yellow and black.

Queensland Railways

Queensland Railways was formed in 1865, and developed as a number of disconnected railway systems that were eventually linked. It remained in government control after other systems had been privatised, and purchased the Northern Rivers Railway, a private NSW operation and later the Western Australian operations of the Australian Railroad Group from Genesee and

Wyoming. The NSW operation was renamed Interail and entered interstate intermodal and intrastate coal traffic, while the operation in WA remained much the same. In the mean time the title QR National was applied in Queensland and NSW. When privatised in 2011, the QR freight operations kept the name QR National, and this name was extended to WA. In 2012 the name Aurizon was adopted. The passenger services in Queensland adopted the name Queensland Rail following the separation.

Queensland Railways had a system of steam locomotive classification which was straightforward but difficult to write down, since it involved fractions. The steam locomotives were numbered in a single series up into the low 1100 series (although early on locomotives were numbered for the separate systems which were not then connected).

Steam locomotives were classified by the number of coupled axles and the cylinder diameter in inches and fractions of inches. This gave:

A for two coupled axles
B for three axles and
C for four coupled axles
So a Baldwin 4-4-0 with 12 inch diameter cylinders was an A12, and a 4-8-0 with 16 inch cylinders was a C16
The US Army 2-8-2 became AC16 ('A' for American to distinguish the type from the 4-8-0)

Tank engines were all type D with a number prefix identifying the number of coupled wheels. A 4-6-4 tank with 16 inch cylinders became 6D16. After a while, the prefix number was ignored, so we had a 4-6-4T class D17, and a later type 4-6-4T became class DD17 to distinguish it.

The US Army locomotives kept their US numbers but other locomotives were basically numbered chronologically (more or less, with numbers being re-used). The first diesel locomotives were very light units for the Etheridge line and were numbered in a separate series from DL1. The main line diesel-electric locomotives were initially numbered upward from 1200 in a single series, but later groups of 100 were allocated to different types. So this gave:
1200 to 1209 English Electric Cab units, became 1200 class
1210 to 1219 GE Hood Units, became 1300 class, later 1150 class
1230 to 1232 Clyde/EMD Hood units, became 1400 class
1270 to 1282 Walkers/GE hood units, later 1500 class, later still 1170 class

Main and branch line diesel locomotives followed in the above sequence from Clyde, Goninan and English Electric:

Classes 1800, 1900 and 2000 were used by diesel railcars
Class 2300 was rebuilt from 1550 and 2400 class, fitting a 2250 HP turbocharged engine.
Class 2250 was rebuilt from 1550 and 2100 class, fitting a 2250 HP turbocharged engine and increasing weight.

There were three groups of QR electric locomotive. Each group was numbered in a single series regardless of the second digit which indicated remote-control capability. In the case of Comeng-Hitachi units, the 3100 series were built as Locotrol command units, 3200 as Locotrol remote units, similarly for the Clyde ASEA Walkers units, 3500 series built as Locotrol command units, the 3600 series as Locotrol remote units and for the Clyde-Hitachi units, the 3300 series built as Locotrol command units, the 3400 series as Locotrol remote units. Freight and passenger locomotives based on the Clyde ASEA Walkers design were numbered in the 3900 series from 3901. The Clyde ASEA Walkers locomotives were rebuilt and renumbered as control units in the 3500 series, with many of the former 3900 series numbered in sequence from 3551.

Sixty-three of the Comeng Hitachi locomotives were rebuilt by Goninan with Siemens AC traction equipment and are being numbered as the 3700 series. A new class of AC traction electric locomotives was built in Germany as the 3800 class.

When QR took over the Northern Rivers Railway, which became Interail, they obtained ex NSW 421 and 422 class locomotives which were not renumbered and after purchasing CRT obtained ex V/Line locomotives of X and G classes. Six 1502 class narrow-gauge locomotives were rebuilt using bogie frames from 49 class as standard-gauge 423 class.

Tasmania

The Tasmanian railways commenced operation in 1871 but the first line was taken over by the government in 1873. The government took over the remaining private railway in 1890, and the system became known as the Tasmanian Government Railways. In 1978, operation of the Tasmanian system was transferred to Australian National. In 1997 the system was privatised and sold to Australian Transport Network, a subsidiary of Wisconsin Central and Tranz Rail (NZ). In 2004, the system was purchased by Pacific National after Toll had been purchased by Toll and Wisconsin Central had been purchased by Canadian National. In 2007 the Tasmanian government re-acquired the rail infrastructure from PN and in 2009 purchased back the rolling stock and operations, ending Pacific National's involvement.

The classification system was a simple alphabetic character, but each class was numbered from 1 rather than in a single series. This system continued up to the end of the TGR's independent existence and for locomotives remained the same until the end of Australian National operation, except that former SAR 830 class locomotives were introduced and not renumbered into the TGR system. Locomotives purchased from QR were renumbered into the TGR system but some operated with their original numbers. After World War

II suffix letters were introduced for modifications of both steam and diesel locomotives, and the two QR types were classified ZB and ZC following the generally similar Z and ZA classes.

With privatisation, a straight numerical system was started, with locomotives numbered in the 2000 and 2100 series. It was common for these locomotives to be referred to by their old letter classes or by previous New Zealand or WA identities, although these didn't appear on the newer locomotives. It appears that the current operators will retain the numerical system, having recently renumbered some further units from Queensland.

Western Australia

The WAGR commenced operation in 1879, but only gained that name on reorganisation in 1890. The title changed again, to Westrail in 1975. The system was privatised in 2000 when it was sold to Genesee and Wyoming and Wesfarmers, becoming the Australia Western Railroad, although this title was changed to Australian Railroad Group. In 2006, the WA assets of ARG were sold to QR who retained the operating title ARG. In 2011, when QR's freight operations were privatised, the title QR National was adopted for WA operations, changing to Aurizon in 2012.

Until 1945, the WAGR used a numbering and classification system common to other state railways, at least NSW and SA in the nineteenth century, a single number series in roughly chronological order and an alphabetical classification system. The WAGR used a number of suffix letters to indicate modifications, often just 'a', but 's' for superheating and 'c' for compound were also used, along with other letters.

In 1945 an effort was made to renumber locomotives into sequential blocks of numbers, and new locomotives were introduced with these numbers which ran from:

U – 4-6-2 – 651–664 to S – 3000 HP Co'Co' – 2101–2111.

When the Midland Railway was taken over, these were added:

E – 250 HP 0-6-0 – 30
F – 730 HP A1A'A1A' – 40–46
G – 1030 HP Co'Co' – 50–51

When standard gauge was introduced, a new series was started:

H – 862 HP Bo'Bo' – 1–5
J – 600 HP Bo'Bo' 101–105
K – 1795 HP Co'Co' 201–210
L – 3000 HP Co'Co' 251–275 (276 ex Comalco)
And much, much later:
Q – 3835 HP Co'Co' 301–319

Two number groups were used for varying types:

A – 1310 HP Co'Co' – 1501–1514

AA – 1500 HP Co'Co' – 1515–1519
AB – 1500 HP Co'Co' – 1531–1536

D – 2000 HP Co'Co' – 1561–1565
DA – 2000 HP Co'Co' – 1571–1577
DB – 2000 HP Co'Co' – 1581–1593
and
T – 660 HP 0-6-0 – 1801–1805
TA – 660 HP 0-6-0 – 1806–1815
M – 650 HP B'B' – 1851–1852
MA – 650 HP B'B' – 1861–1863

N – 2400 HP Co'Co' – 1871–1881
NA 1871–1874 Converted dual brake to air only
NB 1872–1873 Converted to standard gauge

The locomotives in the latter number groups have little in common.

Two former Queensland locomotives are seen at Avon Yard, a major centre for Western Australian grain traffic. These locomotives were given new numbers in the new ARG system, complete with letter classes following the equivalent WAGR classes DB and AB. Both these classes were sold for use in Africa in 2014. (Peter Clark)

The Australian Railroad Group Locomotive Numbering

When part of a single group, ARG started to renumber their locomotives, numbered in the SAR, CR and WAGR series, with some BHP units, into a single uniform series with four digit numbers based generally on the locomotive horsepower rating. Unfortunately, locomotives were only renumbered when they were rebuilt, usually with digital control systems. The system was adopted very slowly as a result, and was far from complete when the WA operation was sold to QR. Despite this, the numbering was continued by ARG in WA, but with the return of the WAGR letter classes to distinguish the WA locomotives from the numerical system used in Queensland. G&WA did not extend the renumbering to classes not already renumbered, and QR didn't apply it to standard-gauge locomotives outside WA, nor to the QR fleet.

Number series	Former class	Locomotive numbers (numbers in italics not used)
500	SAR 500	508,517, 518,527, 532
830	SAR 830	831, 841–844, 846–848, 850–852, 859, 863, 865, 869, 871–873
900	ANR DA	901–906
1000	ANR CK	*1001–1005*
1200	WAGR A	1201–1204
1250	BHP DE	1251
1300	BHP DE	1301–1304
1500	WAGR AB	1501–1504
1600	CR NJ	1601–1606

1800	CR GM	*1801–1811*
1900	WAGR DA	1901–1907
2000	SAR 600	*2001–2003*
2100	SAR 700	*2101–2105*
2200	NSW 422	2201–2216
2300	WAGR DB	2301–2313
2350	WAGR D	*2351–2352*
2500	WAGR P	2501–2517
3000	AN CLF CLP	3001–3016
3100	WAGR L	3101–3118
3200	AN ALF	3201–3208
3300	WAGR S	3301–3311
3400	GM30, Rblt	3401
4000	WAGR Q	4001–4019

The first locomotives renumbered were the eight units rebuilt for the North Australia Railway, which were numbered as 2201–4 and 3101–4 in order of rebuilding from NSW 422 and WAGR L class.

It is possible that the 2000 and 2100 groups were initially left vacant to avoid confusion with the WAGR P and S classes in these series. Additional locomotives from Queensland have been numbered in the 1520, 2350 and 2400 series. A single QR 2800 more or less fitted in but more recently 4100 and 6000 classes have kept their numbers with the addition of a letter code.

Locomotives GWU 002, GWU 001 and GWU 003 haul GWA 006 and GWA 007 through Yarra in April 2012. The identifying features of United and Downer built locomotives can be seen in this view. (Leon Oberg)

AN AUSTRALIAN LOCOMOTIVE GUIDE

Locomotive Recognition

While some locomotives are readily recognised, particularly since privatisation of the former government systems, it is possible for generally similar looking locomotives to be confused. An example shown here is a Goninan-built GE engine EL class and an Islington-built EMD engine RL class, both in CFCLA livery which enhances the general similarity in appearance. In this case, both locomotives have generally similar MLW/Dofasco design bogies, so that isn't a recognition feature in this case.

The EL class, leading in this combination, has the large radiator grilles at the rear characteristic of the GE cooling system with a roof level horizontal radiator with a fan below it. Another feature of GE locomotives since the Dash-7 series is the dynamic brake installation, with two units arranged horizontally blowing left to right with outlets just below roof level just behind the cab.

The RL class has the usual EMD characteristics, with radiators arranged in a vee under three roof-mounted 1220 mm fans, with air intake grilles on the angled section of the roof towards the rear of the unit. The dynamic brakes are above the engine, with two roof-mounted 1220 mm fans and smaller air intake grilles, again on the angled roof section near the centre of the locomotive.

Another very similar locomotive is the AN class, which shared the AN green livery with the EL class when new. The AN class has the distinctive EMD HTC bogies with holes in the sideframe casting under the bolster, but has the later radial dynamic brake installation behind the radiators with an air intake grille on the body sides at the rear. The EMD radiator arrangement is forward of this, and the AN class is somewhat longer than either the EL or RL classes.

It isn't possible to provide such an explanation for every type, and many locomotives are readily recognised by distinctive features. The recent Downer GT 46C-ACe and United C44aci are generally similar but retain the distinctive features described above. An exception to the rule is the GT 42CU-AC which has a horizontal roof level radiator with electric fans below, unlike most larger Downer-EMD design units, and could be confused with a United-GE unit. It does have the distinctive Clyde design steering bogies which help to identify its origin.

The photos used to illustrate the book have been chosen, where possible, to allow the reader to recognise the distinctive features of a locomotive type to allow easy recognition when seen in traffic.

EL 63 and RL 301 at North Dynon Yard in January 2008 on a QR National service to Adelaide. These generally similar locomotives illustrate the difference between locomotives with GE and EMD power equipment. (Peter Clark)

Australian Locomotive Builders in the Diesel Era

The **Clyde Engineering** factory, and that of Hudson Brothers before that, was at Clyde station on the left-hand side of the railway while travelling away from Sydney, while the Commonwealth Engineering factory was on the right-hand side. The Goodwin works was at the other end of Clyde yards on the right-hand side, near the present PN/EDI Locomotive Depot but across Parramatta Road.

Clyde-built steam locomotives at Granville from the mid-1900s until 1951, the last being 2-8-2s intended for China but delivered to the SAR and CR. Clyde became the licensee of GM-Electro-Motive and built diesel locomotives at Granville until the late 1970s when they moved construction to Rosewater (SA) and to Kelso (near Bathurst). Rosewater later closed down, but some locomotives were assembled at Somerton in Victoria, and others at Forrestfield in WA. The 82 class were assembled at the former Comeng plant at Braemar, now owned by Bradken.

In August 2011, a Queensland Rail SMU train waits refurbishment at Downer's Maryborough plant, next to new locomotives for both QR National and Pacific National. The locomotives are used both in Queensland and Western Australia. (Peter Clark)

AN AUSTRALIAN LOCOMOTIVE GUIDE

Clyde was sold to EDI (who also owned Walkers Limited in Maryborough) and this company was later purchased by Downer, who operated both Clyde and Walkers as EDI Rail, and later as just Downer Rail.

EMD locomotives are built at Maryborough (Qld), and at Cardiff (NSW) with components from Downer's plant in Port Augusta (the former CR workshops). Port Augusta has assembled a few locomotives themselves. Major rebuilds have been carried out in the former SAR workshops in Port Lincoln operated by Downer. In June 2012 Downer announced that in future locomotives would be imported from EMD, with no local construction.

A.E. Goodwin became the licensee of Alco Products and from 1955 built locomotives at Auburn and in a leased plant at St Marys in western Sydney. In the late 1960s Goodwin's parent company, A.G. Healing, went into receivership and Goodwin closed down. Comeng took over the licence and built Alco locomotives at Granville and a few at Bassendean for Westrail and Hamersley Iron.

Commonwealth Engineering was formed out of the original company called Waddingtons Limited at Granville in 1947, and afterwards was universally referred to as **Comeng**. Comeng built the first English Electric locomotives for AI&S before Clyde had built its first diesel locomotive. Comeng negotiated patent licensing from the Budd Company in the USA for the fluted stainless-steel construction methods (and a number of other patents). When A.E. Goodwin (just down the road at Auburn) closed, Comeng bought the A.E. Goodwin licenses for diesel engines from MLW-Alco (Montreal Locomotive Works / American Locomotive Company) for use in the new locomotive orders from the big mining companies at Mount Newman, Hamersley and Robe River.

As the company expanded its activities, Comeng was run through the parent company Comeng Holdings Limited. The main operations were:

Commonwealth Engineering (NSW) P/L – Granville – railway rolling stock and general engineering .–

Comeng (NSW) also controlled the branches in WA at Bassendean and Welshpool (spares and service).

Mittagong Engineering – Braemar – freight rolling stock and general engineering.

Comeng (QLD) P/L – Salisbury – railway rolling stock and general engineering.

Comeng (VIC) P/L – Dandenong – railway rolling stock and general engineering, road transportation and automotive components.

The Comeng Granville plant was purchased by ANI who subsequently sold it for redevelopment. ANI sold the Dandenong plant to ABB who became Adtranz and later Bombardier. The Bassendean plant was sold to Goninan. The Braemar plant stayed with ANI and is now known as Bradken (but it was a bit confusing when Clyde leased the Braemar plant to assemble the 82 class). When Comeng formed Union Carriage and Wagon in South Africa in 1957, the combined group became the largest manufacturer of railway rolling stock in the Southern Hemisphere.

To add to the confusion Comeng-built locomotives as a subcontractor to Clyde at Rocklea in Queensland and at Bassendean in WA.

So Bassendean has built:
Comeng design locos – Westrail B class
EMD design locos – Westrail A class
Alco design locos – Westrail N class
GE design locos – Westrail P class

In December 2010 QR National locomotive 5023 stands next to Xtrata XRN010 inside the UGL plant in Broadmeadow, NSW. (Peter Clark)

A. Goninan and Company, normally known as **Goninan**, was a Newcastle heavy engineering company with a plant at Broadmeadow which was a big supplier to the BHP Newcastle Steelworks. They obtained the licence for General Electric locomotives and were quite successful in the early 1950s, building main line locomotives for NSW and Queensland and shunting locomotives for BHP Newcastle. They were unsuccessful in obtaining further main line locomotive orders but continued to build GE shunters for BHP and some other companies until the 1970s.

Goninan did build the 47 class for NSW to a Hitachi design in the early 1970s but these were not considered successful at the time although many are still operating today. In the late 1970s, they began to build large GE locomotives for the Pilbara iron ore railways. These were quite successful after a shaky start,

and many existing Alco locomotives were rebuilt as GE units. A number of GE locomotives were built for the state railways, but the big breakthrough for local construction was obtaining the order from National Rail for the NR class. Sadly although many new GE locomotives have been built for the Pilbara, from the mid-1990s these were all imported from GE in the USA.

Having obtained the Bassendean plant from Comeng, many of the Alco locomotives operated by BHP and Robe River were rebuilt as GE units in Bassendean, and half the National Rail locomotives were built there.

Goninan was sold to the United Group Limited and is now called United Group Rail. UGL now operate the Spotswood workshops where the NR class are maintained and the Chullora workshops. Some locomotives are built at Chullora at times of high demand. UGL also operate a factory in Bohle, near Townsville in Queensland, and all of the QR narrow-gauge GE units were built there. They also rebuilt the shells of the electric locomotives being converted for AC traction, although the installation was carried out in Broadmeadow

English Electric had supplied equipment to the SAR and to Comeng both in Granville and in Rocklea in Queensland, but later began to build its own locomotives in a former Commonwealth factory in Rocklea, adjacent to Comeng. Some 279 locomotives were built there from the late 1950s until the early 1970s, but by that time the work was not regarded as profitable and Clyde, in particular, had taken most of the EE market share. The plant continued to build other GEC products.

Walkers Limited in Maryborough had built steam locomotives for many years and built the first branch line (60-ton) locomotives for QR using GE equipment. They did little further work until they built three locomotives for the Emu Bay Railway, using equipment originally ordered by Tulloch Limited, who gave up the locomotive business in the early 1960s. These diesel hydraulic locomotives were built to North British designs for an Indian metre-gauge locomotive. Realising there was a niche market, a demonstrator was built in 1968 and the DH class were produced in quantity for QR. Similar larger locomotives were built for NSW and WA and more were built for the Emu Bay Railway. They later built the QR electric locomotives of the 3500 and 3900 classes for the Clyde ASEA Walkers consortium. Walkers were purchased by Evans Deakin, another Queensland engineering firm, who in turn purchased Clyde Engineering. This allowed Clyde locomotives to be assembled in Maryborough, the first being the QR 4000 class. Construction of later versions of this type continues for both QR National and Pacific National. The QR Tilt Trains were built at Maryborough as well.

Tulloch Limited at Rhodes in NSW had been building freight and passenger rolling stock for some years but in the late 1950s entered the locomotive field with designs from Krupp in Germany. While these were generally similar to locomotive built in Germany for DB they were new and untested designs and used a Mercedes-Benz diesel with certain design defects and a Krupp hydraulic transmission. Most of these were built for Victorian Railways, which kept them for some years but eventually gave up and withdrew them from service. An order for the Emu Bay Railway was abandoned and the equipment moved to Walkers, who built a different design. Tulloch continued to build rolling stock until the mid-1970s, and struck up an alliance with Sulzer and subsequently with Brush in the UK. The resulting Commonwealth NT class locomotives were a Sulzer design and Brush contributed the WAGR T and TA classes.

Diesel Engines in Australian Locomotives

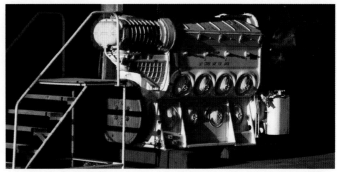

An eight-cylinder EMD blower engine at South Dynon in March 2005. The oval blower and its angled air duct sit above the generator, not present in this view. (Peter Clark)

The great majority of Australian diesel locomotives are equipped with diesel engines from the three large American manufacturers – Alco, Electro-Motive or General Electric – although more than 200 units had the generally equivalent English Electric RK and V series engines. The Electro-Motive engines are two-stroke cycle engines, the original design dating back to 1934 although the first of the improved 567 design appeared in 1939. There were a continuing series of improvements to this engine, with the earliest version in new locomotives being the 567B, in the early GM and B classes. A single 645AC engine was used at Weipa in the NW2 number 1.003. The 567C was used in later locomotives until the larger bore 645E was introduced in the mid-1960s. The first turbocharged engines were the 645E3 engines in the WAGR L class in 1967. The higher speed 645F3 engine was introduced in the SD50 for Hamersley and the longer stroke 710G3 in the Australian National DL class. From the 567C engine onward these engines all looked similar, with distinctive circular access covers. The blower engines had one or two Roots blowers on the output shaft end, above the generator, while the turbocharged engines had a turbocharger, arranged to be driven as a blower at lower engine power.

There were two distinct types of Alco engine used in Australia – the 244, developed from 1944 onward, and the 251 which followed from an initial design in 1951. An earlier type, the 539, only appeared in a second-hand locomotive obtained by Hamersley Iron. The 244 was a very advanced design for its period but was used locally only in the NSW 40 and 43 classes. It suffered from a number of reliability issues, but by the mid-1950s these had been largely overcome. However, the somewhat simpler 251 had been designed to allow for higher power outputs than the 244 and later Alco locomotive designs used this engine. A distinctive feature of the 251 was the long stroke fuel injection pump mounted on the outer face of the crankcase for each cylinder, covered by a small bathtub shaped steel cover. The 244 and the GE FDL had the fuel injection pump mounted between the valve pushrods, and lacked this obvious cover. The designs progressed as far as model 251F, which provided 3600 HP to the alternator from a 16-cylinder engine at 1100 rpm. This engine provided the power to the three large Pilbara mining companies during their formative years, and was only replaced by locomotives with General Electric and Electro-

An Alco12-244H engine stored at the PRHS museum in Karratha, WA. It can be seen that it is significantly different in appearance from the later 251 model. (Peter Clark)

An Alco 16-cylinder 251F engine being rebuilt in Maddington, WA, in August 2007. (Peter Clark)

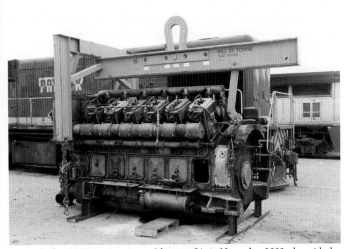

A 12-cylinder GE FDL-12 engine at Islington, SA, in November 2009, also with the alternator removed. (Peter Clark)

Motive engines more than two decades later.

GE was very early to market in Australia, providing the first main line diesel locomotives in Queensland in 1951. The Cooper-Bessemer engine was far from fully developed and was significantly less powerful than the contemporary Alco 244. The QR laboratories at Ipswich were particularly scathing in their criticism of the GE engine, suggesting that QR were being used as a proving ground for GE's designs. But GE was heavy, with a cast crankcase compared to the welded crankcases of Electro-Motive and Alco. The crankcases were subject to cracking, particularly in heavy duty use, and as a result very few GE locomotives are heavily rebuilt for extended use, although Hamersley has fitted new crankcases to its oldest Dash-9 locomotives. A

feature of the FDL is the cross flow head with segmented air ducts from the intercooler along the outside of the engine, with the exhaust in the vee between the cylinder heads. The GE design has the cylinder and head mounted largely outside the crankcase and removable with the piston as a 'power assembly'. The FDL replaced the Alco 251 in the Pilbara, sometimes literally since many existing locomotives were rebuilt to take the GE engine, while many new locomotives were also built. GE produced a new engine in conjunction with Deutz in Germany, the model HDL, which was more powerful, and a number of 6000 HP locomotives were built. These were not successful and GE revised the design to produce the GEVO or V250 engine which was mainly built as a 12-cylinder of 4400 HP, although 16-cylinder replacements were built for the HDL series. The 12-cylinder engines use an air to air intercooler, and possibly because of the size of this device, none have been built for the limited clearances of Australian main line locomotives. As a result the FDL remains in production for this market.

English Electric was also early into the Australian market, with the Australian Iron and Steel locomotives using in line eight-cylinder RK engines and the SAR 900 class using the 16-cylinder SV engine. The first rail application of the original K engine was in a prototype diesel-electric shunter built in 1934. This locomotive was developed into the standard shunter by the addition of double reduction gearing, and these became the Victorian F class, while the same engine appeared in the SAR 350 class, just preceding the larger locomotives indicated above. The locomotive versions of the engine carried the suffix 'T' for traction, and a number of turbocharged 6SRKT engines and a few inline 8SRKT engines were used in Australian locomotives. A Mk II version with a four-valve head was developed, and intercooling was introduced with an additional letter 'C' as an indication. So we now had 6CSRKT Mk II and the equivalent 12CSVT Mk II engines which more or less matched the American engines in power rating at the end of the 1960s. Higher ratings were indicated for the final Mk III versions, but only relatively few of these were delivered. In the UK about this time, the 'V' designation was dropped so that both vee and inline engines became known as the RK type.

A somewhat busy view of a sectioned English Electric 12-SVT engine in a 1250 class locomotive at the Ipswich museum in 2002. (Peter Clark)

AN AUSTRALIAN LOCOMOTIVE GUIDE

Locomotive Diesel Engines

The majority of line haul locomotives in Australia are equipped with one of the types of engine built by the three large American manufacturers, EMD, GE or Alco. The EMD engines were the 567B and 567C, 645E and 710G series, for GE the 7FDL, and from Alco the 244 and 251 series. The other main types of locomotive engine used were the English Electric RK and V series. The EMD engines were two-stroke while the others were all four-stroke engines but they were all generally similar in overall size and weight, and even in the sizes of bore and stroke.

EMD

567B	216 mm x 254 mm	800 rpm	Roots blower
567C	216 mm x 254 mm	835 rpm	Roots blower
567E	216 mm x 254 mm	835 rpm	Roots blower
645E	230 mm x 254 mm	900 rpm	Roots blower
645E3	230 mm x 254 mm	900 rpm	turbocharged, intercooled
645F3	230 mm x 254 mm	950 rpm	turbocharged, intercooled
710G3	230 mm x 279 mm	900 rpm	turbocharged, intercooled
710G3B	230 mm x 279 mm	950 rpm	turbocharged, intercooled

General Electric

FWL	228 mm x 267 mm	1000 rpm	turbocharged
FVL	228 mm x 267 mm	1000 rpm	turbocharged
FDL	228 mm x 267 mm	1050 rpm	turbocharged, intercooled
HDL	250 mm x 320 mm	1050 rpm	turbocharged, intercooled
V250	250 mm x 320 mm	1050 rpm	turbocharged, intercooled
P616	190 mm x 220 mm	1500 rpm	turbocharged, intercooled

Alco

539	317 mm x 330 mm	740 rpm	turbocharged
244	228 mm x 267 mm	1000 rpm	turbocharged
251B	228 mm x 267 mm	1000 rpm	turbocharged
251C	228 mm x 267 mm	1000 rpm	turbocharged, intercooled
251E	228 mm x 267 mm	1050 rpm	turbocharged, intercooled
251F	228 mm x 267 mm	1100 rpm	turbocharged, intercooled

English Electric

H	153 mm x 202 mm	1500 rpm	
K	254 mm x 305 mm	680 rpm	
SRKT	254 mm x 305 mm	750 rpm	turbocharged (Mk I)
SRKT	254 mm x 305 mm	850 rpm	turbocharged (Mk II)
SVT	254 mm x 305 mm	750 rpm	turbocharged (Mk I)
SVT	254 mm x 305 mm	850 rpm	turbocharged (Mk II)
CSRKT	254 mm x 305 mm	850 rpm	turbocharged, intercooled
CSVT	254 mm x 305 mm	850 rpm	turbocharged, intercooled

Smaller locomotives, and more recently large main line locomotives, have used versions of industrial, marine or automotive diesel engines.

Bedford

300BIB	95 mm x 104 mm	2500 rpm	

Caterpillar

D17000	146 mm x 203 mm	1000 rpm		(V-8)
D397	146 mm x 203 mm	1300 rpm		(V-12)
D353 E	159 mm x 203 mm	1400 rpm		(inline 6)
D379 B	159 mm x 203 mm	1300 rpm	turbocharged	(V-8)
D398 B	159 mm x 203 mm	1300 rpm	turbocharged	(V-12)

D399 B	159 mm x 203 mm	1300 rpm	turbocharged (V-16)
3512 C	170 mm x 190 mm	1800 rpm	turbocharged, intercooled

Crossley
HST	267 mm x 343 mm	625 rpm	exhaust pulse compression

Cummins
H	112 mm x 152 mm	1800 rpm	
NHRS	130 mm x 152 mm	1900 rpm	supercharged
NRTO	130 mm x 152 mm	2100 rpm	
VT 12	140 mm x 152 mm	2000 rpm	turbocharged
VT1710L	140 mm x 152 mm	2000 rpm	turbocharged
QSK19	159 mm x 159 mm	2100 rpm	turbocharged, intercooled
QSK60	159 mm x 190 mm	1900 rpm	turbocharged, intercooled
QSK78	170 mm x 190 mm	1800 rpm	turbocharged, intercooled

Fordson
Ford	100 mm x 115 mm	1600 rpm	

Gardner
LW	108 mm x152 mm	1700 rpm	
LX	121 mm x 152 mm	1700 rpm	
L3	140 mm x 197 mm	1200 rpm	

Detroit Diesel
71	108 mm x 127 mm	2100 rpm	Roots blower
110	127 mm x 142 mm	1800 rpm	Roots blower
149	146 mm x 146 mm	1800 rpm	Roots blower

Mack
EN 673	124 mm x 152 mm	1800 rpm	

Maybach
MD 325	185 mm x 200 mm	1600 rpm	turbocharged

Mercedes-Benz
MB 820B	175 mm x 205 mm	1500 rpm	

MTU
396	165 mm x 185 mm	1900 rpm	turbocharged, intercooled
4000	170 mm x 190 mm	2000 rpm	turbocharged, intercooled

National
M4 AA6	152 mm x 216 mm	1350 rpm	

Paxman
RPHL	178 mm x 197 mm	1250 rpm	
RPHX	178 mm x 197 mm	1150 rpm	turbocharged
YHXL	178 mm x 197 mm	1250 rpm	turbocharged
RP200	197 mm x 216 mm	1500 rpm	turbocharged, intercooled
VP185	185 mm x 196 mm	1800 rpm	turbocharged, intercooled

Rolls-Royce
SFL	130 mm x 152 mm	2100 rpm	supercharged
TFL	130 mm x 152 mm	1800 rpm	turbocharged

Ruston
VPHL	137 mm x 203 mm	1500 rpm	

Sulzer
LDA28B	280 mm x 360 mm	750 rpm	turbocharged, intercooled
LDA28C	280 mm x 360 mm	850 rpm	turbocharged, intercooled

The steam railcar NJAB 1 was preserved in Alice Springs as seen in March 1969. (John Beckhaus)

Steam Rail Motor 1

Type	Motor Coach	**Wheel Arrangement**	1A'2'
Boiler Pressure	1170 kPa	**Cylinders**	165 x 254 mm
Grate Area	0.46 m²	**Length**	12.07 m
Heating Surface		**Width**	
Valve Gear	Walschaerts	**Height**	3.36 m
Driving Wheels	724 mm	**Weight**	19.4 t
Tractive Effort	8.9 kN	**Axle Load**	
Maximum Speed	38 km/h	**Gauge**	1067 mm
Builder	Kitson	**Number Built**	2
Introduced	1906		

The South Australian Railways obtained two steam rail motors in an attempt to reduce the costs of passenger operation on branch lines, as were tried on contemporary British railways. One unit was allocated to the Quorn–Hawker line. When the lines through Quorn were transferred to the Commonwealth Railways becoming part of the Trans-Australian and Alice Springs lines, the Hawker rail motor was transferred to the CR, gaining the classification NJAB 1, where the N indicated narrow gauge, and the A and B represented first- and second-class passenger accommodation respectively. The rail car continued in service until 1930 when it was withdrawn and stored at Quorn. After a period on display in Alice Springs it returned to Quorn in 1975, where it was restored to working order and is operated by the Pichi Richi Railway.

STEAM LOCOMOTIVES

Locomotive No. 6, Class A12, in the Ipswich Workshops Museum in 2002. (Peter Clark)

Neilson A12 No. 6

Type	Mixed Traffic	**Wheel Arrangement**	B1′
Boiler Pressure	800 kPa	**Cylinders**	254 x 457 mm
Grate Area	0.65 m²	**Length**	
Heating Surface	36.7 m²	**Width**	
Valve Gear	Stephenson	**Height**	
Driving Wheels	914 mm	**Engine Weight**	13.8 t
Tractive Effort	20 kN	**Tender Weight**	8.5 t
Maximum Speed		**Axle Load**	56 kN
Builder	Neilson	**Gauge**	1067 mm
Introduced	1865	**Number Built**	13

The Queensland government chose the narrow gauge of 1067 mm as a deliberate policy to reduce the cost of construction and operation. In line with this policy, the initial locomotives were very small four-coupled engines. This design was relatively widely used in British colonies but the combination of short wheelbase, outside cylinders and the lack of a leading truck was not conducive to steady running at speed. These locomotives were used on the pioneer section of line from Ipswich to Grandchester. No. 6 was sold in 1895 to Bingera sugar mill, which used 1067 mm gauge for cane transport and continued in use until 1965, when it was handed over to QR in working order to celebrate their centenary. QR had retained a similar locomotive, No. 3, which was displayed in Brisbane and later in Ipswich for many years, but is now in the Ipswich Museum.

The former Mount Lyell Abt locomotive No. 3 at Queenstown in April 2003. (John Beckhaus)

Abt Type Nos 1, 2 ,3, 5

Type	Mixed Traffic	**Wheel Arrangement**	B1'2zt
Boiler Pressure	1240 kPa	**Cylinders**	292 x 508 mm
Grate Area	1.05 m²	**Length**	6.95 m
Heating Surface	42.2 m²	**Width**	
Valve Gear	Walschaerts	**Height**	
Driving Wheels	914 mm	**Weight**	26.9 t
Tractive Effort	45.7 kN	**Axle Load**	94.6 kN
Maximum Speed		**Gauge**	1067 mm
Builder	Dubs	**Number Built**	5
Introduced	1896		

The Mount Lyell Mining and Railway Company built a line from Queenstown to Regatta Point to connect the mine to the port. The mountainous terrain required very steep gradients and a rack railway using the Abt system was adopted. The Abt system used two toothed racks side by side offset by half a tooth pitch, engaged by a similarly offset pair of gear wheels driven by a separate engine to that driving the locomotive wheels. In 1896 Dubs supplied four four-coupled tank locomotives to operate the rack section and they operated all services on that section until 1938 when North British built a fifth locomotive. By 1963, road access had been provided and the railway closed. The rack locomotives were dispersed to museums, but when the line was restored four locomotives were returned to working order and put back in service.

1210

Locomotive 1210 at Queanbeyan in September 2003. (Peter Clark)

Type	Passenger	**Wheel Arrangement**	2'B	
Boiler Pressure	0.96 MPa	**Cylinders**	457 x 609 mm	
Grate Area	1.4 m²	**Length**	14.4 m	
Heating Surface	104 m²	**Width**	2.74 m	
Valve Gear	Stephenson	**Height**	4.09 m	
Driving Wheels	1676 mm	**Weight**	61.9 t	
Tractive Effort	58 kN	**Axle Load**	126 kN	
Maximum Speed	80 km/h	**Gauge**	1435 mm	
Builder	Beyer, Peacock	**Number Built**	68	
Introduced	1877			

This class, originally known as the 79 class, was an improvement on the 1865-built 23 class locomotives. The main change was the substitution of a two-axle Bissel truck for the single-axle truck of the 23 class, and minor changes in dimensions. These became the main passenger locomotives in NSW and by 1889 were the third largest class in the state getting the alphabetic class C following the two largest goods engine types. They were superseded by the larger wheeled 255 class in 1882 and were relegated to secondary service following the introduction of the P class in 1891. Twenty were converted to CC class tank locomotives from 1896 for suburban traffic. The tender engines were used on branch lines and they had a revival of use on fast light passenger trains used to replace rail motors on branch lines from the 1920s, with a number being painted green as were larger passenger locomotives in the mid to late 1930s. The 23 class were rebuilt as class CG, later 14 class, similar to the C class.

1210, 1219 and 1243 were used for historic Vintage Trains from 1960. 1210 was preserved at Canberra station, and was restored by the ARHS (ACT) in 1988. The other two are static exhibits.

Locomotive 1709 was displayed as part of the NSW Rail Sesquicentenary celebrations in September 2005. (Peter Clark)

1709

Type	Passenger	**Wheel Arrangement**	2'B	
Boiler Pressure	0.96 MPa	**Cylinders**	482 × 660 mm	
Grate Area	1.9 m²	**Length**	15.4 m	
Heating Surface	119.4 m²	**Width**	2.74 m	
Valve Gear	Stephenson	**Height**	4.09 m	
Driving Wheels	1676 mm	**Weight**	76.3 t	
Tractive Effort	75 kN	**Axle Load**	156 kN	
Maximum Speed	80 km/h	**Gauge**	1435 mm	
Builder	Vulcan Foundry	**Number Built**	12	
Introduced	1887			

This class, originally known as the 373 class, was introduced at a time of conflict in NSW locomotive affairs, with conflict between Scott and Middleton regarding locomotive design. This was Scott's contribution, favouring British practice. The valve gear followed American ideas, with slide valves located above the cylinders. These became the alphabetic class H in 1889, since there were only 12 engines in the class. They were relegated to secondary service following the introduction of the P class in 1891. When rebuilt with Belpaire boilers, the cylinders were reduced in diameter to 457 mm and the weight reduced and redistributed. Like the 12 class, they were used on branch lines and they had a revival of use on fast light passenger trains used to replace rail motors on branch lines from the 1920s.

1709 was used for historic Vintage Trains from 1960, and was preserved at Thirlmere. It is only run on significant occasions.

The class leader 1801 at Catherine Hill Bay on its last day in service for Coal & Allied in 1963. (Peter Clark) and 1803 as 'Thomas' at Central. (Bruce Belbin)

1803

Type	Passenger Tank	**Wheel Arrangement**	Ct
Boiler Pressure	970 kPa	**Cylinders**	381 × 559 mm
Grate Area	1.2 m2	**Length**	8.54 m
Heating Surface	81.8 m2	**Width**	
Valve Gear	Stephenson	**Height**	
Driving Wheels	1219 mm	**Weight**	38 t
Tractive Effort	54.6 kN	**Axle Load**	62 kN
Maximum Speed		**Gauge**	1435 mm
Builder	Vulcan Foundry	**Number Built**	6
Introduced	1882		

A feature of the railway development in Sydney was the need to run suburban passenger trains, stopping all stations, for which the early locomotives were not well suited. The six-coupled tank locomotive with small driving wheels was suited to this service, and six locomotives numbered from 285, renumbered as the 18 class in 1924, were obtained. These were later used as yard shunting locomotives since their top speed was limited by the small wheels. A number were used as workshops crane engines and one of them, number 1076, retained its crane number when returned to shunting, although others regained their normal numbers. Two, 1801 and 1806, were last used at the Catherine Hill Bay colliery. 1803 was preserved by the Rail Transport Museum, and has been painted to represent Reverend Awdry's character 'Thomas' which if not operational, is at least mobile.

Sister locomotive 1904 in service at Darling Harbour in 1972. (Peter Clark)

1919

Type	Freight	**Wheel Arrangement**	C
Boiler Pressure	1030 kPa	**Cylinders**	457 × 610 mm
Grate Area	1.27 m²	**Length**	14.4 m
Heating Surface	118.9 m²	**Width**	
Valve Gear	Stephenson	**Height**	
Driving Wheels	1219 mm	**Engine Weight**	38.1 t
Tractive Effort	80.7 kPa	**Tender Weight**	22.9 t
Maximum Speed	40 km/h	**Axle Load**	135 kN
Builder	Beyer, Peacock	**Gauge**	1435 mm
Introduced	1877	**Number Built**	77

These locomotives were an improved version of the Stephenson long-boiler goods engine, with a higher boiler pressure and slightly more robust frame construction. In 1889 this type qualified as class 'A' by having more than 70 class members, making it the most numerous type in the state. These locomotives were rebuilt by William Thow with equalised suspension and higher pitched boilers, later with Belpaire fireboxes to suit them for service on lighter branch lines, particularly in mountainous areas. They also were used as shunting locomotives in larger yards, including Darling Harbour. The first locomotive to cross the Sydney Harbour Bridge, 1905, is preserved at Thirlmere, and 1919 was restored to working order by the Glenreagh-Dorrigo Steam Railway.

Y 108, at North Williamstown in 2002, had the same front-end changes and has the same livery as Y 112. (Peter Clark)

Y Class 112

Type	Freight	**Wheel Arrangement**	C
Boiler Pressure	965 kPa	**Cylinders**	457 x 660 mm
Grate Area	1.95 m²	**Length**	15.1 m
Heating Surface	106.9 m²	**Width**	
Valve Gear	Stephenson	**Height**	3.90 m
Driving Wheels	1370 mm	**Engine Weight**	38.9 t
Tractive Effort	77.6 kN	**Tender Weight**	30.4 t
Maximum Speed		**Axle Load**	143 kN
Builder	Phoenix	**Gauge**	1600 mm
Introduced	1888	**Number Built**	31

The Y class was the main line freight locomotive of the four Speight standard locomotive types, which were based on contemporary British practice. As larger locomotives were obtained, they were used on secondary duties until in the 1930s they were mainly used for shunting. With the adoption of knuckle couplers, the surviving locomotives were lengthened by about 450 mm to allow the fitting of a draft gear forward of the inside cylinder casting, which resulted in a long front overhang. Y112 had been used at Ballarat as a shunter, and was displayed there during the 1970s. It is now leased to Steamrail and based at Ballarat and used for excursion trains.

G 233 was extensively used on the Leschenault Lady tourist trains, as here in 1975. (Peter Clark)

G Class 233

Type	Freight	**Wheel Arrangement**	1'C
Boiler Pressure	1103 kPa	**Cylinders**	368 x 508 mm
Grate Area	1.27 m²	**Length**	12.34 m
Heating Surface	72.5 m²	**Width**	2.13 m
Valve Gear	Stephenson	**Height**	3.5 m
Driving Wheels	990 mm	**Engine Weight**	25.6 t
Tractive Effort	61.3 kN	**Tender Weight**	17.2 t
Maximum Speed		**Axle Load**	76 kN
Builder	James Martin	**Gauge**	1067 mm
Introduced	1889	**Number Built**	49

This was a standard Beyer, Peacock design, although the first WAGR locomotives were from Dubs and this locomotive was built by James Martin in South Australia. The G class were used as main line locomotives initially but later were used for branch line and shunting duties. Later G class locomotives had a leading bogie rather than a leading truck. G 233 was used on the Leschenault Lady tourist trains from Bunbury in the 1970s and is now with the Golden Mile Loopline Railway, Boulder.

C 22 represents the original condition of the class at Glenorchy in April 1996. (John Beckhaus)

C Class 22

Type	Freight	**Wheel Arrangement**	1'C	
Boiler Pressure	1000 kPa	**Cylinders**	368 x 508 mm	
Grate Area	1.27 m²	**Length**	12.34 m	
Heating Surface	72.5 m²	**Width**	2.13 m	
Valve Gear	Stephenson	**Height**	3.5 m	
Driving Wheels	990 mm	**Engine Weight**	25.6 t	
Tractive Effort	61.3 kN	**Tender Weight**	17.2 t	
Maximum Speed		**Axle Load**	76 kN	
Builder	Beyer, Peacock	**Gauge**	1067 mm	
Introduced	1885 – 1902	**Number Built**	28	

The Tasmanian C class was a standard Beyer, Peacock design, also used as The SAR Y class and WAGR G class. The C class were the main line goods locomotives of their time, and continued in service in lesser roles until the end of steam. A number were fitted with a larger Belpaire firebox boiler and reclassified CC class. C 22 is in original condition, including the distinctive sloping smokebox front. It is preserved by the Tasmanian Transport Museum.

The CCS was the final development of this type, seen here at the Don River Railway in December 1998. (Peter Clark)

CCS class 23, 25

Type	Freight	**Wheel Arrangement**	1'C	
Boiler Pressure	1206 kPa	**Cylinders**	381 x 508 mm	
Grate Area	1.27 m²	**Length**	12.34 m	
Heating Surface		**Width**	2.13 m	
Valve Gear	Walschaerts	**Height**	3.5 m	
Driving Wheels	990 mm	**Engine Weight**	38.8 t	
Tractive Effort	76.4 kN	**Tender Weight**	17.2 t	
Maximum Speed		**Axle Load**	76 kN	
Builder	Launceston	**Gauge**	1067 mm	
Introduced	1924	**Number Built**	4	

The CCS was the final development of the C type, taken a stage further than the other Australian operators. Starting with the larger diameter Belpaire firebox boiler used on the CC class, this was modified with a superheater. The cylinders were increased in diameter, and fitted with piston valves driven by outside Walschaerts valve gear. Unusually for Tasmania, the CCS retained their numbers in the C class series. The two survivors, 23 and 25, are preserved by the Don River Railway.

2705 is in frequent use at Thirlmere, as seen here in July 2005. (Peter Clark)

2705

Type	Freight	**Wheel Arrangement**	1'C
Boiler Pressure	1030 kPa	**Cylinders**	457 × 610 mm
Grate Area	2.0 m²	**Length**	16.58 m
Heating Surface	120.6 m²	**Width**	
Valve Gear	Walschaerts	**Height**	
Driving Wheels	1232 mm	**Engine Weight**	45.8 t
Tractive Effort	85.6 kN	**Tender Weight**	45.1 t
Maximum Speed	50km/h	**Axle Load**	127 kN
Builder	Hunslet	**Gauge**	1435 mm
Introduced	1913	**Number Built**	8

In the years leading up to World War I, the Public Works Department was responsible for construction of new railway lines in NSW and they had a fleet of older locomotives handed down from the government railways, as well as a number of locomotives obtained new for the task. The largest new locomotives were this Mogul type built in 1913 by the Hunslet engine company. The PWD fleet returned to railway control in 1917 and these locomotives became the G class. They were regarded as too useful to be kept on construction work, but their long coupled wheelbase made them unsuitable for use on many branch lines where sharp curves were common. They were sent to Narrabri West for use on the relatively straight branch lines in the north-west of the state, where they remained until replaced by diesel locomotives. 2705 was retained for use with the Vintage Train, and has passed to the Rail Transport Museum where it is often used on services to Buxton on the loop line.

AN AUSTRALIAN LOCOMOTIVE GUIDE

Locomotive 14A at the head of a train at Belgrave. (Peter Clark)

^{N}A Class 3, 6, 7, 8, 12, 14

Type	Mixed Traffic	**Wheel Arrangement**	1'C1't
Boiler Pressure	1240 kPa	**Cylinders**	330 x 457 mm
Grate Area	0.84 m²	**Length**	9.37 m
Heating Surface	48.7 m²	**Width**	
Valve Gear	Stephenson	**Height**	3.302 m
Driving Wheels	914 mm	**Weight**	37 t
Tractive Effort	54.1 kN	**Axle Load**	93 kN
Maximum Speed	35km/h	**Gauge**	762 mm
Builder	Baldwin, Newport	**Number Built**	17
Introduced	1898		

Late in the nineteenth century, the Victorian government constructed narrow-gauge railways as a means of reducing costs of both building and operation. Two small tank locomotives to a standard design were imported from Baldwin in Philadelphia, USA. One was a Vauclain compound and the other a conventional simple locomotive. Two more were constructed at Newport from spares, again including another compound. Eventually, a total of 17 were obtained, and these were little changed during their service lives, although the compounds were rebuilt as simple locomotives and the side water tanks were enlarged. Although the narrow-gauge lines were closed from the early 1950s, the Gembrook line to the east of Melbourne was preserved under the local name of 'Puffing Billy' and is a great success as a tourist attraction. While three ^{N}A class were retained in service for the Gembrook line, others were restored to service from storage or static preservation.

An F class is seen shunting at Mile End Depot in August 1967. (Peter Clark)

F Class 251

Type	Suburban	**Wheel Arrangement**	2'C1't
Boiler Pressure	1275 kPa	**Cylinders**	445 x 610 mm
Grate Area	1.67 m²	**Length**	12.38 m
Heating Surface	123.9 m²	**Width**	
Valve Gear	Stephenson	**Height**	4.04 m
Driving Wheels	1600 mm	**Weight**	60 t
Tractive Effort	81.5 kN	**Axle Load**	123 kN
Maximum Speed		**Gauge**	1600 mm
Builder	Islington	**Number Built**	43
Introduced	1902		

The F class was the first of the large six-coupled suburban passenger tank locomotives, and since Adelaide did not electrify its suburban system in the 1920s, they were among the last performing their intended duties, being replaced by diesel railcars in the 1950s and 1960s. The 1600 mm driving wheels were large for this duty, but they proved to have good acceleration, even between closely spaced stations. They ended up on shunting work during the 1960s, and a number were statically preserved, including 245 and 255. F 251 was originally preserved at Elizabeth West, but was restored to service by SteamRanger, who operated it on their line to Victor Harbour.

Locomotive 855 in storage at Ipswich Workshops in January 1972. (Peter Clark)

D17 Class 268

Type	Suburban Tank	**Wheel Arrangement**	2′C2′t
Boiler Pressure	1134 kPa	**Cylinders**	432 × 610 mm
Grate Area	1.54 m²	**Length**	11.35 m
Heating Surface	77.4/13.5 m²	**Width**	2.43 m
Valve Gear	Walschaerts	**Height**	3.66 m
Driving Wheels	1295 mm	**Weight**	63 t
Tractive Effort	80.0 kN	**Axle Load**	118 kN
Maximum Speed	80 km/h	**Gauge**	1067 mm
Builder	Ipswich	**Number Built**	
Introduced	1924		

The D17 was a superheated devel-opment of the 6D16 class suburban tank, slightly larger and heavier but generally similar in layout. They were used mainly on the North-side system but appeared on the lines from South Brisbane as well. These were very powerful and quick accelerating locomotives but they were worked very hard and required a lot of maintenance. They were withdrawn from the 1960s. No. 268 is preserved at Ravenshoe.

D^D 592 at Forrestfield in 1998. (Peter Clark)

D^D Class 592

Type	Suburban Tank	**Wheel Arrangement**	2'C2't
Boiler Pressure	1103 kPa	**Cylinders**	457 × 584 mm
Grate Area	1.73 m²	**Length**	13.74 m
Heating Surface	90.2/16.2 m²	**Width**	2.66 m
Valve Gear	Walschaerts	**Height**	3.76 m
Driving Wheels	1372 mm	**Weight**	73.8 t
Tractive Effort	83.5 kN	**Axle Load**	129 kN
Maximum Speed		**Gauge**	1067 mm
Builder	Midland	**Number Built**	10
Introduced	1946		

Two new classes of suburban passenger tank locomotive were built by the WAGR at Midland Junction from 1944, to meet increased demand due to wartime conditions. Ten locomotives were rebuilt from Es class Pacific locomotives, renumbered as 581 to 590, and 10 completely new locomotives, 591 to 600, were built, incorporating all of the then CME, Mr F. Mills' ideas including cylinders with external exhaust steam passages and Y-shaped spokes to the driving wheels and spring side control on the bogies. They were also used on suburban freight trains and as bank engines on the old narrow-gauge line east from Midland Junction. 592 was retained by the ARHS and worked special trains between 1985 and 1995.

AN AUSTRALIAN LOCOMOTIVE GUIDE

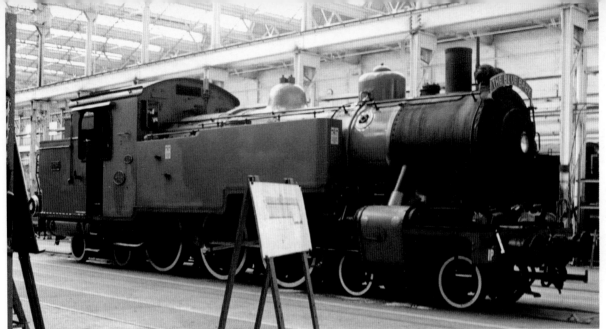

Locomotive 1051 at Ipswich Workshops in September 2002. (Peter Clark)

DD17 Class 1046, 1047, 1049, 1051

Type	Suburban Tank	**Wheel Arrangement**	2'C2't
Boiler Pressure	1200 kPa	**Cylinders**	432 × 610 mm
Grate Area	1.72 m²	**Length**	12.07 m
Heating Surface	84.9/13.9 m²	**Width**	2.40 m
Valve Gear	Walschaerts	**Height**	3.69 m
Driving Wheels	1295 mm	**Weight**	63 t
Tractive Effort	92.5 kN	**Axle Load**	121 kN
Maximum Speed		**Gauge**	1067 mm
Builder	Ipswich	**Number Built**	12
Introduced	1949		

The DD17 class were the last new design of suburban passenger tank locomotive in Australia, and were an enlargement of the 1924 D17 class. Some modern ideas from the Lend Lease AC16 class were incorporated. They were very modern in appearance and were painted blue, a change from the usual black. The blue was later changed to a lighter shade, matching that of the diesel locomotives. They were confined to the North-side system, working primarily between Mayne Junction and Ipswich. They worked mainly the Evans sets of wooden side-door cars and later the stainless steel sets intended for conversion to electric operation. They worked until the late 1960s. 1046, 1047 and 1049 are at Zig Zag, and 1051 is at Ipswich.

Locomotive 3112 at Thirlmere in July 2005. (Peter Clark)

3112

Type	Suburban Tank	**Wheel Arrangement**	2′C2′t	
Boiler Pressure	1100 kPa	**Cylinders**	483 × 610 mm	
Grate Area	2.2 m²	**Length**	12.4 m	
Heating Surface	135 m²	**Width**		
Valve Gear	Allan	**Height**		
Driving Wheels	1397 mm	**Weight**	73 t	
Tractive Effort	90.3 kN	**Axle Load**	147 kN	
Maximum Speed	80 km/h	**Gauge**	1435 mm	
Builder	Beyer, Peacock, NSWGR			
Introduced	1903	**Number Built**	145	

The last and largest tank locomotive designed for Sydney suburban trains was the S class, introduced in 1903 and sharing some similarities with the passenger and goods locomotives also from Beyer, Peacock. These became the 30 class in the 1924 renumbering but shortly afterwards were progressively superseded by the introduction of overhead electrification of the Sydney suburban network. They continued to operate in outer Sydney suburban services and in the Newcastle suburban network and became available for shunting and carriage transfer around Sydney Terminal. From 1928, about half the class was converted to branch line tender locomotives, and these are described separately. A number are preserved, of which 3112, now based in Canberra, is best known from operation on Heritage trains.

G Class 123

Type	Passenger	**Wheel Arrangement**	2′C
Boiler Pressure	1103 kPa	**Cylinders**	368 x 508 mm
Grate Area	1.27 m²	**Length**	12.34 m
Heating Surface	72.5 m²	**Width**	2.13 m
Valve Gear	Stephenson	**Height**	3.5 m
Driving Wheels	990 mm	**Engine Weight**	25.6 t
Tractive Effort	61.3 kN	**Tender Weight**	17.2 t
Maximum Speed		**Axle Load**	76 kN
Builder	Dübs	**Gauge**	1067 mm
Introduced	1894	**Number Built**	24

The WAGR had obtained a number of Mogul type locomotives built to a design originated by Beyer, Peacock. A similar design, but with a leading bogie, was obtained in order to improve the riding and to allow a higher speed for passenger service. For some reason the same class letter was used for both wheel arrangements, which has led to some confusion over the years. Thirteen were lent for use on the North Australia Railway during World War II. The G class remained in use on branch lines and secondary tasks until the end of steam. G123 was used on the Leschenault Lady tourist trains from Bunbury in the 1970s and is now with the Hotham Valley Railway.

The first QR locomotive built by Walkers Limited, 299 was on display at Maryborough station in December 2006. (Peter Clark)

B15 Class 299

Type	Passenger	**Wheel Arrangement**	2′C
Boiler Pressure	1060 kPa	**Cylinders**	381 x 508 mm
Grate Area	1.19 m²	**Length**	13.89 m
Heating Surface	60 m²	**Width**	2.36
Valve Gear	Stephenson	**Height**	3.63 m
Driving Wheels	1143 mm	**Engine Weight**	32.1 t
Tractive Effort	57 kN	**Tender Weight**	24.1 t
Maximum Speed		**Axle Load**	78 kN
Builder	Nasmyth, Walkers	**Gauge**	1067 mm
Introduced	1889	**Number Built**	98

The B15 was introduced as a main line freight locomotive, and after the introduction of the Passenger B15 in 1899 became known as the B15 Goods. With the introduction of the C16 class in 1903, the B15s were being used for more secondary tasks and the driving wheel size was increased from 914 mm to 1143 mm making them closer to the PB15 in capacity. This type became known as the B15 Converted. All but five locomotives were modified. As modified, the locomotives were used for passenger, freight and mixed trains, mainly on branch lines on the Northern and Central Railways. They were withdrawn by the late 1960s, and 299 was restored to working order by Walkers as their first QR locomotive carrying their builder's number 1. No. 290 is also retained by the Ipswich Workshops Museum.

Painted in a colour associated with the larger C17 class, 454 is seen at Belmont Common in 1978. (Peter Clark)

PB15 Class 448, 454

Type	Passenger	**Wheel Arrangement**	2′C
Boiler Pressure	1060 kPa	**Cylinders**	381 x 508 mm
Grate Area	1.23 m²	**Length**	14.47 m
Heating Surface	81 m²	**Width**	2.36 m
Valve Gear	Stephenson	**Height**	3.66 m
Driving Wheels	1219 mm	**Engine Weight**	34.5 t
Tractive Effort	53 kN	**Tender Weight**	24.6 t
Maximum Speed		**Axle Load**	79 kN
Builder	Ipswich, Walkers	**Gauge**	1067 mm
Introduced	1900	**Number Built**	203

The Passenger B15 was an enlargement of the earlier B15, having a longer boiler as well as larger driving wheels, but the general design was similar. The PB15 was relatively soon superseded on main line services but continued on secondary and branch line services up until the end of steam operation. It was said that there were hardly any lines in the state that hadn't seen a PB15 at some stage (with some notable exceptions, of course). They were particularly associated with the South Brisbane to Southport Line. A number have been preserved, 448 by the Queensland Pioneer Steam Railway and 454 by the Bellarine Peninsula Railway. 444 is displayed at Ipswich.

No. 732 in storage at Ipswich Workshops in January 1972. (Peter Clark)

PB15 Class 732, 738

Type	Passenger	**Wheel Arrangement**	2'C	
Boiler Pressure	1060 kPa	**Cylinders**	381 x 508 mm	
Grate Area	1.23 m²	**Length**	14.47 m	
Heating Surface	81 m²	**Width**	2.21 m	
Valve Gear	Walschaerts	**Height**	3.66 m	
Driving Wheels	1219 mm	**Engine Weight**	34.5 t	
Tractive Effort	53 kN	**Tender Weight**	24.6 t	
Maximum Speed		**Axle Load**	80 kN	
Builder	Walkers	**Gauge**	1067 mm	
Introduced	1925	**Number Built**	30	

The PB15 was regarded as so successful that a further batch of 30 was requested during the early 1920s. It was considered that a modernised version with outside Walschaerts valve gear in line with other current locomotives should be built. This was known as the PB15 1924 after the year the design was completed. These were often used on the Southport line, where the more modern valve gear did allow fast running. They all had standard boilers without superheaters and lacked piston valves, which would have allowed even better performance. 732 is preserved at Ipswich and 738 on the Rosewood Railway.

Rx 201 preserved in Tailem Bend in 1994. (Peter Clark)

Rx Class 207, 224

Type	Passenger	**Wheel Arrangement**	2′C
Boiler Pressure	1200 kPa	**Cylinders**	457 x 610 mm
Grate Area	1.88 m²	**Length**	17.67 m
Heating Surface	122/16.5 m²	**Width**	2.43 m
Valve Gear	Stephenson	**Height**	4.05 m
Driving Wheels	1370 mm	**Engine Weight**	
Tractive Effort	95 kN	**Tender Weight**	
Maximum Speed		**Axle Load**	113 kN
Builder	Islington	**Gauge**	1600 mm
Introduced	1899	**Number Built**	84

William Thow introduced the R class, built by Dubs in Glasgow, in 1886 for passenger trains on the Adelaide Hills line. By 1895 a larger boiler was developed and the rebuilt locomotives were given the class Rx. By 1909, additional Rx class were built new in Islington and later by North British. Superheating was applied after some delay. These locomotives were used on major passenger services including the *Overland* until the arrival of Webb's modern locomotives in 1926. They continued in service on secondary duties until the 1960s. A number are preserved, but Rx 207 and Rx 224 were operated by the SteamRanger Tourist Railway on their line to Victor Harbor.

D³ Class 639

Type	Passenger	**Wheel Arrangement**	2′C
Boiler Pressure	1.2 MPa	**Cylinders**	483 × 660 mm
Grate Area	2.3 m²	**Length**	17.76 m
Heating Surface	127.2/21.2 m²	**Width**	
Valve Gear	Stephenson	**Height**	4.14 m
Driving Wheels	1549 mm	**Engine Weight**	58.2 t
Tractive Effort	101 kN	**Tender Weight**	42.9 t
Maximum Speed	96 km/h	**Axle Load**	136 kN
Builder	Newport	**Gauge**	1600 mm
Introduced	1929	**Number Built**	94

The D³ was a development of the Victorian D^D class, using a larger boiler which was a slightly shorter version of the successful K class boiler. This gave a significant improvement in the locomotive's capacity, and provided improved services on light lines where the small turntables restricted the use of the more recent N class locomotives. Conversions continued through World War II until designs were complete for the J class, which could perform similar duties. The larger boiler gave a more modern appearance, but the D³ class were never fitted with the modified draughting arrangements applied to the A2 class and later designs. The locomotives were at first numbered in the high 600 series, and later units had lower numbers, the last conversion being numbered 606. At the end of steam operation, D³ class were used as yard shunters in major rural centres. D³ 639 was allocated to haul the commissioner's inspection train and when it required replacement D³ 658 was substituted, taking the number of that locomotive. That locomotive has been preserved in working order but a number of others are kept as static mementos of the steam era.

3016

Type	Branch Line	**Wheel Arrangement**	2′C
Boiler Pressure	1100 kPa	**Cylinders**	483 × 610 mm
Grate Area	2.2 m²	**Length**	17.57 m
Heating Surface	103.3/25.8 m²	**Width**	
Valve Gear	Allan	**Height**	
Driving Wheels	1397 mm	**Engine Weight**	56.1 t
Tractive Effort	95.3 kN	**Tender Weight**	45.1 t
Maximum Speed	80 km/h	**Axle Load**	147 kN
Rebuilder	Clyde, NSWGR	**Gauge**	1435 mm
Introduced	1928	**Number Built**	77

With the electrification of the Sydney suburban system rendering many of the 30 class tank locomotives surplus to requirements, the opportunity was taken to convert them to branch line tender locomotives by removal of the side tanks, bunker and trailing truck. The conversion was very basic, retaining as much of the original as they could, which included the upper cab sides and the sand boxes, originally fitted to the side tanks. Tenders were obtained from

obsolete locomotives being withdrawn, although a number of six-wheel 32 class tenders that had been replaced by larger bogie tenders were used on the rebuilt tank locomotives. One problem was the classification. Before the 1924 renumbering, such a modification would have been indicated by a suffix letter, while under the current system a new numerical class was required. The next available number was from 3701, but in the event a suffix letter 'T' was added clumsily to the numerical class, becoming 'C30T'. Despite the unsatisfactory numbering, these became excellent branch line locomotives and were seen all over the state. In 1940, No. 3100 was rebuilt with a superheater and new piston valves in place of the flat valves. This increased the power to almost that of the larger 32 class and made the C30T even more useful. Many were superheated during World War II and afterwards until half the class were so fitted. 3016, based in Canberra, is a superheated locomotive and 3102, currently out of service, retains its original saturated type of boiler.

3265 in Junee on 8 March 2014 while operating a heritage train service. (Peter Clark)

3237, 3265

Type	Passenger	**Wheel Arrangement**	2′C
Boiler Pressure	1 100 kPa	**Cylinders**	533 × 660 mm
Grate Area	2.5 m²	**Length**	18.39 m
Heating Surface	137.9/39.9 m²	**Width**	
Valve Gear	Allan	**Height**	
Driving Wheels	1524 mm	**Engine Weight**	59.6 t
Tractive Effort	115.6 kN	**Tender Weight**	42.1 t
Maximum Speed	100 km/h	**Axle Load**	145 kN
Builder	Beyer, Peacock, Clyde	**Gauge**	1435 mm
Introduced	1891	**Number Built**	191

These P class were very large passenger locomotives for the period, but with relatively small driving wheels for the steeply graded main lines in NSW at that time. They were equipped with Richardson balanced slide valves which improved efficiency. The first 50 locomotives had six-wheeled tenders but later locomotives had larger bogie tenders. After 190 locomotives had been built both in Britain and in Australia, a single prototype superheated locomotive, P 937, was built by Beyer, Peacock in 1911. The superheater turned a good locomotive into an outstanding one but the superheater required piston valves, so only a few were fitted, since new valve and cylinder castings were required. In 1924 they were renumbered as the 32 class. It wasn't until 1929 that the majority of the class were superheated as the cylinders fell due for replacement. It was at this time that the class was selected to power lightweight express passenger trains since they were more reliable than later designs. They continued in secondary passenger service until the end of steam passenger trains in NSW.

AN AUSTRALIAN LOCOMOTIVE GUIDE

3526

Type	Passenger	**Wheel Arrangement**	2'C
Boiler Pressure	1240 kPa	**Cylinders**	572 × 660 mm
Grate Area	2.83 m²	**Length**	19.2 m
Heating Surface	207.6/50.8 m²	**Width**	
Valve Gear	Stephenson	**Height**	
Driving Wheels	1752 mm	**Engine Weight**	82.8 t
Tractive Effort	130 kN	**Tender Weight**	47.3 t
Maximum Speed	115 km/h	**Axle Load**	206 kN
Builder	Eveleigh	**Gauge**	1435 mm
Introduced	1914	**Number Built**	35

The NN class were an enlargement of Thow's N class which was in turn an enlarged P class. E.E. Lucy introduced a tapered boiler based on those on the GWR in England, from where he had been recruited. The cab design also reflected practice at Swindon. In 1924 they were renumbered as the 35 class.

While they were substantially more powerful than the P class they were not really successful locomotives. The boiler did not reach expectations and the plate frames were not sufficiently rigid. The latter problem was addressed by the fitting of thicker frames from 1937 and the footplate was lowered to act as a stiffener, particularly at the rear. This also allowed easier access to the inside Stephenson valve gear from above. At the same time a new more enclosed cab was fitted. The 35 class were concentrated on the Northern and North Coast lines and ended up working between Gosford and Newcastle after electrification to Gosford. After World War II, the 35 class were to be rebuilt with a standard Belpaire boiler fitted to the 36 class, but although the boilers were built, no 35 class were fitted. Only 3526 was retained for preservation.

3642

Type	Passenger	**Wheel Arrangement**	2′C
Boiler Pressure	1380 kPa	**Cylinders**	584×660 mm
Grate Area	2.83 m²	**Length**	20.7 m
Heating Surface	186/60.4 m²	**Width**	
Valve Gear	Walschaerts	**Height**	
Driving Wheels	1752 mm	**Engine Weight**	87.6 t
Tractive Effort	151 kN	**Tender Weight**	74.9 t
Maximum Speed	115 km/h	**Axle Load**	209 kN
Builder	Clyde, Eveleigh	**Gauge**	1435 mm
Introduced	1925	**Number Built**	75

An outstanding order existed for 25 NN class locomotives, 1324 to 1348, to be built by Eveleigh workshops. Locomotive design had moved on and E.E. Lucy adopted Walschaerts valve gear and a new boiler design based on American ideas. The appearance of the locomotive was influenced by Forster, who had spent some time in Germany prior to World War I. Designated the NN2 class, the locomotives emerged after the 1924 renumbering as the C36 class. Eveleigh were to build the first 25 and Clyde Engineering another 35. Owing to delays Eveleigh only built 10, with 3611 to 3625 being built by Clyde. Clyde also gained an additional order for a further 15 locomotives. The firebox design with a copper inner firebox and radial staying proved unsatisfactory. By 1931, only 12 of the 75 were 'counted working' and only in 1934 when new direct stayed steel fireboxes were fitted did the 36 class fulfil its potential. However, they were then used on all the heaviest passenger duties and remained the mainstay of NSW passenger services until the withdrawal of steam. In the early 1950s, a new Belpaire boiler was fitted to all but two locomotives. One loco, 3616, was fitted with the Austrian Giesl ejector exhaust system with some increase in power. 3609, 3616 and 3642 are preserved.

4079

Type	Passenger	**Wheel Arrangement**	2′C
Boiler Pressure	1956 kPa	**Cylinders**	406 x 660 mm
Grate Area	2.81 m²	**Length**	20 m
Heating Surface	190/24.4 m²	**Width**	2.59 m
Valve Gear	Walschaerts	**Height**	4.04 m
Driving Wheels	2045 mm	**Engine Weight**	81.1 t
Tractive Effort	140 kN	**Tender Weight**	47.5 t
Maximum Speed	160 km/h	**Axle Load**	181 kN
Builder	Swindon	**Gauge**	1435 mm
Introduced	1923	**Number Built**	179

This Castle class was the first passenger design of C.B. Collett, the successor to G.B. Churchward and was an improvement on the existing Star class. This locomotive 'Pendennis Castle' was lent to the London and North Eastern Railway for demonstration purposes, where it proved capable of the heaviest duties on that line. It remained in service until the end of steam operation and in 1977 it was brought to Australia for operation out of Dampier in Western Australia on excursions on the Hamersley Iron railway. In 1989 it was transferred to Perth where it operated with *Flying Scotsman* on excursion trains. Sadly, changes to the signalling and the reduction of a local workforce meant that the locomotive fell into disuse in Dampier. In 1999, the locomotive was returned to England, where it is being restored at the Didcot Railway Centre.

Pmr 729, preserved at Coolgardie in August 2007. (Peter Clark)

Pmr Class 706, 721

Type	Passenger	**Wheel Arrangement**	2'C1'
Boiler Pressure	1206 kPa	**Cylinders**	483 x 660 mm
Grate Area	3.25 m²	**Length**	19.39 m
Heating Surface	139.8/33 m²	**Width**	2.69 m
Valve Gear	Walschaerts	**Height**	3.81 m
Driving Wheels	1370 mm	**Engine Weight**	64.3 t
Tractive Effort	115 kN	**Tender Weight**	44.5 t
Maximum Speed		**Axle Load**	138 kN
Builder	North British	**Gauge**	1067 mm
Introduced	1949	**Number Built**	35

In 1924, the WAGR introduced the P class Pacific type, built by North British, which was typical of British colonial designs of the period. WAGR later built a group of similar class Pr at Midland workshops with higher pressure boilers. Following World War II, an order was placed with North British for 35 similar locomotives. Unfortunately, many of the features that had made the P class a success were not included. Critically the equalising of the suspension of the coupled wheels, and the pivoted trailing truck, also equalised, was replaced by the less effective Cartazzi axle, which moved in angled axle guides. The new Pm class, or Pmr for 16 fitted with roller bearings, proved to be less well adapted to the track conditions and was soon confined to secondary or freight service rather than the faster passenger trains. They lasted until the end of the steam era. As well as the two preserved in working order, P508, Pr521 and Pm 701 are preserved at Bassendean, and three others are statically preserved in rural WA.

AN AUSTRALIAN LOCOMOTIVE GUIDE

No. 1072 at Zig Zag in 1990. (Peter Clark)

BB18¼ 1072, 1079, 1089

Type	Passenger	**Wheel Arrangement**	2′C1′
Boiler Pressure	1200 kPa	**Cylinders**	464 × 610 mm
Grate Area	2.3 m²	**Length**	18.34 m
Heating Surface	141/31 m²	**Width**	2.56 m
Valve Gear	Walschaerts	**Height**	3.81 m
Driving Wheels	1293 mm	**Engine Weight**	58.9 t
Tractive Effort	100.7 kN	**Tender Weight**	43.9 t
Maximum Speed		**Axle Load**	120 kN
Builder	Vulcan Foundry, Walkers	**Gauge**	1067 mm
Introduced	1950	**Number Built**	55

Following the connection of the individual railways with the North Coast line through to Cairns, it was realised that a more modern and capable passenger locomotive was required. In 1926, the first of 23 B18¼ class locomotives were built. In 1930 a revised version with an enlarged cab with glazed side windows was introduced, of which 60 were built. A further modernised version, fitted with roller bearings and with long travel valve gear was introduced in 1951, with 35 locomotives built by Vulcan Foundry in England. These proved to be more capable than the earlier locomotives, and were identified as the BB18¼ class. A further order for 20 locomotives was built by Walkers between 1955 and 1958. The last of these, 1089, was the last new steam locomotive built for the QR. A number are preserved, 771 being the last B18¼ at Ipswich. However, 1072 is operated by the Zig Zag Railway, and 1079 and 1089 are operated by the Ipswich Workshops.

M4 at East Tamar in April 1996. Note the distinctive SCOA-P wheels. (John Beckhaus)

M Class 4, 5, 6

Type	Passenger	**Wheel Arrangement**	2′C1′
Boiler Pressure	1240 kPa	**Cylinders**	406 x 610 mm
Grate Area	2.15 m²	**Length**	18.05 m
Heating Surface	102.9/24.6 m²	**Width**	
Valve Gear	Walschaerts	**Height**	
Driving Wheels	1397 mm	**Engine Weight**	55.1 t
Tractive Effort	76 kN	**Tender Weight**	43.1 t
Maximum Speed		**Axle Load**	105 kN
Builder	Stephenson	**Gauge**	1067 mm
Introduced	1952	**Number Built**	10

The M class were obtained after World War II to modernise the TGR fleet. To expedite construction, the M class were built to a pre-war standard Indian metre-gauge design, the YB type, although modified to take advantage of the larger Tasmanian loading gauge. The driving wheels are the distinctive SCOA-P type with U-shaped spokes. However, the earlier arrival of the X class diesel locomotives, small as they were, meant that the M class were obsolete on arrival and were never used to their full potential. They continued in use to the end of steam operation in freight and secondary passenger duties. M4 is preserved at the Don River Railway, M5 is at the Tasmanian Transport Museum and M6 at the Bellarine Peninsula Railway.

MA2 at East Tamar in April 1996. Note the distinctive Y-spoke wheels. (John Beckhaus)

MA Class 2

Type	Freight	**Wheel Arrangement**	2′C1′	
Boiler Pressure	1240 kPa	**Cylinders**	406 x 610 mm	
Grate Area	2.15 m²	**Length**	18.05 m	
Heating Surface	102.9/24.6 m²	**Width**		
Valve Gear	Walschaerts	**Height**		
Driving Wheels	1219 mm	**Engine Weight**	55.1 t	
Tractive Effort	87 kN	**Tender Weight**	43.1 t	
Maximum Speed		**Axle Load**	105 kN	
Builder	Launceston	**Gauge**	1067 mm	
Introduced	1957	**Number Built**	4	

As indicated under the M class description, following the introduction of the X class diesel locomotives, the M class were primarily used on freight working. To improve their performance in this role, they were modified using coupled wheel sets from withdrawn Australian Standard Garratt locomotives which were smaller in diameter but shared the same piston stroke. This resulted in a higher nominal tractive effort which improved their performance on freight trains. Because all Tasmanian classes were numbered from 1, a complex renumbering involving both converted and original M class locomotives followed. All four converted MA class are preserved, but MA 2 is operated by the Don River Railway.

621 in Mile End Locomotive Depot in April 1978. (Peter Clark)

621

Type	Passenger	**Wheel Arrangement**	2′C1′	
Boiler Pressure	1400 kPa	**Cylinders**	470 × 710 mm	
Grate Area	3.10 m²	**Length**	21.23 m	
Heating Surface	161.3/39.1	**Width**		
Valve Gear	Baker	**Height**		
Driving Wheels	1.676 m	**Engine Weight**		
Tractive Effort	110 kN	**Tender Weight**		
Maximum Speed		**Axle Load**	159 kN	
Builder	Islington	**Gauge**	1600 mm	
Introduced	1936	**Number Built**	10	

The 620 class was the first of the post-Webb locomotives, a modern design but suitable for use on lighter lines than the heavier American-style locomotives. The first was built in time to be displayed at the South Australian Centenary exhibition, and was streamlined with a chromium plated grille over the smokebox front, but later locomotives had a conventional appearance, although the smokebox front was still at an angle. They proved to be fast and efficient, but a little too small for many duties, and only the initial 10 were built. They were the first locomotives in Australia to use Baker valve gear, which allowed long valve travel that increased efficiency. They lasted until the 1960s, and two are preserved. No. 621 is operated by the SteamRanger Tourist Railway.

3801 climbing eastbound towards Cullerin in November 2006. (Peter Clark)

3801, 3830

Type	Passenger	**Wheel Arrangement**	2'C1'
Boiler Pressure	1.68 MPa	**Cylinders**	546 x 660 mm
Grate Area	4.4 m²	**Length**	23.28 m
Heating Surface	240.4/69.5 m²	**Width**	2.74 m
Valve Gear	Walschaerts	**Height**	4.09 m
Driving Wheels	1752 mm	**Weight**	198.3 t
Tractive Effort	161 kN	**Axle Load**	227 kN
Maximum Speed	115 km/h	**Gauge**	1435 mm
Builder	Clyde, NSWGR	**Number Built**	30
Introduced	1942		

The 38 class resulted from lobbying by Ray Purves of Clyde Engineering for an order for additional locomotives to maintain workload during the economic depression. Five 36 class were considered but Harold Young decided that a more modern design should be built. The new design drew very heavily on US practices. Much of the locomotives' frames and running gear were designed and built in the USA, including cast one-piece locomotive beds including the cylinders, the coupled and trailing wheels and even the roller bearings were imported from Sweden.

The planned delivery of the locomotives in 1939 was not met due to delays in obtaining overseas components, and the introduction of wartime restrictions further delayed the completion of the first locomotive until December 1942. To meet wartime traffic, 25 further locomotives were ordered and the cast frames for these arrived in 1943. The first of the additional batch, built in railway workshops to avoid wartime controls, emerged in 1946. Even-numbered locomotives were built at Eveleigh and odd-numbered locomotives at Cardiff.

Locomotives entered service in grey until 1946, when a verdant green livery was adopted. Locomotives were painted black with red lining from 1955.

3801 is retained by the RTM and 3830 by the Powerhouse Museum.

R 707 stored at Newport Workshops in 1995. (Peter Clark)

R Class 707, 711, 761, 766

Type	Passenger	**Wheel Arrangement**	2'C2'
Boiler Pressure	1.45 MPa	**Cylinders**	546 × 711 mm
Grate Area	3.9 m²	**Length**	23.55 m
Heating Surface	208/42.9 m²	**Width**	
Valve Gear	Walschaerts	**Height**	4.26 m
Driving Wheels	1854 mm	**Engine Weight**	109.4 t
Tractive Effort	142.7 kN	**Tender Weight**	81.1 t
Maximum Speed		**Axle Load**	194 kN
Builder	North British	**Gauge**	1600/1435 mm
Introduced	1951	**Number Built**	70

The R class was designed as a replacement for the A2 class which was Victoria's most numerous main line type and responsible for most country passenger train services. The R class had bar frames, set at a spacing suitable for standard gauge, and roller bearings and long travel valve gear that resulted in an efficient and fast locomotive, but the arrival of main line diesel locomotives soon after their delivery meant that they were soon restricted to freight and secondary services. Seventy locomotives were built, but many were withdrawn after a relatively short time. Two were fitted for oil firing and one was equipped to burn pulverised brown coal but it was soon restored to conventional coal burning.

Two locomotives were modernised by the private West Coast Railway, and were used on some regular trains as well as excursions. These have since been restored to more or less standard condition but R766 has since been converted to standard gauge although to date hasn't operated in its modified condition.

No. 8 standing in the Don Valley depot in November 1988. (Peter Clark)

EBR 8

Type	Mixed Traffic	Wheel Arrangement	2'D	
Boiler Pressure	1205 kPa	Cylinders	432 x 558 mm	
Grate Area	1.48 m²	Length	16.0 m	
Heating Surface		Width		
Valve Gear	Stephenson	Height	3.73 m	
Driving Wheels	1143 mm	Engine Weight		
Tractive Effort	97.4 kN	Tender Weight		
Maximum Speed		Axle Load	88 kN	
Builder	Dübs	Gauge	1067 mm	
Introduced	1900	Number Built	4	

These Dübs locomotives were the heaviest power on the Emu Bay Railway for 30 years until the introduction of the Beyer Garratt locomotives in 1930. They were remarkably similar in dimensions to the later SAR T class locomotives. They continued in service until the end of steam, and two, numbers 6 and 8, were modernised with smoke deflectors and converted to oil burning to operate the West Coaster tourist train in 1960. Both 6 and 8 were preserved and the latter was restored by the Don River Railway in time for the EBR centenary in 1997.

T251 operating at Belmont Common in 1978. (Peter Clark)

T Class 186, 251

Type	Freight	**Wheel Arrangement**	2'D	
Boiler Pressure	1275 kPa	**Cylinders**	419 x 558 mm	
Grate Area	1.60 m²	**Length**	16.43 m	
Heating Surface	97.3/10 m²	**Width**		
Valve Gear	Stephenson	**Height**	3.53 m	
Driving Wheels	1051 mm	**Engine Weight**		
Tractive Effort	97.4 kN	**Tender Weight**		
Maximum Speed		**Axle Load**	90 kN	
Builder	Islington	**Gauge**	1067 mm	
Introduced	1903	**Number Built**	78	

The T class was the heaviest freight locomotive on the SAR narrow gauge until the introduction of Garratt locomotives on the Broken Hill Port–Pirie line after World War II. Conceptually it was an enlargement of the successful Beyer, Peacock Mogul types including the SAR Y class. All were built in Australia, at Islington, James Martin and Walkers. Five were converted to broad gauge in 1923, and remained there until 1949 when they were rebuilt to narrow gauge. These were among the last in service. After the Commonwealth Railways took over the Alice Springs line, six were sold to Tasmania. They lasted in secondary duties until 1970, when the Broken Hill line was converted to standard gauge. T186 is operated by the Pichi Richi Railway and T251 by the Bellarine Peninsula Railway.

No. 965 at Gympie undergoing restoration in 2002. (Peter Clark)

C17 Class 45, 720, 802, 812, 934, 967, 971, 974, 1000 NM Class 25

Type	Freight	**Wheel Arrangement**	2'D
Boiler Pressure	1207 kPa	**Cylinders**	432 × 559 mm
Grate Area	1.72 m²	**Length**	16.29 m
Heating Surface	70.9/13.5 m²	**Width**	2.56 m
Valve Gear	Walschaerts	**Height**	3.81 m
Driving Wheels	1143 mm	**Engine Weight**	48.8 t
Tractive Effort	93.4 kN	**Tender Weight**	35.5 t
Maximum Speed		**Axle Load**	89 kN
Builder	Ipswich, Clyde, Walkers	**Gauge**	1067 mm
Introduced	1920	**Number Built**	227

The C16 class was introduced in 1903 and 157 were built up until 1918. These were used for freight traffic, but also for passenger trains on steeper grades. In 1920, a superheated version with larger diameter cylinders, the C17, was introduced. This was equally successful and 227 were built up until 1953. From 1938, a larger cab with glazed side windows was fitted. Some post World War II locomotives also had roller bearings. These C17s were used on secondary main lines for both freight and passenger service. They remained in service until the late 1960s. Even for a large class, many have been preserved and several are in operational condition. 45 and 802 and 967 are operated by the Mary Valley Heritage Railway. 720 is with the Rosewood Railway. 812 is at Atherton. 934 is at the Zig Zag Railway. 971 is at Warwick. 974 and 1000 are at Ipswich. The Commonwealth Railways also used this design, built by Thompsons in Victoria, on the narrow-gauge line from Port Augusta to Alice Springs. NM 25 and NM34 survive, the former operating on the Pichi Richi Railway.

K 153 shunting at Newport Workshops in March 2005. (Peter Clark)

K Class 153, 160, 163, 190

Type	Freight	**Wheel Arrangement**	1'D
Boiler Pressure	1207 kPa	**Cylinders**	508 x 660 mm
Grate Area	2.39 m²	**Length**	18.36 m
Heating Surface	133.9/22.1 m²	**Width**	
Valve Gear	Walschaerts	**Height**	4.25 m
Driving Wheels	1397 mm	**Engine Weight**	63.4 t
Tractive Effort	127 kN	**Tender Weight**	42.9 t
Maximum Speed		**Axle Load**	134 kN
Builder	Newport	**Gauge**	1600 mm
Introduced	1922	**Number Built**	53

The K class was the first modern locomotive built for the extensive network of lightly laid rural branch lines. As built, they had a typical British colonial appearance with the pressed steel Canadian-style cab. The boiler proved to be very successful, and the K class was regularly used on the steeply graded Cudgewa line as well as the many more easily graded lines in grain growing areas. Only 10 locomotives were built before the requirement for future locomotives to be convertible to standard gauge resulted in the development of the N class which replaced the K class in production. The K class received the boiler improvements applied to larger VR locomotives in the 1930s which changed the appearance significantly. In 1940 further K class locomotives were built to assist with the war effort. The 10 original locomotives were renumbered from 140 upward to align with the new locomotives numbered from 150. Forty-three additional locomotives had been built by 1946. The K class remained in service until the end of regular steam operation in Victoria and many were preserved, some in working order.

J515 on display at Spencer Street station in 1980. (Peter Clark)

J Class 515, 541, 549

Type	Freight	**Wheel Arrangement**	1'D	
Boiler Pressure	1241 kPa	**Cylinders**	508 x 660 mm	
Grate Area	2.9 m²	**Length**	18.42 m	
Heating Surface	134/22 m²	**Width**		
Valve Gear	Walschaerts	**Height**		
Driving Wheels	1397 mm	**Engine Weight**	68 t	
Tractive Effort	127 kN	**Tender Weight**	46.5 t	
Maximum Speed		**Axle Load**	134 kN	
Builder	Vulcan Foundry	**Gauge**	1600/1435 mm	
Introduced	1954	**Number Built**	60	

The J class was designed as a successor to the K class which would be suitable for conversion to standard gauge. The greater length of the N class limited its use on many branch lines owing to the small turntables used on these lines. The J class had a shallower wide firebox above the frames and a higher pitched boiler which allowed the frame spacing to be reduced for standard-gauge operation. The basic dimensions of the frames and cylinders were standard with the K class. Half the class was equipped to burn fuel oil. The J class was introduced after main line diesel locomotives had entered service and shortly before branch line diesel locomotives arrived and so were effectively obsolete on delivery. J 559 was the last steam locomotive introduced in Victoria and J 515 was the last in service. They lasted until the end of steam operation and a number were preserved.

Former SMR 18 at Bradken Braemar following an overhaul in March 2006. (Peter Clark)

10, 18

Type	Freight	**Wheel Arrangement**	1'D1't
Boiler Pressure	1270 kPa	**Cylinders**	508 x 660 mm
Grate Area	2.87 m²	**Length**	9.55 m
Heating Surface	171 m²	**Width**	
Valve Gear	Allan	**Height**	
Driving Wheels	1295 mm	**Weight**	84.9 t
Tractive Effort	142 kN	**Axle Load**	134 kN
Maximum Speed		**Gauge**	1435 mm
Builder	Beyer, Peacock	**Number Built**	14
Introduced	1912		

The South Maitand Railways had Beyer, Peacock design a heavy freight tank locomotive based on the NSW T (later 50) class, adding a radial axle to support the bunker. The remainder of the chassis was common with the T class, but the boiler was smaller, based on the P (later 32 class) passenger locomotives to reduce the weight to allow for the full-length water side tanks while maintaining an acceptable axle load. They were used between East Greta Junction and Cessnock for many years until NSWGR diesel locomotives took over, and were used for some years more on the former J. & A. Brown lines to Hexham well after other commercial steam operations had finished in NSW. Most of the class have been preserved, but numbers 10 and 18 are in working order at East Greta, although 18 was restored and used on the Cockatoo run by 3801 Limited.

AC16 No. 218A at the Zig Zag Depot. (Leon Oberg)

AC16 Class 218A, 221A

Type	Freight	**Wheel Arrangement**	1'D1'
Boiler Pressure	1230 kPa	**Cylinders**	406 x 610 mm
Grate Area	2.57 m²	**Length**	17.97 m
Heating Surface	127.3/34.7 m²	**Width**	2.54 m
Valve Gear	Walschaerts	**Height**	3.42 m
Driving Wheels	1219 mm	**Engine Weight**	54.3 t
Tractive Effort	89.5 kN	**Tender Weight**	41.4 t
Maximum Speed		**Axle Load**	102 kN
Builder	Baldwin	**Gauge**	1067 mm
Introduced	1943	**Number Built**	15

The AC16 was a standard US Army wartime design, provided to Queensland under Lend Lease terms, entering service in 1943.

The Queensland locomotives were all built by Baldwin in Philadelphia. Because of their status, they were not renumbered into QR stock but retained their US army allocated numbers, to which an 'A' was appended as a suffix to distinguish them from QR locomotives with those numbers. Poor damping in the tender springing meant the tenders oscillated at speed, and these locomotives were limited to freight service. It was realised that standard QR tenders could be fitted, and these locomotives took over operation of the *Midlander* train on the Central line. They were also used west of Toowoomba on the South Western division. They were all withdrawn by 1969, but 218A is operated on the Zig Zag and 221A is at the Ipswich Museum.

5917 on a tour train working at Cootamundra, June 2008. (Peter Clark)

5910, 5917

Type	Freight	Wheel Arrangement	1'D1'
Boiler Pressure	1379 kPa	Cylinders	533 × 711 mm
Grate Area	4.4 m²	Length	20.56 m
Heating Surface	199.6/57.9 m²	Width	2.97 m
Valve Gear	Walschaerts	Height	4.11 m
Driving Wheels	1524 mm	Engine Weight	93.54
Tractive Effort	156 kN	Tender Weight	59.94
Maximum Speed	90 km/h	Axle Load	169kN
Builder	Baldwin	Gauge	1435 mm
Introduced	1952	Number Built	20

The 59 class were ordered as oil burners during a period of coal strikes. The expected fast delivery didn't occur owing to material shortages due to the Korean War. They used the basic design of locomotives built for the British Army for use in the Middle East, but had one-piece cast frames with integral cylinders in place of bolted bar frames and other detail improvements. The use of oil firing limited the range of the 59 class and they were largely used between Sydney and Broadmeadow until 1962, when most of the class were converted to coal fuel. This change saw the 59s used between Sydney and Goulburn as well as the north. The surviving oil burners were based at Casino and South Grafton where they were able to burn diesel fuel, simplifying logistics on an otherwise all-diesel operated line, but later were used as stationary boilers at Broadmeadow. 5910 is preserved by the Rail Transport Museum and 5917 by the Lachlan Valley Railway. The surviving oil burners, 5908 and 5916, are on display in Goulburn.

AN AUSTRALIAN LOCOMOTIVE GUIDE

V 1213 in storage at Forrestfield during 1994. (Peter Clark)

V Class 1209, 1213

Type	Freight	**Wheel Arrangement**	1'D1'
Boiler Pressure	1480 kPa	**Cylinders**	483 × 660 mm
Grate Area	3.7 m²	**Length**	21.24 m
Heating Surface	168.7/45.7 m²	**Width**	2.89 m
Valve Gear	Walschaerts	**Height**	3.86 m
Driving Wheels	1295 mm	**Engine Weight**	82 t
Tractive Effort	149.5 kN	**Tender Weight**	55 t
Maximum Speed		**Axle Load**	142 kN
Builder	Stephenson	**Gauge**	1067 mm
Introduced	1955	**Number Built**	24

The V class was from a family of designs intended for eventual conversion to standard gauge, and was the largest WAGR steam locomotive design. Designed by Beyer, Peacock, pressure of work meant that the locomotives were built by Robert Stephenson and Hawthorns under subcontract. This was the last new steam design for WA but when standard gauge became a reality some 10 years later, locomotives of much greater power were obtained and this type finished its days on narrow gauge. The V class were largely confined to the south west on coal trains and other freight services. 1209 is preserved by the Bellarine Peninsula Railway and 1213 by the Pemberton Tramway.

N407 at Maryborough Loco Depot in 1964. N441 will be very similar to this locomotive regarding frame type and boiler pattern. (Peter Clark)

N Class 441

Type	Freight	**Wheel Arrangement**	1'D1'
Boiler Pressure	1207 kPa	**Cylinders**	508 x 660 mm
Grate Area	2.9 m²	**Length**	20.55 m
Heating Surface	134.9/30.1 m²	**Width**	
Valve Gear	Walschaerts	**Height**	4.25 m
Driving Wheels	1397 mm	**Engine Weight**	75.1 t
Tractive Effort	127 kN	**Tender Weight**	50.5 t
Maximum Speed		**Axle Load**	138 kN
Builder	Newport	**Gauge**	1600/1435 mm
Introduced	1925	**Number Built**	83

The N class was a modification of the K class, sharing the major dimensions but with a wide firebox and a trailing truck to allow for future conversion to standard gauge. These were numbered from 110 in sequence from the K class. The first 20 had a KW pattern trailing truck but in 1930 N 110 was fitted with a Delta trailing truck with a booster engine which provided an additional 25 kN tractive effort at starting. Locomotives from N130 onward had the Delta truck to allow for fitting a booster. The original boiler had very long tubes and

a revised design with a combustion chamber and a steel inner firebox was adopted for post World War II construction. Fifty new locomotives designed for easy conversion to standard gauge were ordered from Scotland with the new boiler and Delta trucks, numbered 450 to 499. N 111 to N 129 were renumbered 400 to 418 and to keep the Delta trucks together 110 became 419 and 130 onward became 420 to 429. Three further locomotives were built at Newport, 430 to 432. Ten locomotives were sold to South Australia, becoming 750 to 759, of which 752 is preserved, as is N 432, the last new steam locomotive built at Newport.

An 84th locomotive to be numbered N 441 is currently being constructed using a spare post-war N class boiler and a modified K class frame.

Class 24 No. 3696 shunting the coal stage at Beaconsfield, Kimberley, South Africa, in April 1983. (H.G. Graser)

3620

Type	Freight	**Wheel Arrangement**	1'D2'
Boiler Pressure	1740 kPa	**Cylinders**	483 x 660 mm
Grate Area	3.34 m²	**Length**	22.79 m
Heating Surface	151.9/35.3 m²	**Width**	
Valve Gear	Walschaerts	**Height**	3.93 m
Driving Wheels	1295 mm	**Engine Weight**	74 t
Tractive Effort	123 kN	**Tender Weight**	57.5 t
Maximum Speed		**Axle Load**	114 kN
Builder	North British	**Gauge**	1067 mm
Introduced	1948	**Number Built**	100

This Class 24 locomotive was built for the South African Railways and was intended as a modern locomotive for secondary lines, slightly smaller and lighter than the Class 19D. The 24 was fitted with one-piece cast steel frames incorporating the cylinders, and other modern features. Despite its design, it had to be modified slightly to fit the QR loading gauge and is the largest non-articulated steam locomotive in Queensland. It was purchased with other South African locomotives and transferred to Auckland, New Zealand, in 1996, and moved to Cairns in 2001 for operation on the Kuranda line by the Cairns Kuranda Steam Railway.

No. 903 at Pinjarra in July 2006. (Peter Clark)

W Class 901, 903, 908, 916, 920, 924, 933, 934, 945

Type	Mixed Traffic	**Wheel Arrangement**	2'D1'
Boiler Pressure	1380 kPa	**Cylinders**	406 × 610 mm
Grate Area	2.50 m²	**Length**	18.87 m
Heating Surface	104/28 m²	**Width**	2.49 m
Valve Gear	Walschaerts	**Height**	3.77 m
Driving Wheels	1219 mm	**Engine Weight**	94.4 t
Tractive Effort	96.79 kN	**Tender Weight**	39.6 t
Maximum Speed		**Axle Load**	103 kN
Builder	Beyer, Peacock	**Gauge**	1067 mm
Introduced	1951	**Number Built**	60

The W class were originally designed as a lighter version of the Pm class Pacific type for use on secondary lines. A change in senior design staff resulted in changes to the design, and equalisation of the axles and a conventional trailing truck were added.

The boiler design was revised to take account of the characteristics of Collie coal, resulting in the addition of a combustion chamber and a radially stayed round-top firebox in place of the Belpaire. Beyer, Peacock were able to adapt the cylinders and valve gear from one of their wartime standard Garratt locomotives. The result was a good steaming locomotive with a good capacity for speed. Despite the intention for mixed traffic on secondary lines, the W class were used on the Australind, the fastest main line train in WA. Such a flexible and useful locomotive, the whole class lasted into the 1970s and a large number have been preserved, either static or operational. Four locomotives are operated by the Hotham Valley Railway and three by the Pichi Richi Railway, one of which, 916, has been modified to represent Silverton W22.

AN AUSTRALIAN LOCOMOTIVE GUIDE

S 542 is preserved at Perth Terminal. (Peter Clark)

S Class 549

Type	Freight	**Wheel Arrangement**	2'D1'
Boiler Pressure	1380 kPa	**Cylinders**	483 x 611 mm
Grate Area	3.71 m²	**Length**	22.09 m
Heating Surface	155.4/41.6 m²	**Width**	2.74 m
Valve Gear	Walschaerts	**Height**	3.74 m
Driving Wheels	1219 mm	**Engine Weight**	76.5 t
Tractive Effort	136 kN	**Tender Weight**	44.7 t
Maximum Speed		**Axle Load**	129 kN
Builder	Midland	**Gauge**	1067 mm
Introduced	1943	**Number Built**	10

The S class was the first large freight locomotive for Western Australia since the F class, and had a number of features associated with later Western Australian locomotives. The most visible was the external main steam pipe from the dome to the superheater, which was enclosed in a streamlined casing along the top of the boiler. Later, the rear section of this casing, which was purely cosmetic, was removed. Two types of tender were provided, the later locomotives having greater water capacity but less coal space. Each locomotive was named after a mountain in Western Australia. These locomotives were used extensively in the South West, particularly after diesels took over the Kalgoorlie line. They lasted until the end of steam operation in 1971. S 549 is owned by RHWA but operated by Hotham Valley.

Preserved locomotive H 7, with M 3 alongside, at the Don River Railway in March 2010. (Chris Walters)

H Class 2

Type	Freight	**Wheel Arrangement**	2'D1'
Boiler Pressure	1379 kPa	**Cylinders**	457 x 610 mm
Grate Area	3.16 m²	**Length**	19.12 m
Heating Surface	150.8/27.7 m²	**Width**	
Valve Gear	Walschaerts	**Height**	3.78 m
Driving Wheels	1219 mm	**Engine Weight**	69.4 t
Tractive Effort	122.5 kN	**Tender Weight**	43.1 t
Maximum Speed		**Axle Load**	124 kN
Builder	Vulcan Foundry	**Gauge**	1067 mm
Introduced	1951	**Number Built**	8

When locomotives were needed for post World War II reconstruction, the TGR accepted the builder's suggestion of an existing design, used on the then Gold Coast railway in Africa. This design was generally equivalent to the existing Q class in use for heavy freight trains. These locomotives, known as the H class, arriving at the same time as the X class diesel-electric locomotives, were never used to their full potential and were largely withdrawn by the mid-1960s. Two were restored to traffic for the centenary of Tasmanian railways in 1971, and one of these, H 2, remains serviceable with the Derwent Valley Railway.

520 on a special train at Keswick, 1994. (Peter Clark)

520

Type	Passenger	**Wheel Arrangement**	2′D2′
Boiler Pressure	1480 kPa	**Cylinders**	520 × 710 mm
Grate Area	4.2 m²	**Length**	26.62 m
Heating Surface	227.9/60.5 m²	**Width**	
Valve Gear	Walschaerts	**Height**	4.18 m
Driving Wheels	1.676 m	**Engine Weight**	113.1 t
Tractive Effort	145 kN	**Tender Weight**	90.8 t
Maximum Speed		**Axle Load**	158 kN
Builder	Islington	**Gauge**	1600 mm
Introduced	1943	**Number Built**	12

The 520 class was an enlarged development of the 620 class Pacific, more powerful but retaining the capability to operate on secondary lines. The 520 included a Belpaire firebox, not seen in SA after Webb's designs abandoned it, and introduced a lateral motion device on the leading coupled axle, effectively reducing the rigid wheelbase. The locomotive was streamlined, reflecting Raymond Loewy's design for the Pennsylvania T-1 duplex. The tender was a large 12-wheel design which allowed long non-stop runs. During coal shortages, these locomotives were fitted for auxiliary oil firing to aid the burning of poor quality coal. They were all withdrawn from regular service by the late 1960s, although a few were used for special trains. 520 is operated by the SteamRanger Tourist railway, and 523 is in the National Railway Museum.

K 1 at Caernarfon, Wales in May 2008. (Andrew Burnham)

K Class 1

Type	Freight	**Wheel Arrangement**	B+B
Boiler Pressure	1695 kPa	**Cylinders**	279, 432 x 406 mm
Grate Area	1.37 m²	**Length**	9.8 m
Heating Surface	58.3 m²	**Width**	
Valve Gear	Walschaerts	**Height**	
Driving Wheels	800 mm	**Weight**	34 t
Tractive Effort	72.4 kN	**Axle Load**	83 kN
Maximum Speed		**Gauge**	610 mm
Builder	Beyer, Peacock	**Number Built**	2
Introduced	1909		

K 1 is the first Beyer Garratt locomotive built. It (and its sister K 2) differed from every subsequent Garratt in that it was a compound, and the cylinders on the inner end of the engine units shortened the length of the steam pipes between the high and low pressure cylinders. The Garratts were required to provide locomotives of greater power on the North East Dundas tramway in the remote West Coast area of Tasmania where it served the mining industry. A downturn in business meant the locomotives were withdrawn and stored in 1938. In 1947, Beyer, Peacock purchased K 1, restored it using some parts of K 2, and placed it on display at their Gorton Foundry. After the factory closed, it passed to the National Railway Museum in York. They in turn made K 1 available to the Ffestiniog Railway where it has been restored to operation

G Class 42

Type	Freight	**Wheel Arrangement**	1'C+C1'
Boiler Pressure	1280 kPa	**Cylinders**	337×457 mm
Grate Area	2.10 m²	**Length**	13.56 m
Heating Surface		**Width**	
Valve Gear	Walschaerts	**Height**	
Driving Wheels	914 mm	**Weight**	70.1 t
Tractive Effort	122.9 kN	**Axle Load**	94 .kN
Maximum Speed		**Gauge**	762 mm
Builder	Beyer, Peacock	**Number Built**	2
Introduced	1925		

When more powerful locomotives were required on the Victorian Railways narrow-gauge lines, Beyer, Peacock offered a locomotive generally similar to the WA M class, one of the very early Beyer Garratt designs. One locomotive each was allocated to the narrow-gauge lines radiating from Moe and Colac, where they replaced double heading of NA class locomotives. They operated until the lines closed in the 1960s. G 42 was preserved by the Puffing Billy Preservation Society and was returned to service in March 2004 and operates on the Gembrook line.

A Beyer, Peacock builder's photo of a QR Garratt. (Beyer, Peacock)

1009

Type	Freight	**Wheel Arrangement**	2′D1′+1′D2′
Boiler Pressure	1740 kPa	**Cylinders**	349 x 610 mm
Grate Area	3.62 m²	**Length**	27.4 m
Heating Surface	136.6/16.5 m²	**Width**	
Valve Gear	Walschaerts	**Height**	3.73 m
Driving Wheels	1295 mm	**Weight**	139.2 t
Tractive Effort	145.7 kN	**Axle Load**	95.6 kN
Maximum Speed		**Gauge**	1067 mm
Builder	Beyer, Peacock	**Number Built**	29
Introduced	1950	**Maximum Speed**	

The Queensland Railways were irrevocably opposed to the Australian Standard Garratt built during World War II, and contributed to its failure by imposing unnecessary constraints. Despite this, the operational advantages of such locomotives became obvious and QR ordered some heavier, less powerful Garratts from Beyer, Peacock soon after the war and these were delivered from 1950. They were based at Rockhampton, as had been the ASGs, and were initially used on the North Coast line as well as the Central line. With the introduction of main line diesel locomotives, they were confined to the Central line and mainly used on coal traffic from the Dawson valley and from Blair Athol. They were withdrawn by 1970, and 1009 was preserved at Redbank. It was restored to operation in 1992 and is based at the Ipswich Railway Workshops.

6029 is seen in Canberra yard on 3 September 2014 while undergoing trials. (Peter Clark)

6029

Type	Freight	**Wheel Arrangement**	2'D2'+2'D2'	
Boiler Pressure	1.38 MPa	**Cylinders**	505 × 660 mm	
Grate Area	6.0 m²	**Length**	33.1 m	
Heating Surface	281.5/70 m²	**Width**		
Valve Gear	Walschaerts	**Height**		
Driving Wheels	1397 mm	**Weight**	264 t	
Tractive Effort	282.4 kN	**Axle Load**	179 kN	
Maximum Speed		**Gauge**	1435 mm	
Builder	Beyer, Peacock	**Number Built**	47	
Introduced	1952			

The 60 class Beyer Garratt was designed to provide high power on secondary lines, but was designed so that by simply removing spacer discs from the bogie centres the coupled axle load could be increased for use on main lines. The Garratts were unpopular with crews and were banned from operation in single-track tunnels because exiting from the cab in an emergency would be difficult. The government tried to cancel the remainder of the contract in 1955, but were obliged to accept 47 complete locomotives and three pairs of cast frames, with no substantial saving in cost. Only 42 locomotives were placed in service but the other five were used by swapping numbers as locomotives came in for overhaul and interchanging the central boiler units when boiler repairs were required. As a result, the real identity of individual locomotives became confused. 6042 was the last in service in 1973, but 6029 operated for some years later in preservation. 6029 is operating, based in Canberra, but 6040 is on display at Thirlmere. 6039 and 6042 remain in storage.

4821 running around a train at Goulburn, September 2006. (Peter Clark)

4801 – 4885

Type	DL-531	**Wheel Arrangement**	Co'Co'
Engine	Alco 251B	**Length**	13.49 m
Cylinders	Inline 6	**Width**	2.74 m
Power	670 kW	**Height**	4.09 m
Generator	GE GT 584	**Weight**	75.2 t
Motors	GE 761	**Axle Load**	128 kN
Builder	A.E. Goodwin	**Tractive Effort**	179 kN
Introduced	1959	**Maximum Speed**	120 km/h
Number Built	85	**Gauge**	1435 mm

The DL-531 was the most numerous diesel locomotive type in Australia. They had generally simple lines, with the cab roofs flush with the hood tops. The end of the short hood was slightly pointed but the end of the long hood was flat. The bogies are of the equalised Trimount type, with cast frames. No dynamic braking equipment is installed. Tall tapered exhaust stacks are used. Units 4823, 4826, 4827, 4829 and 4830 were fitted in 1962 to supply train heating power for the Cooma Mail overnight train. 4820 – 4822 and 4824 – 4825 were also converted for this service later. The second group built, from 4846, had engines rated at 710 kW and AEI TG 3602 generators but were originally fitted with GE 761 traction motors removed from 44 class locomotives. The 48 class were used on all NSW divisions, on both main and branch lines and also for shunting in large goods yards and passenger stations. They were, at their peak, widely distributed and were based at many country depots as well as in Sydney. Many of the first and second groups are still in secondary service, some with smaller private operators.

DIESEL LOCOMOTIVES WITH ALCO ENGINES

847 standing on a loaded train at Iron Knob Junction, June 2006. (Peter Clark)

830 – 874

Type	DL-531	**Wheel Arrangement**	Co'Co'
Engine	Alco 251B	**Length**	13.49 m
Cylinders	Inline 6	**Width**	2.74 m
Power	670 kW	**Height**	4.09 m
Generator	GE GT 584	**Weight**	70 t
Motors	GE 761	**Axle Load**	117 kN
Builder	A.E. Goodwin	**Tractive Effort**	179 kN
Introduced	1959	**Maximum Speed**	120 km/h
Number Built	45	**Gauges**	all

The 830 class are generally similar to the NSW 48 class, but lacked the buffing plates originally fitted to NSW locomotives. Units with narrow-gauge bogies have projecting rubbing pads on the bogie frame. AN has applied double cab roofs and air-conditioning. Locomotives 830–846 and 850–855 were equipped as per the tabulation. Other units had AEI TG 3602 generators, AEI 253 motors and were rated at 710 kW. They were once used on all SAR gauges and all divisions. Locomotive 874 was purchased from the Silverton Tramway in 1970. A large number were transferred to Tasmania after the formation of AN, but only 852 remains there in preservation. Numbers have been reduced by conversion to DA class, as well as by sale and scrapping. To clear the 'class number', unit 830 was renumbered as 875 by AN. Units 847 to 849 spent several years working in NSW on lease. The locomotives are listed below in building order with their builder's numbers.

830 – 839	83721 – 83730	1959 Broad gauge
850 – 851	84136 – 84137	1962 Port Lincoln
840 – 844	84138 – 84142	1962 Broad gauge
856 – 867	84702 – 84713	1963 Peterborough
845 – 846	84714 – 84715	1963 Broad gauge
852 – 855	84716 – 84719	1963 Port Lincoln
871 – 873	G3422-1 –G3422-3	1966 Port Lincoln
847 – 849	G6016-1 –G6016-3	1969 Standard gauge
868 – 870	G6016-4 –G6016-6	1969 Standard gauge

DIESEL LOCOMOTIVES WITH ALCO ENGINES

27 – 36, later 48s28 – 48s36

Silverton 32 at Broken Hill Locomotive Depot, November 1998. (Peter Clark)

Type	DL-531	**Wheel Arrangement**	Co'Co'	
Engine	Alco 251B	**Length**	13.49 m	
Cylinders	Inline 6	**Width**	2.74 m	
Power	670 kW	**Height**	4.09 m	
Generator	GE GT 584	**Weight**	75.2 t	
Motors	GE 761	**Axle Load**	128 kN	
Builder	A.E. Goodwin	**Tractive Effort**	179 kN	
Introduced	1960	**Maximum Speed**	120 km/h	
Number Built	10	**Gauge**	1435 mm	

Silverton originally purchased three DL-531s for use on the Silverton Tramway connecting Broken Hill with the SAR 1067 mm line to Port Pirie at Cockburn. They were originally used as main line locomotives on this section. When the SAR standard-gauge line was completed in 1970, the first locomotive, No. 27, was sold to the SAR and converted to standard gauge, becoming AN No. 874. Nos 28 and 29 were converted to standard gauge and are still in use shunting industrial sidings in Broken Hill. While No. 28 was undergoing conversion, Silverton hired SAR 859 and ran it in multiple with No. 29. The other locomotives were obtained from AN in Tasmania or from the NSWSRA as they became surplus. Former NSW locomotives may be identified by the frame openings provided for staff exchangers. The original Silverton colour scheme was crimson, with white lining and company name, but this scheme was only carried by the first three units. This was replaced by a scheme officially called Tramway Gold with blue lining. Most of these units ended up with Greentrains.

AN AUSTRALIAN LOCOMOTIVE GUIDE

4886 – 48165, 48201 - 48218

Type	DL-531	**Wheel Arrangement**	Co'Co'
Engine	Alco 251C	**Length**	13.49 m
Cylinders	Inline 6	**Width**	2.74 m
Power	710 kW	**Height**	4.09 m
Generator	AEI TG3602	**Weight**	77.8 t
Motors	AEI 253	**Axle Load**	128 kN
Builder	A.E. Goodwin	**Tractive Effort**	189 kN
Introduced	1966	**Maximum Speed**	120 km/h
Number Built	80	**Gauge**	1435 mm

These two orders, each of 40 units, had a 40% increase in fuel capacity, obtained by moving the air reservoirs to the short hood, allowing an increase in the size of the fuel tank. The batteries then had to be relocated to the footplate in front of the driver beside the short hood. The final order, from 48126, had only minor changes, paired marker lights and five-chime horns being the most visible. These locomotives were obtained to complete the replacement of steam locomotives. They were used interchangeably with the earlier units. The locomotives remaining with Pacific National are often equipped with cab air-conditioning and outside handrails are being fitted. The GPS antenna required for safe working is usually fitted on a raised mount to clear the cab air-conditioner. Eighteen locomotives were transferred to Grain Corp and were renumbered 48201–48218.

901 – 907, ex DA 1 – DA 7, T 01, T 02

Type	DL-531m	**Wheel Arrangement**	Co'Co'
Engine	Alco 251C	**Length**	13.49 m
Cylinders	Inline 6	**Width**	2.74 m
Power	710 kW	**Height**	4.09 m
Generator	AEI TG3602	**Weight**	71t
Motors	AEI 253	**Axle Load**	115 kN
Builder	A.E. Goodwin	**Tractive Effort**	189 kN
Introduced	1992	**Maximum Speed**	120 km/h
Number Built	8	**Gauges**	all

To improve visibility and permit single crewing, AN converted 849 by cutting down the short hood, and by moving both doors to the rear of the cab. To indicate the change, 849 was renumbered DA 1 shortly after conversion. Further conversions followed, with some progressive changes. DA 3 had a raised mansard cab roof, to provide more room for cab air-conditioning. To further increase visibility, EL class cab windows were applied to DA 4 and

following units. Although DA 1 – DA 3 were initially on standard gauge, DA 4 went to Port Lincoln on narrow gauge and DA 5 was first allocated to Tailem Bend on the broad gauge. All these locomotives carried the standard AN green and yellow when new. DA 7 was converted from ex-NSWR 4813, and carried the Australia Southern colours from new. 874 was modified using the cab from damaged DA 3 and was transferred to Albany numbered T 01. DA 1 was also transferred and renumbered T 02, the change in class being required since Australia Western already had a different DA class in service, but all of their previous (different) T class had been withdrawn. All remained with Genesee and Wyoming Australia at the split from ARG.

901	DA 1	ex 849	to T 02	904	DA 5	ex 830/875
902	DA 2	ex 832		905	DA 6	ex 836
	DA 3	ex 835	wdn 11/1997	906	DA 7	ex 4813
903	DA 4	ex 839		907	(DA 8)	ex 874 to T 01 (briefly 901)

AN AUSTRALIAN LOCOMOTIVE GUIDE

PL 1 – PL 7

Type	DL-531
Engine	Alco 251B
Cylinders	Inline 6
Power	670 kW
Generator	AEI TG3602
Motors	GE 761
Builder	A.E. Goodwin
Introduced	2000
Number Built	7

Wheel Arrangement	Co'Co'
Length	13.49 m
Width	2.74 m
Height	4.09 m
Weight	75.2 t
Axle Load	128 kN
Tractive Effort	179 kN
Maximum Speed	120 km/h
Gauge	1435 mm

The PL conversion was generally similar to the earlier DA conversions to permit single crew operation, but included radio remote control so that a locomotive could run either end of dedicated intermodal shuttle trains in the Sydney Metropolitan Area. These were known as PortLink trains and this resulted in the PL class designation being adopted. These container services were later passed to other operators and several PL class were used in Pelton coal traffic with unmodified 48 class, until replaced in 2011. PL 1 is allocated as the shunter in Adelaide Keswick passenger terminal.

4848	Rebuilt as PL1	4881	Rebuilt as PL5
4871	Rebuilt as PL2	4867	Rebuilt as PL6
4870	Rebuilt as PL3	4856	Rebuilt as PL7
4868	Rebuilt as PL4		

DIESEL LOCOMOTIVES WITH ALCO ENGINES

HI 007 at Six Mile PRHS Museum, April 1994. (Peter Clark)

007

Type	S-2	**Wheel Arrangement**	Bo'Bo'
Engine	Alco 539	**Length**	12.65 m
Cylinders	Inline 6	**Width**	2.92 m
Power	750 kW	**Height**	4.45 m
Generator	GE GT 556	**Weight**	102.5 t
Motors	GE 731	**Axle Load**	256 kN
Builder	Alco New York	**Tractive Effort**	152 kN
Introduced	1965	**Maximum Speed**	106 km/h
Number Built	1	**Gauge**	1435 mm

This is the only example in Australia of a pre World War II pattern Alco switcher. It was built in April 1940 for the Spokane Portland and Seattle Railroad, who returned it as a trade-in on a later Alco locomotive. It was purchased by Hamersley Iron and shipped to Dampier (WA) with the C-628s in 1965. It is identified as an S-2 type by the bogies of the 'Blunt' design. When introduced it was used as the shunter at Dampier. With the introduction of the more powerful C-415 it was transferred to Mount Tom Price where it performed general shunting. There was little work for it, and it was withdrawn and presented to the Pilbara Railway Historical Society. The first Hamersley number carried was 003, which was a blank in the series, but it was soon renumbered 007.

HI 1000, carrying the number 2000, at Six Mile PRHS Museum, April 1994. (Peter Clark)

1000

Type	C-415	**Wheel Arrangement**	Bo'Bo'	
Engine	Alco 251C	**Length**	14.78 m	
Cylinders	V-12	**Width**	3.03 m	
Power	1120 kW	**Height**		
Generator	GE GT 581	**Weight**	109 t	
Motors	GE 752	**Axle Load**	267 kN	
Builder	Alco New York	**Tractive Effort**	kN	
Introduced	1968	**Maximum Speed**	106 km/h	
Number Built	1	**Gauge**	1435 mm	

This locomotive is of the centre-cab design and has the engine and generator mounted under one hood and the radiators and fan under the other. It is fitted with dual controls mounted centrally in the cab as it is intended for one-man operation. This locomotive has the distinction of being the first locomotive in Australia to use US 'AAR type B' bogies. This locomotive was built by Alco in 1966 as a demonstrator and toured the American railroads fairly extensively before returning to Alco where it was offered for sale. Hamersley Iron purchased the locomotive and had it shipped to the A.E. Goodwin plant at Sydney for checking, modification and repainting in the HI colours. Shipped to Dampier with the first order of C-636s in mid-1968, it was used to handle the heavy shunting work at Dampier but is now used by the Pilbara Railway Historical Society.

4001 at Sydney Central, December 2010. (Peter Clark)

4001 – 4020

Type	RSC-3	**Wheel Arrangement**	A1A'A1A'
Engine	Alco 244B	**Length**	15.85 m
Cylinders	V-12	**Width**	3.03 m
Power	1190 kW	**Height**	4.28 m
Generator	GE GT 581	**Weight**	113 t
Motors	GE 752	**Axle Load**	185 kN
Builder	Montreal LW	**Tractive Effort**	204 kN
Introduced	1951	**Maximum Speed**	130 km/h
Number Built	20	**Gauge**	1435 mm

These locomotives were the first road-switcher or hood type mainline locomotive in Australia. They are single-ended, having only one set of controls, and a cowcatcher under the short hood end. (The RSC 3 type was normally run with the long hood leading.) The cab layout was basically identical to the North American locomotive, only the brake pedestal position being changed for left-hand operation. The main point of identification on this locomotive is the pronounced inward cant of the cab side above the waist. Also notable is

the large transverse exhaust stack which indicates a water-cooled turbocharger, upgrading the engine to model 244H. During the Royal Tour of 1954, locomotives 4001 and 4002 were assigned to the Royal Train, and for this duty were specially painted in 'Royal' Caledonian blue with buff lining. Locomotive 4017 was the first NSWR diesel locomotive to cover a million miles while 4014 was the first of the class to be withdrawn from service, after an electrical fire on 27 May 1968. They were based at Enfield (Sydney), and were usually operated on the Northern and Southern divisions of the system, particularly on the North Coast line and the 'Short North' between Gosford and Newcastle. The 40 class were traded in to A.E. Goodwin and certain components were used in the construction of 20 type DL500G (442 class) cab units. 4001 was obtained for preservation by the NSWRTM at Thirlmere.

AN AUSTRALIAN LOCOMOTIVE GUIDE

9405 shunting at Cape Lambert, November 1976. (Peter Clark)

9401 and 9405

Type	RSC-3m	Wheel Arrangement	Bo'Bo'
Engine	Alco 244H	Length	15.85 m
Cylinders	V-12	Width	3.03 m
Power	1190 kW	Height	4.28 m
Generator	GE GT 581	Weight	110 t
Motors	GE 752	Axle Load	275 kN
Builder	Montreal LW	Tractive Effort	204 kN
Introduced	1971	Maximum Speed	45 km/h
Number Built	2	Gauge	1435 mm

Two former NSW 40 class were sold by A.E. Goodwin to Cliffs Robe River for their mining project railway between Cape Lambert and Pannawonica. 4006 and 4002 became 261-001 and 261-002 respectively and later 1701 and 1705. They were in use as shunting locomotives at Cape Lambert until withdrawal in 1983. In Robe River service, the idler axles were removed. Their appearance suffered when an air-conditioning unit was installed above the short hood during 1975. The colour scheme used at Robe River was yellow, with black bogies and black lettering. One is preserved as 4002 at Dampier, and the other as a static exhibit at Karratha. The Pilbara Railway Historical Society has restored 4002 to operation with the original wheel arrangement using components from scrapped Hamersley C 628 locomotives.

4306 at Queanbeyan in 1996. (Peter Clark)

4301 – 4306

Type	Cab	**Wheel Arrangement**	Co'Co'
Engine	Alco 244H	**Length**	16.41 m
Cylinders	V-12	**Width**	2.91 m
Power	1190 kW	**Height**	4.19 m
Generator	GE GT 581	**Weight**	107.6 t
Motors	GE 761	**Axle Load**	176 kN
Builder	Goninan NSW	**Tractive Effort**	191 kN
Introduced	1956	**Maximum Speed**	114 km/h
Number Built	6	**Gauge**	1435 mm

These locomotives are unusual in having Alco power units in GE-designed bodies. The cab profile is similar to four US General Electric prototypes numbered 750 (as a single four-unit locomotive) built in 1954 which, however, had Cooper-Bessemer prime movers. The class may be recognised by their squared-off appearance. The large vertical radiator vents (originally with shutters) and the flush headlight mounting provide recognition features, as do the oval buffers, fitted at both ends. The bogies are of a cast frame, inside equalised, equally spaced axle type. The drop equalisers have a distinctive channel section. Hostler controls only are fitted at the rear end of the locomotive. Initially used on the Western division from Sydney to Orange, prior to electrification, they were later based at Broadmeadow (Newcastle) and worked on the North Coast and Main North routes as well as to Gosford on the 'Short North'. The last survivor in traffic, 4306, did considerable work on the Main South. 4306 is held by the NSWRTM, and was restored to trafficable condition in June 1996.

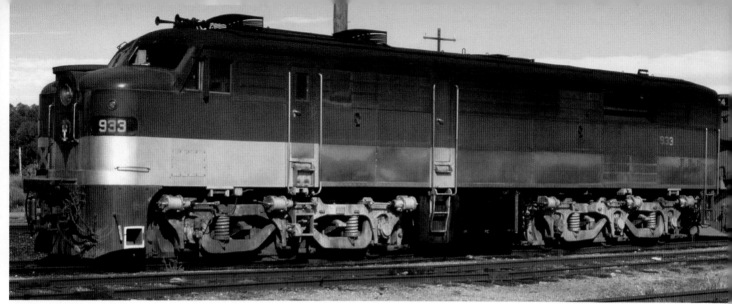

930 – 935

Type	DL-500B	**Wheel Arrangement**	Co'Co'	
Engine	Alco 251B	**Length**	16.90 m	
Cylinders	V-12	**Width**	2.85 m	
Power	1190 kW	**Height**	4.01 m	
Generator	GE GT 581	**Weight**	103.2 t	
Motors	GE 761	**Axle Load**	170 kN	
Builder	A.E. Goodwin	**Tractive Effort**	191 kN	
Introduced	1955	**Maximum Speed**	114 km/h	
Number Built	6	**Gauge**	1600 mm	

The then SAR 930 class were the first Alco 'World' type cab units to use the 251 engine, and the first Alco design built in Australia. These first six had only one cab at the streamlined end, but all later locomotives had the standard double-cab design. The first six had pressed steel gratings along the radiator grilles. All had dynamic braking. Staff exchangers were placed on the right side in the direction of travel, at the front of single ended locomotives. The original colour scheme was maroon with silver bands. The silver band along the body sides was achieved by leaving the natural stainless steel finish on the panels. 930 was renumbered 967, to clear the 'class' number. These units were widely used on the 1600 mm gauge lines in South Australia and particularly the Northern and Eastern lines. 930 is preserved at the NRM in Adelaide, restored to the original colours and number.

936 – 966

Type	DL-500B	Wheel Arrangement	Co'Co'
Engine	Alco 251B	Length	16.90 m
Cylinders	V-12	Width	2.85 m
Power	1190 kW	Height	4.01 m
Generator	GE GT 581	Weight	105.9 t
Motors	GE 761	Axle Load	175 kN
Builder	A.E. Goodwin	Tractive Effort	191 kN
Introduced	1956	Maximum Speed	114 km/h
Number Built	31	Gauges	1435/1600 mm

Alone amongst the users of this type the SAR, and later AN, retained the 1600 HP (1190 kW) rating for most of the locomotives' operating lives. The first six units were single ended, originally numbers 930 – 935, but numbers 936 – 966, supplied over the 12 years 1956–67, were all double ended. All of these later units had illuminated numbers applied to the

blunt cab end. 936 to 957 (built 1957–62) had GE electrical equipment, as indicated in the table above. The last two orders (units 958 to 966), delivered from 1965 to 1967, had AEI electrical equipment. The generators were the AEI 5302 type and AEI 253 traction motors were used. These were used all over the former SAR broad-gauge system, and worked into Melbourne in later years. Several were converted to standard gauge when Adelaide was connected to the standard-gauge network, and the last survivor, 961, with a special blue and yellow colour scheme, intended for tourist trains, was working on standard gauge from 1996. This unit was sold to Silverton in 2001 and was renumbered 44s1. CFCLA purchased the locomotive during 2005.

4401 at Broadmeadow, June 2004. (Peter Clark)

4401 – 4460

Type	DL-500B	Wheel Arrangement	Co'Co'
Engine	Alco 251B	Length	16.90 m
Cylinders	V-12	Width	2.85 m
Power	1340 kW	Height	4.01 m
Generator	GE GT 581	Weight	108.1 t
Motors	GE 761	Axle Load	177 kN
Builder	A.E. Goodwin	Tractive Effort	205 kN
Introduced	1957	Maximum Speed	108 km/h
Number Built	60	Gauge	1435 mm

From their introduction, the 44 class became the standard road locomotives on the NSWR and was widely used on all divisions, being allocated to Enfield (Sydney) and Bathurst. They were used on all types of trains ranging from local goods working to the crack *Southern Aurora* and *Indian Pacific*. The class remained in passenger traffic until withdrawal in mid-1994. With such a large class built over an extended period (1957–68) there were detail differences between early and later locomotives. Dynamic braking is fitted to all locomotives. 4401 – 4460 lacked the illuminated numbers at the non-streamlined end. Mechanical staff-exchanging equipment was mounted on left front and right rear. Standard buffing plates were fitted at the front and the rear, and remained in place until withdrawal. Owing to speed restrictions with the GE 761 motors, 11 sets of heavier GE731 motors were obtained in the early 1960s, and these were fitted to locomotives 4403–4, 4407–8, 4421/3/6, 4430/2/4/5. The remainder were later fitted with AEI 253 motors in exchange for the GE 761 motors which were fitted to 48 class locomotives 4846 – 4885. Units 4430, 4431, 4436 and 4437 were equipped in 1962 to provide train heating power for the Cooma Mail.

4477 at Junee Locomotive Depot, March 2006. (Peter Clark)

4461 – 44100

Type	DL-500B	**Wheel Arrangement**	Co'Co'
Engine	Alco 251B	**Length**	16.90 m
Cylinders	V-12	**Width**	2.85 m
Power	1340 kW	**Height**	4.01 m
Generator	AEI 5302	**Weight**	112.1 t
Motors	AEI 254	**Axle Load**	184 kN
Builder	A.E. Goodwin	**Tractive Effort**	195 kN
Introduced	1965	**Maximum Speed**	130 km/h
Number Built	40	**Gauge**	1435 mm

A fourth order was placed, for 40 locomotives, giving a total of 100. The first of these arrived in October 1965, and the last in January 1968, 11 years after the first order was placed. These had AEI electrical equipment, with the AEI 5302 generator replacing the GE GT 581 of the first 60 locomotives, and with AEI 254 motors, an upgraded version of the AEI253 that the first group gained as a retrofit. Externally the only visible differences were the illuminated numbers at the rear end, and Koyo bearings instead of the distinctive old pattern Timken bearings. The last 20 locomotives lacked the decorative mesh grille between the cab window and the cab door at the number one end. The last group of 44 class were sent to work the interstate traffic from Lithgow to Broken Hill in 1970. They remained there until replaced by the 80 class in the early 1980s, and gained a visual distinction by having the pilots repainted from Indian red to silver, to improve their visibility. All were withdrawn in 1994, but 4490 has been retained as a Heritage unit for special duties and CFCLA and a number of private owners operate units in a variety of colour schemes.

4501 – 4540

Type	DL-541	**Wheel Arrangement**	Co'Co'
Engine	Alco 251C	**Length**	16.61 m
Cylinders	V-12	**Width**	2.96 m
Power	1340 kW	**Height**	4.24 m
Generator	AEI 5301	**Weight**	111.8 t
Motors	AEI 165	**Axle Load**	184 kN
Builder	A.E. Goodwin	**Tractive Effort**	302 kN
Introduced	1962	**Maximum Speed**	120 km/h
Number Built	40	**Gauge**	1435 mm

Although the 45 class appeared quite long, they were actually shorter over the body than the similarly powered 44 class cab units. The four horns were positioned above the cab, which had two sliding and one fixed window and one drop window each side. The exhaust stack is mounted crosswise (unlike that of the DL 531). Twin multiple unit receptacles were mounted each end, just above the buffer beam. Unequally spaced Trimount bogies with equalising beams are used. Dynamic braking was fitted inside the short hood. Staff exchangers were originally mounted on both sides and buffing plates were originally mounted on each end. The second 20 units were originally fitted with GE 752 motors. GE GT 586 generators were fitted in the early 1970s to about half the class. In 1988, six units were fitted with rubber sandwich secondary suspensions and minor cab improvements. These were reclassified as 35 class, retaining the last two digits of their original number. After a period on the West, they were mainly allocated to Broadmeadow, working the North Coast and Northern lines but they did work into Sydney and were used on Illawarra and Southern divisions as well. Locomotive 4525 was the first withdrawn and condemned in June 1972. Many were stored, but the class as a whole was withdrawn in 1994. 4520 is retained as a Heritage unit and is restored to the original colour scheme. Silverton operate a 35 as 45s1 and other private owners operate units.

600 – 606

Type	DL-541	Wheel Arrangement	Co'Co'
Engine	Alco 251C	Length	16.61 m
Cylinders	V-12	Width	2.96 m
Power	1340 kW	Height	4.24 m
Generator	AEI 5301	Weight	111.8 t
Motors	AEI 165	Axle Load	184 kN
Builder	A.E. Goodwin	Tractive Effort	310 kN
Introduced	1965	Maximum Speed	120 km/h
Number Built	7	Gauge	1435 mm

The 600 class differed only slightly from the NSWR 45 class locomotives. At first, the cab had only three windows each side, but a fourth was added in AN days. There were no buffing plates and only a single MU receptacle was provided, mounted higher above the footplate. No staff exchangers were fitted. Locomotives 600 and 601 originally had GE 752 traction motors. From 1975, the dynamic brake intakes were enlarged, and other changes made to reduce sound levels in the cab. Later, AN fitted the class with double roofs and eventually, roof-mounted air-conditioners. 600 was renumbered 607 to clear the 'class' number. The 600 class were originally allocated to the Peterborough division standard-gauge line, and were used on construction trains before commencing work on revenue trains between Broken Hill and Port Pirie. They later worked between Adelaide and Whyalla, and after standardisation, to Tailem Bend. This is the only former SAR class that has only operated on standard gauge. Four units were stripped and rebuilt as slug units for use with ALF class locomotives. These were not a success, but the three remaining, 602, 603 and 607, are still in traffic, and were sold during 2005 to South Spur, now Greentrains.

BU 3 at Dry Creek, 1994. (Peter Clark)

BU 1 – BU 4

Type	Road Slug	**Wheel Arrangement**	A1A'A1A'
Engine	None	**Length**	16.61 m
Cylinders		**Width**	2.96 m
Power		**Height**	4.24 m
Generator	None	**Weight**	120 t
Motors	EMD D78	**Axle Load**	200 kN
Builder	MKA Whyalla	**Tractive Effort**	180 kN
Introduced	1994	**Maximum Speed**	115 km/h
Number Built	4	**Gauge**	1435 mm

These units were rebuilt to operate as 'road slugs', unpowered locomotives drawing power from an adjacent locomotive, to provide additional tractive effort at low speed where the locomotive was otherwise unable to operate at full power owing to traction motor and adhesion restrictions. This principle has been used frequently and successfully in the USA, but this particular attempt was not successful. Rather than use the slug coupled to a single locomotive, the BU was intended to be coupled between a pair of ALF class locomotives which had special power cables fitted to allow them to operate as 'slug mothers', each powering two traction motors on the nearer bogie, so at lower speed, each ALF powered a total of eight traction motors. The BU units were also fitted with dynamic brakes, two EMD type resistor and cooling fan units being mounted near the centre of the body, each serving one bogie. It was found that the additional power load caused problems with the ALF locomotives and the BU class never entered regular service. They were stored at Islington for some years but were eventually scrapped.

44211 at Bowral in April 2011. (Peter Clark)

44201 – 44240

Type	DL-500G	**Wheel Arrangement**	Co'Co'
Engine	Alco 251C	**Length**	17.40 m
Cylinders	V-12	**Width**	2.96 m
Power	1490 kW	**Height**	4.24 m
Generator	AEI 5302	**Weight**	111.8 t
Motors	GE 752	**Axle Load**	184 kN
Builder	A.E. Goodwin/Comeng	**Tractive Effort**	232 kN
Introduced	1970	**Maximum Speed**	120 km/h
Number Built	40	**Gauge**	1435 mm

These first twenty 442 class were replacements for the 40 class, from which class certain components were reused – in particular, air reservoirs and the GE 752 traction motors. A new design of underframe with integral fuel tanks was used. The first three locomotives used GE GT 586 generators, and the next two units had AEI 5301 generators, the remainder of the first 20 being equipped as in the tabulation. A second order for 20 specified AEI 5301 generators and AEI 165 motors, but the final six were built by Comeng with Mitsubishi BZ288P alternators and MB451AVR motors. The bogies are of the high-adhesion Dofasco type, with rubber sandwich secondary suspension. Standard NSWR buffing plates were originally fitted at both ends, but removed in the 1980s. A five-chime horn is mounted above each cab. The 442 class were used mainly on interstate traffic on the South to Albury, and North Coast to Brisbane, but they were later relegated to secondary tasks. Several were rebuilt into GL and RL types, and the survivors are operated by Greentrains and CFCLA. 44211 is operated by the NSWRTM.

700 – 705

Type	DL-500G	**Wheel Arrangement**	Co'Co'
Engine	Alco 251C	**Length**	17.40 m
Cylinders	V-12	**Width**	2.96 m
Power	1490 kW	**Height**	4.24 m
Generator	AEI 5301	**Weight**	114.8 t
Motors	AEI 165	**Axle Load**	188 kN
Builder	A.E. Goodwin	**Tractive Effort**	311 kN
Introduced	1971	**Maximum Speed**	120 km/h
Number Built	6	**Gauge**	1435/1600 mm

The SAR locomotives were substituted for an existing order for an equal number of 930 class units, and were offered at a better price owing to the simultaneous construction of the NSW units. The SAR units differed only in the lack of buffers, and in having wider bogie frames to allow operation on the broad gauge. This latter feature exceeded the NSW loading gauge, and prevented through operation into NSW. AN fitted cab air-conditioners, but only at the No. 1 end. 700 – 702 originally operated on the Peterborough division on standard gauge, while 703 – 705 were on the broad gauge. After the standardisation from Crystal Brook to Adelaide, the 700s were all moved to the broad gauge, and worked through to Melbourne. After that line was standardised in 1995, some units moved back to the standard gauge. In line with other types AN renumbered the locomotives 701 to 706.

N 1871 – N 1881

Type	CE 618	**Wheel Arrangement**	Co'Co'
Engine	Alco 251E	**Length**	17.89 m
Cylinders	V-12	**Width**	2.90 m
Power	1790 kW	**Height**	3.99 m
Alternator	GE GTA 11	**Weight**	98 t
Motors	GE 761	**Axle Load**	163 kN
Builder	Comeng WA	**Tractive Effort**	241 kN
Introduced	1977	**Maximum Speed**	105 km/h
Number Built	11	**Gauge**	1067 mm

The N class was the first Alco-engined design on Westrail, and the last. It was the first Comeng design, and the only narrow-gauge design with Century series features such as a pressurised carbody and a centralised air system. These

were the first Australian narrow-gauge locomotives with the Dofasco-style bogies. The sealed body resulted in some ventilation problems, particularly with the combined air compressor and vacuum exhauster. These problems were sufficiently severe for 1871 – 1874 to be converted to air braking only, using a conventional Westinghouse air compressor, and these were reclassified NA. As a small group of orphans, the N class seemed destined for a relatively short life, although the locomotives are quite capable when in working order. Due to a shortage of locomotives on the standard gauge, 1872 and 1873 of the air braked NA class were fitted with modified standard-gauge bogies and reclassified as class NB. One unit, NA 1874, survived on narrow gauge until early 2006, operated by South Spur. It too was converted to standard gauge.

AN AUSTRALIAN LOCOMOTIVE GUIDE

NB 1872 – NB 1873, 1874

Type	CE 618	**Wheel Arrangement**	Co'Co'
Engine	Alco 251E	**Length**	17.89 m
Cylinders	V-12	**Width**	2.90 m
Power	1790 kW	**Height**	4.19 m
Alternator	GE GTA 11	**Weight**	118 t
Motors	GE 752	**Axle Load**	193 kN
Builder	Comeng WA	**Tractive Effort**	374 kN
Introduced	1995	**Maximum Speed**	113 km/h
Number Built	3	**Gauge**	1435 mm

Two of the NA class units, equipped only with Westinghouse brakes, were converted to meet a locomotive shortage on the standard gauge, and were reclassified as class NB by Westrail. These units were fitted with standard-gauge bogies surplus from withdrawn BHP Iron Ore M636 locomotives, complete with their larger GE 752 motors, resulting in an increase in tractive effort and locomotive weight. The overall height was increased, resulting in a minor fouling of the loading gauge in NSW, which required a slight rounding-off of the previously flat cab roof. These two units were delivered to Austrac in February 1998, for use in NSW based in Junee. They retained their original numbers, but the letter classification was dropped, becoming known as '18 class' units. They remained in service until Austrac ceased operations in August 2002. The two NB class are currently with El Zorro. The two units differ in that 1873 had a single number board on the cab end, while 1872 had the more conventional two. These units did not have illuminated numbers in Westrail service.

In early 2006, NA 1874 was also converted by South Spur to standard gauge using M636 bogies, losing the classification letters.

8005 and 8050 in Canberra, April 2008. (Peter Clark)

8001 – 8050

Type	CE 615	Wheel Arrangement	Co'Co'
Engine	Alco 251CE	Length	17.73 m
Cylinders	V-12	Width	2.96 m
Power	1490 kW	Height	4.24 m
Alternator	MB BZ 288P	Weight	121 t
Motors	MB 451 BVR	Axle Load	198 kN
Builder	Comeng NSW	Tractive Effort	273 kN
Introduced	1978	Maximum Speed	130 km/h
Number Built	50	Gauge	1435 mm

The 80 class resulted from a call for tenders in 1976 for a 2000 HP main line locomotive. The design selected was a development of the 442 class built by A.E. Goodwin. The contract was awarded to their successors as Alco/MLW licensees, Commonwealth Engineering. The first contract was for 30 units, and a number of new features were incorporated, not least the 251CE engine with a larger turbocharger and uprated Mitsubishi electrical equipment. The 80s

were the first NSW units to be delivered with cab air-conditioning. The class was the first not to have the distinctive buffing plates, and the first locomotive to use captive 48 pin MU cables (later removed) in addition to 27 pin sockets and jumper leads. Deliveries commenced in 1978, but because of delays to the Clyde 81 class a second order was placed in 1980 for a second batch of 20 machines. They were initially allocated to the main south, but soon transferred to the west. They were also used on coal trains in the Newcastle area. To reduce the need for repainting, the body used pre-coloured fibreglass panels, so the class retained the original colour schemes longer than might have been expected after the 1982 scheme was introduced. The first unit withdrawn was 8009, which was badly damaged in late 1990 in an accident at Narromine. They were extensively used on interstate services by National Rail working through to Melbourne and Brisbane. The survivors are largely used on secondary services by PN, QUBE and Greentrains.

2001 – 2005

2003 on a train loading at Mount Tom Price, 1978. (Peter Clark)

Type	C 628	**Wheel Arrangement**	Co'Co'
Engine	Alco 251C	**Length**	19.66 m
Cylinders	V-16	**Width**	3.02 m
Power	2050 kW	**Height**	4.75 m
Generator	GE GT 586	**Weight**	176 t
Motors	GE 752	**Axle Load**	290 kN
Builder	Alco New York	**Tractive Effort**	374 kN
Introduced	1965	**Maximum Speed**	113 km/h
Number Built	5	**Gauge**	1435 mm

When delivered, these were the largest locomotives ever exported from the USA. They also represented a major change in Australia, as the first use of the largest US domestic locomotive designs. They were in most respects identical to a standard US domestic locomotive but had the largest available fuel capacity (4000 gallons). All were equipped with slow speed controls for loading and tippling the iron ore vehicles. The bogies were of the Trimount type and were double equalised. They were initially used to construct the line from Dampier to Mount Tom Price, and later in normal ore traffic. The first unit was numbered 2000 on arrival, but was renumbered to 2003 early in its service life. All were withdrawn by the early 1980s, but 2003, restored as 2000, forms a static exhibit at Dampier. The colour scheme was dark green with yellow nose and hood end. The bogies and the fuel tank were silver and black, respectively.

9417 at Cape Lambert, 1978. (Peter Clark)

9417 – 9420

Type	C-630u	**Wheel Arrangement**	Co'Co'	
Engine	Alco 251F	**Length**	19.74 m	
Cylinders	V-16	**Width**	3.02 m	
Power	2680 kW	**Height**	4.65 m	
Alternator	GE GTA 9	**Weight**	190.5 t	
Motors	GE 752	**Axle Load**	316 kN	
Builder	Alco New York	**Tractive Effort**	403 kN	
Introduced	1975	**Maximum Speed**	113 km/h	
Number Built	4	**Gauge**	1435 mm	

These locomotives were built by Alco at their Schenectady Works, New York State, USA, in 1967 for the Chesapeake and Ohio Railway as numbers 2100 – 2103. They were purchased from the C&O by Morrison Knudsen for the company and arrived at Cape Lambert in January 1975. They were the only C-630 locomotives built with the Hi-Ad bogie. 9417 and 9420 had been modified to provide 2680 kW before shipment to Australia. The high Pilbara temperatures resulted in their getting larger radiators, which extended over the side walkways. The C-630s carried the then standard yellow and black colour scheme. In February 1979 locomotive 9417 was involved in a head-on collision involving a total of six locomotives. Locomotive 9417 was too extensively damaged to be economically repaired and was scrapped. The remainder were rebuilt as GE CM40-8ms in 1990 and 1991.

3006 – 3017

3014 at Seven Mile Locomotive Depot, 1978. (Peter Clark)

Type	C 636	**Wheel Arrangement**	Co'Co'
Engine	Alco 251F	**Length**	19.74 m
Cylinders	V-16	**Width**	3.02 m
Power	2680 kW	**Height**	4.65 m
Alternator	GE GTA 9	**Weight**	190 t
Motors	GE 752	**Axle Load**	316 kN
Builder	A.E. Goodwin	**Tractive Effort**	403 kN
Introduced	1968	**Maximum Speed**	113 km/h
Number Built	12	**Gauge**	1435 mm

These were the largest and most powerful diesel locomotives built in Australia up to that time, and are still amongst the largest and heaviest. Although the C-636s are generally similar to the earlier C-628s, the former may be distinguished by several features: a new design of bogie using helical secondary springs but without drop equalisers known as the Hi-Ad; intercooler radiator shutters on the air intake nearer the cab in place of a simple mesh cover; a different ('W') shape of cab front and a more angular hood profile. The locomotives also carried ploughs, mounted on the front headstock. The C-636s were often used in threes, on iron ore trains of up to 240 vehicles weighing just under 30,000 tons. The arduous conditions took their toll and the whole class were extensively rebuilt as C-636Rs by Comeng in Perth, from 1981 onward.

DIESEL LOCOMOTIVES WITH ALCO ENGINES

5461 at the Nelson Point Locomotive Depot, 1976. (Peter Clark)

5452 – 5468, 9424, 9425

Type	C636	**Wheel Arrangement**	Co'Co'
Engine	Alco 251F	**Length**	19.74 m
Cylinders	V-16	**Width**	3.02 m
Power	2680 kW	**Height**	4.65 m
Alternator	GE GTA 9	**Weight**	190 t
Motors	GE 752	**Axle Load**	316 kN
Builder	A.E. Goodwin	**Tractive Effort**	403 kN
Introduced	1968	**Maximum Speed**	113 km/h
Number Built	18	**Gauge**	1435 mm

The Mount Newman locomotives, apart from the colour scheme, were, as delivered, much the same as the contemporary Hamersley units. On Mount Newman, different policies resulted in the enlarging of the radiators, by one third, which improved reliability and allowed the locomotives to be rebuilt in kind for a longer service life in their original form. The first four Mount Newman locomotives were originally numbered from 001-0001 upwards but were soon given the numbers listed above. The remaining units were rebuilt as CM36-7m or CM40-8m by Goninan in Perth. The last Newman C636 unit built, 5468, was sold to Robe River in 1982. The first of the Robe C636 units, 9424, was from the Burlington Northern railroad, who had used it as their No. 4369. It had been built in 1968 for the Spokane, Portland and Seattle Railway, which was later absorbed into BN. This was the only US-built C636 to operate in Australia in its original form. The two Robe units were rebuilt as type CM40-8m by Goninan in Perth in 1989.

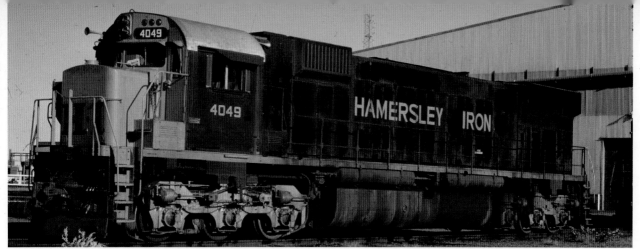

4049 at Seven Mile Locomotive Depot, 1978. (Peter Clark)

4030 – 4056

Type	M636	**Wheel Arrangement**	Co'Co'
Engine	Alco 251F	**Length**	19.82 m
Cylinders	V-16	**Width**	3.10 m
Power	2680 kW	**Height**	4.64 m
Alternator	GE GTA 11	**Weight**	190 t
Motors	GE 752	**Axle Load**	318 kN
Builder	A.E. Goodwin	**Tractive Effort**	403 kN
Introduced	1971	**Maximum Speed**	113 km/h
Number Built	27	**Gauge**	1435 mm

After Alco decided to leave the US market in early 1969 a strong market still existed in Canada and in various export markets, including Australia. The design work was transferred to the Montreal Locomotive Works, which had previously been an Alco subsidiary. MLW developed a new bogie design to reduce lateral forces in curves. It had a very short wheelbase, and used rubber metal sandwich secondary suspension. In Canada, this bogie was cast by Dofasco, and in Australia this became the name of the MLW design. Applied to Alco's C-636 design along with changes to the central air system and the frame, the type became the M-636. In Australia, the modified design also introduced a contraflow radiator system of much greater capacity to address the high operating temperatures in the Pilbara, which allowed the elimination of separate intercooler radiators. Hamersley Iron immediately adopted the design, and A.E. Goodwin built units 4030 to 4048. Later, Comeng WA built units 4049 to 4056 to a slightly modified design in Bassendean. Twelve of the Goodwin units were rebuilt with the modified cab, but the other 15 remained in service as built until superseded by the imported GE C44-9s in 1995.

5469 – 5495

5471 at the Nelson Point Locomotive Depot, 1976. (Peter Clarke)

Type	M636C	**Wheel Arrangement**	Co'Co'
Engine	Alco 251F	**Length**	19.82 m
Cylinders	V-16	**Width**	3.10 m
Power	2680 kW	**Height**	4.64 m
Alternator	GE GTA 11	**Weight**	191 t
Motors	GE 752	**Axle Load**	318 kN
Builder	A.E. Goodwin	**Tractive Effort**	403 kN
Introduced	1971	**Maximum Speed**	113 km/h
Number Built	27	**Gauge**	1435 mm

Mount Newman had an easier track profile than Hamersley Iron, both in curvature and gradients, and the line had originally been built with heavier rail. This allowed a more conservative view of the advantages of the Dofasco bogie and the Alco Hi-Ad bogie was retained for most of Mount Newman's locomotives, which were thus known as model M-636C. Two orders were built by A.E. Goodwin in their Auburn factory, and one order by Comeng at nearby Granville. The last Comeng M-636C, 5495, was fitted as a Locotrol command unit, and led some world record trains, but the system was not adopted at that time. Some units received the scheme with large hood side lettering and a diagonal white flash on the cab, and a few were repainted in BHP's corporate blue scheme. These units have stayed in the Newman–Port Hedland ore traffic. However, the majority were rebuilt progressively as CM-40ms operating under the new title of BHP Iron Ore but 5495 was scrapped, its cab going to the PRHS.

9410 – 9416, 9421 – 9423

Robe River 9413 at Cape Lambert, showing the air to air intercooler modification. (Peter Clark)

Type	M636	**Wheel Arrangement**	Co'Co'
Engine	Alco 251F	**Length**	19.82 m
Cylinders	V-16	**Width**	3.10 m
Power	2680 kW	**Height**	4.64 m
Alternator	GE GTA 11	**Weight**	190 t
Motors	GE 752	**Axle Load**	318 kN
Builder	A.E. Goodwin	**Tractive Effort**	403 kN
Introduced	1971	**Maximum Speed**	113 km/h
Number Built	10	**Gauge**	1435 mm

The fourth of the Pilbara mining railways, Robe River, adopted the same design the other two large systems were buying, and A.E. Goodwin delivered five M-636s in late 1971. These were painted overall yellow, with black fuel tanks and silver trucks. The cab side carried the company initials, and the numbers, which were 262-001 to 005. They were renumbered, initially to 1710

– 1714, and later became 9410 – 9414. They were repainted into a yellow and black scheme in Cape Lambert. Owing to a locomotive shortage, an additional unit on order from Goodwin in 1971 was supplemented by new Hamersley 4045, which was shipped new directly to Cape Lambert in HI green and yellow. These two became 9415 and 9416. Three more units were built by Comeng in Bassendean, two in 1977 and the last in 1980. Two of these units, 9411 and 9414, were rebuilt to the CM40-8m design. Locomotives 9410, 9413, 9415 and 9416 were rebuilt with an air to air intercooler, to reduce the temperature of intake air. This resulted in a distinctive appearance with air ducting above the engine compartment. Locomotives 9413, 9415 and 9416 also had the later Montreal design 251 Plus engine. These units were stored for use in periods of high traffic, but were not used after the merger with Hamersley. They were sold to GTSA in Maddington.

5496 – 5505

Type	M636	**Wheel Arrangement**	Co'Co'
Engine	Alco 251F	**Length**	19.82 m
Cylinders	V-16	**Width**	3.10 m
Power	2680 kW	**Height**	4.64 m
Alternator	GE GTA 11	**Weight**	191 t
Motors	GE 752	**Axle Load**	318 kN
Builder	Comeng NSW	**Tractive Effort**	403 kN
Introduced	1975	**Maximum Speed**	113 km/h
Number Built	10	**Gauge**	1435 mm

Comeng were less flexible than Goodwin, and pushed hard for the adoption of the Dofasco bogie, reflecting this in their tender pricing. They also strove hard to have the MLW version of the 'Canadian cab' adopted, but this would not fit through Mount Newman's car dumper at Port Hedland, and these efforts were in vain. The Dofasco bogie was adopted for two batches of locomotives numbered 5496 – 5505. These straight M-636s were never as popular as the M-636C, and 5498, 5500 and 5503 – 5505 were sold and placed in storage in Perth. One of these has now become a CM-40m, becoming Robe River second 9410. The remaining units stayed in the Newman–Port Hedland ore traffic, operating under the new title of BHP Iron Ore, although none were required for traffic with completion of the CM40-8m program. Three units are preserved, in Port Hedland, Karratha and Bassendean.

AN AUSTRALIAN LOCOMOTIVE GUIDE

3006–3017

Type	C636R	**Wheel Arrangement**	Co'Co'
Engine	Alco 251F	**Length**	19.74 m
Cylinders	V-16	**Width**	3.02 m
Power	2680 kW	**Height**	4.67 m
Alternator	GE GTA 9	**Weight**	190 t
Motors	GE 752	**Axle Load**	318 kN
Builder	Comeng WA	**Tractive Effort**	403 kN
Introduced	1981	**Maximum Speed**	113 km/h
Number Built	12	**Gauge**	1435 mm

In 1981, Hamersley Iron began to have their C-636 locomotives rebuilt by Comeng in Bassendean to an upgraded configuration. Firstly, the successful M-series contraflow radiators were incorporated, as was a new cab design specifically to meet local conditions. A feature of the cab was a toilet compartment, which had to be located clear of the electrical cabinet and behind the crew, resulting in a very long cab. Minor changes were made during the period of reconstruction, particularly in the air intakes and the shape of the hood at the rear. The C-636 dynamic brakes with integral electric cooling fans were retained on these units. These units all remained in service until replaced by GE C44-9Ws in 1995. Except for 3017, operated by the PRHS, these units were partly dismantled for parts by NREC. Two units, 3007 and 3013, were refurbished and leased to Fortescue Metals as DR 8402 and 8404 for construction of their line from Port Hedland to Cloudbreak. 3008 was rebuilt as DR 8405 but was not used. All were scrapped.

Only the MLW-Dofasco bogies indicate 4034's origin as an M-636. (Peter Clark)

4031 – 4037, 4039 – 4041, 4043, 4047

Type	M636R	**Wheel Arrangement**	Co'Co'
Engine	Alco 251F	**Length**	19.82 m
Cylinders	V-16	**Width**	3.10 m
Power	2680 kW	**Height**	4.67 m
Alternator	GE GTA 11	**Weight**	190 t
Motors	GE 752	**Axle Load**	318 kN
Builder	Comeng WA	**Tractive Effort**	403 kN
Introduced	1987	**Maximum Speed**	113 km/h
Number Built	12	**Gauge**	1435 mm

After the success of the C-636R program, those M-636s requiring major attention were also rebuilt at Bassendean from 1985. These were known as the M-636R type, and were distinguished from the C-636R by the Dofasco pattern bogies. Body modifications were similar to those on the last versions of the C-636R, resulting in a squarer hood profile. This was at least consistent with the very functional design of the Pilbara cab. These locomotives also remained in service until replaced by the GE C44-9Ws in 1995. These units were partly dismantled for parts by NREC.

DR8401 on a ballast train on the approach to the West Turner River, July 2008. (Peter Clark)

9426 – 9427

Type	CE 636R	**Wheel Arrangement**	Co'Co'
Engine	MLW 251 Plus	**Length**	19.74 m
Cylinders	V-16	**Width**	3.10 m
Power	2680 kW	**Height**	4.67 m
Alternator	GE GTA 9	**Weight**	190 t
Motors	GE 752	**Axle Load**	318 kN
Builder	Comeng WA	**Tractive Effort**	403 kN
Introduced	1986	**Maximum Speed**	113 km/h
Number Built	2	**Gauge**	1435 mm

These were the last examples of the Comeng rebuild, and incorporated all the design changes developed to meet Pilbara conditions. The 251 Plus engine, fitted later by Robe River, incorporated a modified structure to eliminate fatigue cracking of the camshaft mounts, which had proved to be the Achilles heel of the 251 engine in heavy duty use. The Pilbara cab was applied, as was a totally new design of radiator, mounted vertically in each side of the hood rather than horizontally above the fan. This new design was applied to two of the oldest C-636 underframes around, from Conrail units 6781 and 6782, built for the Penn Central Railroad by Alco in 1968. While they have operated successfully, these two units were the last new Alco design in the Pilbara, and further C-636 underframes would all be rebuilt with GE engines and carbodies. These two units carried a new image with large lettering on the hood sides and more use of red lining, still on the basic yellow body colour. These units saw limited use after the Hamersley merger. They were sold to GTSA in Maddington, refurbished and leased to Fortescue Metals as DR 8401 and 8403 for construction of their line from Port Hedland to Cloudbreak. They have since been scrapped.

Y142 at South Dynon, May 2008. The 'Broad Gauge' sign is unusual. (Peter Clark)

Y 101 – Y 150

Type	G6B	**Wheel Arrangement**	Bo'Bo'
Engine	EMD 567C	**Length**	12.19 m
Cylinders	V-6	**Width**	2.92 m
Power	445 kW	**Height**	4.19 m
Generator	EMD D-25	**Weight**	65 t
Motors	GE 237	**Axle Load**	160 kN
Builder	Clyde NSW	**Tractive Effort**	79 kN
Introduced	1963	**Maximum Speed**	73 km/h
Number Built	50	**Gauge**	1435/1600 mm

This group of locomotives is unusual in using power bogies formerly used under suburban electric power cars. The motors were modified and upgraded for locomotive duty by using improved insulation and forced ventilation. The motors were originally self-ventilated.

The end cab and hood resemble those of the later T class, but no short hood is fitted and a central door and large windows flanking it alter the appearance of the cab end. Single headlights only are fitted at each end and cast number plates are mounted on each end (in lieu of illuminated number boards) and on each cabside. The cast bogies are inside equalised and fitted with spoked driving wheels and only leave room for air tanks between them. The fuel tank forms part of the hood, adjacent to the cab. As with several other VR locomotives, a single set of controls facing along the hood was fitted. The Y class can run in multiple unit with other types fitted with EMD control, but are not fitted for dynamic braking. The surviving members of the Y class are still used for shunting in the larger yards but the class was also used for secondary freight and passenger trains. One unit is used by One Steel at Westernport and two by Downer at Newport and Cardiff.

DIESEL LOCOMOTIVES WITH EMD ENGINES

Y161 at Dudley Street sidings, March 2005. (Peter Clark)

Y 151 – Y 175

Type	G6B	**Wheel Arrangement**	Bo'Bo'
Engine	EMD 645E	**Length**	12.19 m
Cylinders	V-6	**Width**	2.92 m
Power	560 kW	**Height**	4.19 m
Generator	EMD D-25	**Weight**	65 t
Motors	GE 237	**Axle Load**	160 kN
Builder	Clyde NSW	**Tractive Effort**	79 kN
Introduced	1968	**Maximum Speed**	73 km/h
Number Built	25	**Gauge**	1600 mm

With the changeover to the larger bore EMD 645E engine, the last group of 25 Y class locomotives were fitted with this engine, and had a small increase in power as a result. EMD policy was to add the number 10 to the model number (based on the number of cylinders) of export locomotives. This could not be done for the G 6B, since it would conflict with the 16-cylinder 567C engined model. These locomotives were used interchangeably with the 567C engine versions. Locomotive Y 175, especially re-geared for 100 km/h maximum speed, was at one time used as the commissioner's train locomotive.

DIESEL LOCOMOTIVES WITH EMD ENGINES

121

J103 at Creek Sidings, July 2004. (Peter Clark)

J 101 – J 105

Type	G6B		
Engine	EMD 567C	**Wheel Arrangement**	Bo'Bo'
Cylinders	V-6	**Length**	13.03 m
Power	445 kW	**Width**	2.90 m
Generator	EMD D-25	**Height**	4.23 m
Motors	EMD D-29	**Weight**	65 t
Builder	Clyde NSW	**Axle Load**	160 kN
Introduced	1966	**Tractive Effort**	118 kN
Number Built	5	**Maximum Speed**	100 km/h
		Gauge	1435 mm

This class was purchased for shunting in large Western Australian standard-gauge yards, and was a modification of the G 6B as supplied to the VR as their Y class. Differences include EMD export-style Flexicoil bogies with EMD motors, and an underframe hung fuel tank. A curved cab roof and the hood pressurising filter box alter the appearance considerably. Dual sealed-beam headlights and full length outside handrails are fitted. They were used at Leighton, Forrestfield and Avon yards. In 1995 four units were sold to Great Northern and Rail Technical Services for use in Melbourne. Two units were leased to National Rail, and were painted in NR colours for shunting duties in Dynon yards. Two are now used by FreightLink as class FJ and the other two are operated by SCT.

AN AUSTRALIAN LOCOMOTIVE GUIDE

T 320 – T 346, T 413

Type	G 8	**Wheel Arrangement**	Bo'Bo'
Engine	EMD 567C	**Length**	13.56 m
Cylinders	V-8	**Width**	2.87 m
Power	650 kW	**Height**	3.80 m
Generator	EMD D-15	**Weight**	69 t
Motors	EMD D-19	**Axle Load**	170 kN
Builder	Clyde NSW	**Tractive Effort**	125 kN
Introduced	1955	**Maximum Speed**	100 km/h
Number Built	28	**Gauge**	1600 mm

These locomotives (V/Line Diagram T-1) were eight-cylinder versions of the 'Model G', used by QR and BHP Whyalla in the 12-cylinder form. There are only minor differences in appearance in items such as steps, and head and marker lights. The general appearance was of a square, boxy hood unit with cab roof flush with the hood top, and sloping down to the top of the cabside windows. These units were fitted with a narrow oval 'stovepipe' exhaust. The earliest units had fabricated bogie frames. These 'first series' T class were based at South Dynon depot, Melbourne, and were used to haul secondary freight and passenger trains on main and branch lines. They were commonly seen over the whole system. They were painted in the standard blue and gold VR colour scheme. The last addition to this group, the second T 413 (formerly the Australian Cement unit, D 1), was used between the quarry and crushers at Fyansford, near Geelong, until replaced by a conveyor belt in 1967. This locomotive was 1067 mm gauge and was fitted with dynamic braking. D 1's original colour scheme was slightly modified from that of the VR, but was altered to standard, along with minor changes to the steps and headstock. These locomotives did not get the V/Line livery. Thirteen were converted to P class, and the remainder withdrawn. A number are preserved in working order. T 344 is operated by SCT at Penfield, SA.

DE 01 – DE 02, T 414

T414 in the SCT Depot at Parkes, NSW, in January 2009. (Peter Clark)

Type	G 8	**Wheel Arrangement**	Bo'Bo'
Engine	EMD 567C	**Length**	13.56 m
Cylinders	V-8	**Width**	2.87 m
Power	650 kW	**Height**	3.80 m
Generator	EMD D-15	**Weight**	69 t
Motors	EMD D-19	**Axle Load**	170 kN
Builder	Clyde NSW	**Tractive Effort**	125 kN
Introduced	1955	**Maximum Speed**	100 km/h
Number Built	2	**Gauge**	1067 mm

These two locomotives were used on the open cut mine railways at Iron Knob, but were replaced in 1968 by 50-ton road trucks more suited to the pit mining method then introduced. DE 01 and DE 02 were fitted with dynamic brakes, and the original 1067 mm gauge bogies were of fabricated construction. They were originally painted in the same maroon and silver colour scheme as their later 12-cylinder sisters, and DE 02 was never repainted. The two units were converted to operate at Port Lincoln on the standard-gauge lime sands railway, and DE 02 remained there until the line's closure. When traffic at Port Lincoln did not reach expectations, DE 01 was returned to Whyalla to work on the standard-gauge steelworks network. DE 01 was repainted in the salmon and brown and later in the yellow and blue liveries at Whyalla. In 1993, DE 01 was rebuilt by Morrison Knudsen as a G 14M and went into ore haulage on the main line. DE 02 was rebuilt with a raised cab and low nose for SCT, and was used as T 414 as a shunter in Parkes and later in Penfield.

AN AUSTRALIAN LOCOMOTIVE GUIDE

P 16 in the Dudley Street sidings, January 2004. (Peter Clark)

P 11 – P 23

Type	G18HB-R	**Wheel Arrangement**	Bo'Bo'
Engine	EMD 645E	**Length**	13.56 m
Cylinders	V-8	**Width**	2.85 m
Power	746 kW	**Height**	4.21 m
Generator	EMD D-15E-R	**Weight**	74 t
Motors	EMD D-29	**Axle Load**	181 kN
Builder	Clyde Victoria	**Tractive Effort**	152 kN
Introduced	1984	**Maximum Speed**	100 km/h
Number Built	13	**Gauge**	1600 mm

This class was rebuilt from the first group of T class locomotives for outer suburban and shorter country passenger service, in conjunction with air-conditioned passenger cars rebuilt from steel suburban electric stock. They were equipped with a separate GM Detroit 6V-71T diesel alternator set of 105 kW for train power, allowing the full locomotive power to be used for traction. A 645E main engine was substituted for the original 567C, giving a small increase in power, and a vertical radiator was substituted for the original horizontal unit, which allowed the engine and generator to be moved back. This provided room for the auxiliary engine and alternator just behind the cab. A new raised cab was provided with a low short hood with a flat nose end. This, and the greater length, is the main differentiation point from the later T class locomotives. The P class were originally almost exclusively used on passenger services with the matching H car sets. The auxiliary power is really only enough for one set, particularly since many of the sets are now four cars in length. The H sets are fitted with multiple unit cables and use of two sets with a locomotive at each end with one crew is quite common. Locomotives P 11 to P 18 were retained by V/Line Passenger, but units P 19 and P 20 passed to Freight Australia, although these are sometimes made available for passenger use at peak times. These units were rebuilt from T class units 336, 329, 340, 330, 344, 332, 327, 339, 331, 331, 337, 338, 328 and 326.

T 356 at South Dynon, January 2004. (Peter Clark)

T 347 – T 356

Type	G 8B	**Wheel Arrangement**	Bo'Bo'	
Engine	EMD 567CR	**Length**	12.40 m	
Cylinders	V-8	**Width**	2.87 m	
Power	650 kW	**Height**	4.24 m	
Generator	EMD D-15	**Weight**	69 t	
Motors	EMD D-29	**Axle Load**	170 kN	
Builder	Clyde NSW	**Tractive Effort**	151 kN	
Introduced	1959	**Maximum Speed**	100 km/h	
Number Built	10	**Gauge**	1600 mm	

This group (Diagram T-2) is a modification of the earlier T class locomotives. They were introduced with cast bogies and a shorter underframe which eliminated the rear-end platform of earlier units. As V/Line hood units were each equipped with only a single set of controls the cab roof and floor were raised by approximately 440 mm to give the driver improved visibility when operating with the short hood leading, since the controls face along the long hood. Also, the cab roof gained some overhang, the shape of the hood ends was improved and the radiator intake was reduced to half the size of that of the first group on one side. A wide, transverse exhaust stack was used. This group used the original horizontal radiator and right-angle fan drive. These units were used interchangeably with other T class locomotives. They are now all withdrawn, but T356 has been preserved by Steamrail and is sometimes used in regular traffic.

AN AUSTRALIAN LOCOMOTIVE GUIDE

T 357 at South Dynon, March 2005. (Peter Clark)

T 357 – T 398

Type	G 8B	**Wheel Arrangement**	Bo'Bo'
Engine	EMD 567CR	**Length**	12.40 m
Cylinders	V-8	**Width**	2.87 m
Power	650 kW	**Height**	4.24 m
Generator	EMD D-25	**Weight**	69 t
Motors	EMD D-29	**Axle Load**	170 kN
Builder	Clyde NSW	**Tractive Effort**	151 kN
Introduced	1961	**Maximum Speed**	100 km/h
Number Built	42	**Gauge**	1435/1600 mm

These locomotives are described on V/Line diagrams T-3 and T-4. While generally similar to the immediately preceding group, they adopted the vertical radiator developed for the EMD export model GL-8. This eliminated the right-angle gearbox for the cooling fan, saving weight and cost and reducing

maintenance. Numbers 357 to 366 originally had valances below the footplates and curved fillets at the footplate/cabside join. Units 367 to 398 lack the valances, have a lower, sloping short hood and number boards above the cab windows at the short end. On these units the radiator air intake was revised for the new arrangement of radiator and consists of a vertical grid the full height of the hood. These locomotives were used interchangeably with other T class locomotives. T 358 and T 359 were delivered as standard-gauge locomotives. T 360 was very heavily damaged at Portland in March 1970 and rebuilt from the frame up at Clyde by November 1970, reappearing with the low nose of the later units. Some of these units are still in service, with El Zorro, CFCLA and Southern Shorthaul and some preserved units available for hire.

T 400 at South Dynon, May 2008. (Peter Clark)

T 399 – T 412, H 1 – H5

Type	G 18B	**Wheel Arrangement**	Bo'Bo'
Engine	EMD 645E	**Length**	12.40 m
Cylinders	V-8	**Width**	2.87 m
Power	745 kW	**Height**	4.24 m
Generator	EMD D-25	**Weight**	69 t
Motors	EMD D-29	**Axle Load**	170 kN
Builder	Clyde NSW	**Tractive Effort**	151 kN
Introduced	1967	**Maximum Speed**	100 km/h
Number Built	19	**Gauge**	1435/1600 mm

This group (V/Line diagrams T-5 and H-1) is externally similar to the low-nose version of the 567CR-engined T class. The first deliveries had paired exhaust stacks, but later engines reverted to the single exhaust. Mesh is used on the radiator inlet in place of the vertical bars on earlier units. These T class locomotives were used interchangeably with the lower powered versions of the T class; however, H 1 to H 5 cannot be used on light lines as they were intended for hump shunting in Melbourne Yard and are ballasted to 81 t. They were also modified for 'inching' trains through the hump by the fitting of special low-speed controls. H 1 to H 5 were to be numbered T 413 to T 417 and all appeared with these numbers. Although they were restricted from branch line use, the H class proved very popular because of their good adhesion resulting from the 200 kN axle load, and this continued after use of the hump yard was discontinued. The H class are all still in traffic and were equipped with cab air-conditioning before the others. Five of the T-5 series were sold to AN, becoming their CK class.

CK 1 – CK 5

Type	G 18B	**Wheel Arrangement**	Bo'Bo'
Engine	EMD 645E	**Length**	12.40 m
Cylinders	V-8	**Width**	2.87 m
Power	745 kW	**Height**	4.24 m
Generator	EMD D-25	**Weight**	69 t
Motors	EMD D-29	**Axle Load**	170 kN
Builder	Clyde NSW	**Tractive Effort**	151 kN
Introduced	1993	**Maximum Speed**	100 km/h
Number Built	5	**Gauge**	1600 mm

V/Line had a number of the T-5 series surplus to requirements, and some of these were stored adjacent to Spencer Street station. AN had converted some standard-gauge 830 class to DA class to improve visibility, but there was a need for similar locomotives on the broad gauge. AN purchased five of these units, giving them the numbers CK 1 to CK 5. They were found to require work on the bogies, and spent some time out of use as a result. They were used as bank engines to Tailem Bend until the standardisation of this line, and are now used in local work around Adelaide and on the Angaston stone traffic. They were progressively repainted in AN green and yellow, but operated in V/Line colours and with their old numbers at first, although the cast number plates had been removed before sale. CK 2 was sold to SCT and renumbered as T 404.

CK 1	T401	CK 3	T405	CK 5	T407
CK 2	T404	CK 4	T406		

4902 in the short-lived green colour scheme at Delec Depot, 1990. (Peter Clark)

4901 – 4918

Type	G 8C	**Wheel Arrangement**	Co'Co'
Engine	EMD 567CR	**Length**	14.10 m
Cylinders	V-8	**Width**	2.79 m
Power	650 kW	**Height**	4.19 m
Generator	EMD D-25	**Weight**	81 t
Motors	EMD D-29	**Axle Load**	133 kN
Builder	Clyde NSW	**Tractive Effort**	166 kN
Introduced	1960	**Maximum Speed**	124 km/h
Number Built	18	**Gauge**	1435 mm

This class is a variation of the type G 8 intermediate between the second and third types of G 8B. The cab is raised and is equipped with dual controls, but a high short hood was retained. Three orders each for six units were placed.

Valances were fitted only to the first 12 units, and all locomotives have the vertical-grille radiator vents resulting from the GL 8 cooling system. End access platforms are provided, but overhang the couplers. The whole class was originally allocated to Parkes, and could be seen working on most of the Western Division on freight and passenger trains, including the severe Tarana to Oberon line. The survivors finished up in the Sydney Metropolitan area. Two units were sold to Manildra Flour Mills and were converted to low nose configuration by Clyde. Two were similarly converted for use by Patricks on their Portlink services, and the NSWRTM has 4916 and 3801 Limited has 4918. Three now operate with CFCLA.

MM 01   4907   MM 02   4913

1711D at Mayne Junction, September 1994. (Peter Clark)

1700 – 1711

Type	GL-8C	**Wheel Arrangement**	Co'Co'	
Engine	EMD 567CR	**Length**	12.34 m	
Cylinders	V-8	**Width**	2.79 m	
Power	650 kW	**Height**	3.81 m	
Generator	EMD D-25	**Weight**	60 t	
Motors	Clyde CD-36	**Axle Load**	100 kN	
Builder	Clyde Qld	**Tractive Effort**	150 kN	
Introduced	1963	**Maximum Speed**	113 km/h	
Number Built	12	**Gauge**	1067 mm	

These engines are of the end-cab hood design, and of extremely lightweight construction. This can be seen particularly in the slender construction of the Flexicoil bogies. The wheels also are of 950 mm diameter; most other Clyde/EMD locomotives have 1015 mm wheels. These locomotives can operate in multiple unit with each other, and with other Clyde and GE locomotives suitably equipped. When modified for driver-only operation, a short hood containing the air-conditioning equipment was mounted right of centre in front of the cab. The 1700 class worked mainly in the South Western district being based at Roma, but they were later seen in other areas. Locomotive 1706 was destroyed by fire at Bindango in November 1987. The remaining units were withdrawn and scrapped by late 2002.

1771D at Kuranda Station, May 2010. (Peter Clark)

1720 – 1775

Type	GL-18C	**Wheel Arrangement**	Co'Co'
Engine	EMD 645E	**Length**	12.34 m
Cylinders	V-8	**Width**	2.79 m
Power	745 kW	**Height**	3.81 m
Generator	EMD D-25	**Weight**	62.5 t
Motors	Clyde CD-36	**Axle Load**	103 kN
Builder	Clyde Qld	**Tractive Effort**	150 kN
Introduced	1966	**Maximum Speed**	113 km/h
Number Built	56	**Gauge**	1067 mm

The 1720 class were a development of the 1700 class, not intended for branch lines like their predecessors, but instead they were largely intended to work Brisbane suburban trains. A modification to the excitation control allowed optional elimination of the delay required when accelerating a heavy freight train to allow quick acceleration between closely spaced suburban stations. They also had integral frame fuel tanks, indicated by brown patches on the headstocks, and were built with automatic couplers. The only external difference of significance was a small raised section of hood adjacent to the radiator. The same changes for driver-only operation have been made as for the 1700 class. A number received strengthened cabs, starting with 1764 in 2000. These have tinted side windows and lack the ribbed side panels of the original cabs. Following the Brisbane suburban electrification in 1979, the 1720s replaced the former English Electric branch line units and were often used as assistant locomotives north of Rockhampton on the North Coast line. Locomotive 1770 was named 'James Cook' in 1970, and 1723 was painted green and yellow for the Australian Bicentennial from 1988 until 1993. Three units, 1734, 1771 and 1774, were repainted in a blue colour scheme with an Indigenous theme for the Kuranda Tourist Train during 2002.

AN AUSTRALIAN LOCOMOTIVE GUIDE

1.003

Type	NW-2	**Wheel Arrangement**	Bo'Bo'
Engine	EMD 567A	**Length**	12.34 m
Cylinders	V-12	**Width**	3.10 m
Power	745 kW	**Height**	4.42 m
Generator	EMD D-4D	**Weight**	112 t
Motors	EMD D-27	**Axle Load**	280 kN
Builder	EMD	**Tractive Effort**	135 kN
Introduced	1976	**Maximum Speed**	100 km/h
Number Built	1	**Gauge**	1435 mm

This locomotive was formerly a Canadian National Railway unit, but was purchased from a dealer to operate as a shunting locomotive at the wagon repair centre at Weipa. It was the first standard General Motors shunting locomotive to operate in Australia. The characteristic high arched cab roof was cut down, resulting in a mansard appearance like many Clyde designs. The locomotive first operated in a blue livery similar to that on the Comalco GT 26C locomotives. It was later painted in orange and black.

DIESEL LOCOMOTIVES WITH EMD ENGINES

1405 at Mayne Junction, 1982. (Peter Clark)

1400 – 1412

Type	G 12	**Wheel Arrangement**	A1A'A1A'
Engine	EMD 567C	**Length**	13.56 m
Cylinders	V-12	**Width**	2.81 m
Power	980 kW	**Height**	3.71 m
Generator	EMD D-12	**Weight**	77 t
Motors	EMD D-19	**Axle Load**	150 kN
Builder	Clyde NSW	**Tractive Effort**	125 kN
Introduced	1955	**Maximum Speed**	100 km/h
Number Built	13	**Gauge**	1067 mm

These standard EMD 'export models' formed the first class of mainline hood units built in Australia. Of simple appearance, they had flat-sided and square-topped hoods ending at the front in panels flush with the buffer beam, and a cab roof of mansard pattern aligned with the hood roof. The hood ends have only a projecting headlight numberboard assembly, two marker lights and the rungs of an access ladder. Four cab windows are provided each side, and entrance doors in diagonally opposite corners. No dynamic braking is fitted. The driving wheels were of 1015 mm diameter, but the idler wheels were of 760 mm diameter giving the bogies a drop-centre appearance. The prototype, numbered 1230, was placed in service on the Northern and Western lines from Brisbane, but after the first three, the following locomotives were numbered into the 1400 series, and 1230 – 1232 were renumbered to 1400 – 1402. The 1400 class were last based at Mayne (Brisbane) and tended to be used on North Coast line trains. Ten similar locomotives were supplied new to New Zealand, with cabs designed for tighter clearances.

Sister locomotive 4421 at Westfield Depot, Auckland, in January 2001. On 4588 only the lettering was changed to read 'Tasrail'. (Peter Clark)

DC 4588

Type	G 22-AR	**Wheel Arrangement**	A1A'A1A'
Engine	EMD 645E	**Length**	13.11 m
Cylinders	V-12	**Width**	2.78 m
Power	980 kW	**Height**	3.64 m
Generator	EMD D-32	**Weight**	82.5 t
Motors	EMD D-29	**Axle Load**	150 kN
Builder	GM Canada/Clyde SA	**Tractive Effort**	151 kN
Introduced	1999	**Maximum Speed**	100 km/h
Number Built	1	**Gauge**	1067 mm

This is a single unit transferred from New Zealand to provide an additional locomotive suitable for driver-only operation. This unit was equipped with advanced wheelslip controls, but this did not make up for the restricted adhesion of only four driven axles. As a Canadian-built locomotive, this unit was built on a shorter frame than Australian-built G 12 locomotives, and this resulted in a smaller fuel tank, which is also regarded as a disadvantage. This locomotive was built in London, Ontario, by General Motors Diesels in October 1964, with a builder's number of A2070, and entered service with New Zealand Railways as Da 1489. It was equipped with a 567E type engine as built, which was upgraded to a 645E type at rebuilding. It was sent to Clyde at Rosewater, SA, in October 1979 for rebuilding as a model G 22-AR, and re-entered service with NZR as DC 4588 in June 1980, carrying Clyde builder's number 80-945. This locomotive has thus crossed the Tasman three times, but has been withdrawn from service and will not to return to New Zealand.

DE 04 and DE 06 at Iron Knob. (David Griffiths

DE 03 – DE 09

Type	G 12	**Wheel Arrangement**	Bo'Bo'
Engine	EMD 567C	**Length**	13.56 m
Cylinders	V-12	**Width**	2.81 m
Power	980 kW	**Height**	3.71 m
Generator	EMD D-12	**Weight**	74 t
Motors	EMD D-19	**Axle Load**	181 kN
Builder	Clyde NSW	**Tractive Effort**	125 kN
Introduced	1955	**Maximum Speed**	100 km/h
Number Built	7	**Gauge**	1067 mm

This class worked iron ore trains on the tramway from Iron Knob and Iron Baron to Whyalla, and performed shunting duties at Whyalla on 1067 mm gauge. The last two locomotives, purchased for lime sand trains on the 1435 mm gauge Coffin Bay to Port Lincoln tramway, joined them, after exchanging bogies with the two G 8s. The class resembled the QR 1400 class but was fitted with dynamic braking, so grids are visible at the top of the short hood, which has a fan recessed into its roof. The last two locomotives purchased, DE 08 and DE 09, differed in details and lacked ventilation louvres on the side of the hood, as air was drawn through a Farr Dynavane filter. This was contained in a box-like assembly above and behind the cab. These two lacked a rear platform. Box-like mufflers were fitted above the hood over the engine on all units. The cab roofs were reshaped to provide more headroom and air-conditioning was fitted. A number of these units were rebuilt by Morrison Knudsen in 1993 to a new design described as G 14M. The last survivor, DE 07, was renumbered 1251 and transferred to Forrestfield, WA, where it operated as the narrow gauge workshops shunter. In 2014 it was sold for use in Africa.

TL 154, the first in service in Australia, at South Dynon in January 2008. (Peter Clark)

TL 152 – 155

Type	G 12	**Wheel Arrangement**	Bo'Bo'
Engine	EMD 567C	**Length**	13.56 m
Cylinders	V-12	**Width**	2.81 m
Power	980 kW	**Height**	3.71 m
Generator	EMD D-12	**Weight**	74 t
Motors	EMD D-19	**Axle Load**	181 kN
Builder	Clyde NSW	**Tractive Effort**	125 kN
Introduced	1955	**Maximum Speed**	100 km/h
Number Built	4	**Gauge**	1435 mm

These locomotives were built by Clyde Engineering and exported to Hong Kong as Kowloon–Canton Railway 51 – 55. The first two units had a smaller generator, the D-15, the type used in the eight-cylinder model G 8, best known in Australia as the VR T class (320 to 346). These were the only G 12s built with this option, which limited the engine power to 1125 HP compared to 1310 HP for all other G 12 units. All units had welded steel bogie frames similar to those of the earliest VR T class. Locomotive 51 has been preserved in the Hong Kong Railway Museum, but the remaining four units were purchased by CFCLA and were unloaded in Adelaide in December 2005 and were hauled to Islington for overhaul and modification by RTS. A small auxiliary diesel generator was added at the long hood end in Hong Kong to run the air-conditioner. This has been removed. These have been used mainly in Victoria and South Australia, but TL 154 was used constructing the Fortescue Metals line in the Pilbara.

1301 – 1304, ex DE 1, DE 3, DE 4, DE 7 – DE 9

Type	G 14M	**Wheel Arrangement**	Bo'Bo'
Engine	EMD 645E	**Length**	13.56 m
Cylinders	V-12	**Width**	2.72 m
Power	1040 kW	**Height**	4.28 m
Alternator	EMD AR-10	**Weight**	72 t
Motors	EMD D-29	**Axle Load**	180 kN
Builder	MK Whyalla	**Tractive Effort**	151 kN
Introduced	1993	**Maximum Speed**	100 km/h
Number Built	6	**Gauge**	1067 mm

Apart from the conversion to microprocessor control and the addition of radio remote-control equipment, the technical side of this rebuild was fairly modest. The 567 engine, a V-8 in DE 1 or a V-12 in the other units, was replaced with a 645E with increased power and the generator was replaced by an alternator. The traction motors were replaced by later versions. The body was altered out of all recognition, a much taller hood incorporating the BHP design of muffler was substituted, and a new design of cab and a low nose were provided. Desktop type controls were provided. A new striped yellow, black and red livery was carried after rebuilding. These units operated on both 1067 mm and 1435 mm gauges. After the transfer of rail operations to ARG, the survivors (two were lost in accidents) were repainted in the G&W orange and black livery and renumbered from 1301.

1301	DE 1	1302	DE 3	1303	DE 4	1304	DE7

1459 is seen at Rockhampton Locomotive Depot, 1980. (Peter Clark).

1450 – 1459

Type	G 12C	**Wheel Arrangement**	Co'Co'
Engine	EMD 567C	**Length**	15.04 m
Cylinders	V-12	**Width**	2.79 m
Power	980 kW	**Height**	3.71 m
Generator	EMD D-12	**Weight**	91.5 t
Motors	EMD D-19	**Axle Load**	150 kN
Builder	Clyde NSW	**Tractive Effort**	214 kN
Introduced	1957	**Maximum Speed**	100 km/h
Number Built	10	**Gauge**	1067 mm

These locomotives were an adaptation of the model G 12, with six traction motors giving a greater adhesive weight. This required longer bogies and body to accept three motors on each bogie, and the extra length of body is noticeable in the longer short hood. Other identification features were the Flexicoil bogies, with unequally spaced axles. The original EMD model type classification for these locomotives was GR-12 but these locomotives are only generally similar to the GR-12, which is substantially different in dimensions and detail design. The Clyde model number now used is G 12C. The class was used for both passenger and freight on QR lines available for 150 kN axle loads. They could not run in multiple unit, however, and were not fitted for dynamic braking. They were based at Mayne (Brisbane) and worked in the Brisbane suburban area and on the North Coast and Western lines. After the main line electrification, the 1450s were no longer required and all were withdrawn.

A 1502 on a loaded grain train at Avon Yard, 1975. (Peter Clark)

A 1501 – A 1502

Type	G 12C	**Wheel Arrangement**	Co'Co'
Engine	EMD 567C	**Length**	15.04 m
Cylinders	V-12	**Width**	2.79 m
Power	980 kW	**Height**	3.82 m
Generator	EMD D-15	**Weight**	91.5 t
Motors	EMD D-29	**Axle Load**	150 kN
Builder	Clyde NSW	**Tractive Effort**	226 kN
Introduced	1960	**Maximum Speed**	100 km/h
Number Built	2	**Gauge**	1067 mm

The problems of the X class locomotives, many related to the operation of the Crossley engine, resulted in an approach to Clyde to re-engine two units to see if the X class could be made more reliable. Clyde were doubtful that the unconventional chassis would be worth rebuilding, and suggested that they build a pair of locomotives to a conventional design. These two locomotives were the result. They could be identified from the earlier GR-12 type by the shaped hood ends, smaller short hoods, and the cab roofs, which were raised above the tops of the hoods. These first two had mansard-shaped cab roofs, only slightly raised above the hood tops. Connections for multiple unit operation were provided. No illuminated numbers were fitted, but brass numbers and class letters were mounted on the cab sides. These units were immediately placed in main line freight and passenger traffic. They continued in more secondary roles, but were withdrawn and A 1502 was sold to Tranz Rail New Zealand and later to NREC in the USA. A 1501 has been preserved.

AN AUSTRALIAN LOCOMOTIVE GUIDE

A 1202 at Forrestfield Locomotive Depot, June 2008. (Peter Clark)

1202 – 1204, ex A 1503 – A 1514

Type	G 12C	**Wheel Arrangement**	Co'Co'
Engine	EMD 567C	**Length**	15.04 m
Cylinders	V-12	**Width**	2.79 m
Power	980 kW	**Height**	4.01 m
Generator	EMD D-25	**Weight**	91.5 t
Motors	EMD D-29	**Axle Load**	150 kN
Builder	Clyde NSW	**Tractive Effort**	226 kN
Introduced	1962	**Maximum Speed**	100 km/h
Number Built	12	**Gauge**	1067 mm

In 1962 Clyde delivered three more units, A 1503 – A 1505, with a higher cab roof and additional windows in the cab end plates, and all of these later locomotives retained this arrangement. In the earlier locomotives, air for the engine and auxiliaries was drawn in through louvres on the sides of the long hoods, near the cab. Later locomotives lacked these louvres and the air entered through filters arranged in a box structure above the hood, behind the cab. An air motor driven pressurising fan, mounted in this box, delivered the air to the sealed hood. Earlier locomotives had deep valances below the running board. Nos A 1506, A 1513 and A 1514 were fitted with dynamic braking, an external fan and angled grids being visible on the short hoods. All of these locomotives use cast frame Flexicoil bogies. A 1513 and A 1514 were purchased by Western Mining Corporation, and were originally operated by the WAGR on iron ore trains from Koolanooka to Geraldton. The majority of these units were sold to Tranz Rail New Zealand, and A 1507 was sent to Tasmania to provide spare parts for their DQ class. The few remaining A class units have been overhauled and continue in service, 1203/4 ex 1513/4 now on the Eyre Peninsula in South Australia, and 1202 ex 1511 was in Western Australia until sold for use in Africa in 2014.

1501, the last of its class and one of five units fitted with dynamic brakes, at Mackay, September 1994. (Peter Clark)

1460 – 1501

Type	G 12C	**Wheel Arrangement**	Co'Co'
Engine	EMD 567C	**Length**	15.04 m
Cylinders	V-12	**Width**	2.79 m
Power	980 kW	**Height**	3.82 m
Generator	EMD D-25	**Weight**	91.5 t
Motors	EMD D-29	**Axle Load**	150 kN
Builder	Clyde Qld	**Tractive Effort**	187 kN
Introduced	1964	**Maximum Speed**	100 km/h
Number Built	42	**Gauge**	1067 mm

The QR 1460 class had arched cab roofs, as required by the QR loading gauge. They also had end platforms with inter-unit drop plates, illuminated end numbers and, on later locomotives, destination boxes. None of them were fitted with valances. The 1460 class had only two exhaust stacks. Nos 1470 – 1471 and 1498 – 1501 are fitted with dynamic braking with the fan and grids on the short hood. 1461 was painted gold and named 'Centennial' for the QR centenary in 1965. All 1460 class were originally based at Mayne (Brisbane), and were used on North Coast freight and passenger trains including the Sunlander, on the Western line and certain local services. Several units of this class were sold to New Zealand, and the remainder were withdrawn.

AA 1515 – AA 1519

Type	G 22C	**Wheel Arrangement**	Co'Co'
Engine	EMD 645E	**Length**	15.04 m
Cylinders	V-12	**Width**	2.79 m
Power	1120 kW	**Height**	4.01 m
Generator	EMD D-25	**Weight**	91.5 t
Motors	EMD D-29	**Axle Load**	150 kN
Builder	Clyde NSW	**Tractive Effort**	226 kN
Introduced	1967	**Maximum Speed**	100 km/h
Number Built	5	**Gauge**	1067 mm

The AA class were basically similar to the A class but had the 1120 kW 645E engine in place of the older 567C type. Visually, the AA class could be distinguished by a slightly longer air filter box above the hood behind the cab. All five AA class were sold to the metre-gauge Antofagasta and Bolivia Railway in Chile and entered service in their Westrail orange colour scheme.

1502 – 1530

Type	G 22C	**Wheel Arrangement**	Co'Co'
Engine	EMD 645E	**Length**	15.04 m
Cylinders	V-12	**Width**	2.79 m
Power	1120 kW	**Height**	3.82 m
Generator	EMD D-32	**Weight**	91.5 t
Motors	EMD D-29	**Axle Load**	150 kN
Builder	Clyde Qld	**Tractive Effort**	226 kN
Introduced	1967	**Maximum Speed**	100 km/h
Number Built	29	**Gauge**	1067 mm

Apart from the three exhaust stacks, compared to the two on the 1460, there was little to show for the additional power from the 645 engine. The more significant change was the reversion to the larger D-32 generator which allowed simplification of the traction circuitry, and perhaps increased reliability. Other minor changes included automatic couplers, and additional fuel tanks integral with the frames. The colour scheme was the same as the 1460 class. Some 1502 class were based at Mayne (Brisbane), and were used on North Coast freight and passenger trains including the Sunlander. The remainder of the 1502 class were based at Toowoomba and worked the Western line. They were withdrawn, and some units was sold to New Zealand for further service. Two units, 1513 and 1514, were rebuilt for used in WA and renumbered AD 1521 and 1522, after briefly operating as class AC. The control stands were moved to the left side of the cab for this service.

2001 new at East Tamar Locomotive Depot, November 1998. (Peter Clark)

2001 – 2012

Type	G 22C	**Wheel Arrangement**	Co'Co'
Engine	EMD 645E	**Length**	15.04 m
Cylinders	V-12	**Width**	2.79 m
Power	1120 kW	**Height**	3.82 m
Generator	EMD D-32	**Weight**	91.5 t
Motors	EMD D-29	**Axle Load**	150 kN
Builder	Clyde Qld	**Tractive Effort**	226 kN
Introduced	1998	**Maximum Speed**	100 km/h
Number Built	12	**Gauge**	1067 mm

ATN, having taken over Tasrail from Australian National, decided to introduce General Motors motive power and decided to transfer a number of former Queensland 1460 and 1502 class locomotives, after rebuilding, and service in some cases, in New Zealand. These locomotives were rebuilt in Tranz Rail's Hutt workshops near Wellington. In all cases, the short hood was lowered and large windows added to make these units suitable for driver-only operation. Dynamic brake grids were added in the radiator inlet ducts, cooled by the radiator fan, in the manner of General Electric U series locomotives. The locomotives rebuilt from 1502 class locomotives (2001 – 2004) retained their original (refurbished) engines and electrical equipment. The other locomotives, which were rebuilt from 1460 class units, had the 567C engines upgraded to 645CE series by the substitution of the larger bore power assemblies, which provided the same power output as the former 1502 series. These units retained their smaller D-25 main generators and more complex switchgear, however. The first two units were delivered in a striking bright red livery, but later units arrived in the standard Wisconsin Central maroon and cream colours.

42301 – 42306

Type	G 22C	**Wheel Arrangement**	Co'Co'
Engine	EMD 645E	**Length**	15.04 m
Cylinders	V-12	**Width**	2.79 m
Power	1120 kW	**Height**	
Generator	EMD D-32	**Weight**	95 t
Motors	EMD D-29	**Axle Load**	155 kN
Builder	Clyde Qld	**Tractive Effort**	226 kN
Introduced	2002	**Maximum Speed**	100 km/h
Number Built	6	**Gauge**	1435 mm

These locomotives were rebuilt to standard gauge from QR 1502 class, using bogies from the less powerful NSW 49 class obtained with the purchase of the Northern Rivers Railroad. A new cab, based on the reinforced driver-only cabs, applied to narrow-gauge Clyde units, but with a higher profile and a new sloping low nose were fitted. No changes were made to the power equipment, but new mufflers and sound screens were applied to meet NSW requirements

since these were effectively new locomotives in NSW. The first two conversions retained the QR right-hand-driving station, but the subsequent locomotives were completed with left-hand drive. The first four were completed in the Interail scheme, based on the NRR colours, but the final two carried QR National colours from new. These units have been mainly used in the Newcastle area on coal traffic.

Old and new numbers are as below:

42301	1504	42304	1524
42302	1507	42305	1526
42303	1518	42306	1520

AC 1520, later class AD, at Avon Yard Locomotive Depot, June 2008. (Peter Clark)

AD 1520 – AD 1521

Type	G 22C	**Wheel Arrangement**	Co'Co'
Engine	EMD 645E	**Length**	15.04 m
Cylinders	V-12	**Width**	2.79 m
Power	1120 kW	**Height**	3.82 m
Generator	EMD D-32	**Weight**	91.5 t
Motors	EMD D-29	**Axle Load**	150 kN
Builder	Clyde Qld	**Tractive Effort**	226 kN
Introduced	1967/2008	**Maximum Speed**	100 km/h
Number Built	2	**Gauge**	1067 mm

Following the QR purchase of ARG's Western Australian operations, it was realised that some QR locomotives that were surplus to requirements could be transferred to WA to help meet the expanding traffic due to the mineral boom. The smallest of these units were QR 1502 class numbers 1513 and 1514, which

had been stored at Redbank. One unit was modified at Redbank and the other by EDI at Port Augusta. The conversions were not given a low nose, as was done in the rebuilds for New Zealand and Tasmania, but the control stand was moved to the left side, as was standard in WA, and the cab entry doors were altered to provide access from the rear. A roof-mounted air-conditioner was provided, along with full side handrails. Originally given class AC, this was changed to AD to free that class for standard-gauge locomotives. The AD are very similar to the AB class but are on a shorter frame and have a lower profile to meet the more restrictive QR loading gauge. Both these units were sold for use in Africa in 2014.

1520	1513
1521	1514

AB 1501 at Forrestfield, February 2010. (Peter Clark)

AB 1531 – AB 1536, later AB 1501 – AB 1504

Type	G 22C	**Wheel Arrangement**	Co'Co'
Engine	EMD 645E	**Length**	15.49 m
Cylinders	V-12	**Width**	2.79 m
Power	1120 kW	**Height**	4.01 m
Generator	EMD D-32	**Weight**	94.5 t
Motors	EMD D-29	**Axle Load**	158 kN
Builder	Clyde NSW	**Tractive Effort**	226 kN
Introduced	1969	**Maximum Speed**	100 km/h
Number Built	6	**Gauge**	1067 mm

The AB class was the version of the G 22C with the larger D-32 generator, a lengthened frame, a larger fuel tank and a slightly higher all up weight. It was most easily recognised by the larger pressurising box above the long hood. The colour schemes and duties were the same as those for the A class. AB 1532 was sold to the FCAB in Chile and AB 1533 was sold to New Zealand but it was subsequently scrapped. Renumbered AB 1501 and AB 1502 were sold for use in Africa in 2014.

NJ 1602 and NJ 1605 at Albany, July 2006. (Peter Clark)

1601 – 1606 ex NJ 1 – NJ 6

Type	JL-22C	**Wheel Arrangement**	Co'Co'
Engine	EMD 645E	**Length**	13.96 m
Cylinders	V-12	**Width**	2.90 m
Power	1120 kW	**Height**	4.16 m
Generator	EMD D-25	**Weight**	67 t
Motors	Clyde CD-36	**Axle Load**	118 kN
Builder	Clyde NSW	**Tractive Effort**	159 kN
Introduced	1971	**Maximum Speed**	103 km/h
Number Built	6	**Gauge**	1067 mm

This type resembles the larger standard-gauge J-26 (NSWR 422 class) but has only one flat-fronted cab and has ribbed body side panels. Another distinctive feature is the radiator air intake, at the rear on the left side only. Lightweight bogies, like those of the GL-8C, are used. The first locomotive of the class is named 'Ben Chifley' after a former prime minister. The NJ class locomotives were originally used on the narrow-gauge portion of the Central Australian Railway, but after standardisation they settled down on the Eyre Peninsula lines out of Port Lincoln. Two units, 1602 and 1605, were transferred to Albany, WA, to operate the woodchip service. This required minor changes to reduce the overall height. These units were repainted in G&W orange and black, as were the others after overhaul. NJ 1602 and NJ 1605 were sold for use in Africa.

1550 – 1576

Type	GL 22C-AC	**Wheel Arrangement**	Co'Co'
Engine	EMD 645E	**Length**	17.04 m
Cylinders	V-12	**Width**	2.77 m
Power	1120 kW	**Height**	3.85 m
Alternator	EMD AR10	**Weight**	91.5 t
Motors	EMD D-29	**Axle Load**	150 kN
Builder	Clyde Qld	**Tractive Effort**	225 kN
Introduced	1972	**Maximum Speed**	100 km/h
Number Built	27	**Gauge**	1067 mm

The 1550 class were a lighter version of the 2100 series for use on the main lines, since the 2100 could not operate with full fuel tanks except on the Special class mineral lines. They had the smaller 12-cylinder engine, and a lower power rating. The radiators were smaller and lighter as a result, and the radiator cooling fans consisted of one large and one small unit, which provided the best means of differentiating between the two types, apart from the number series. The first 16 locomotives were built for general traffic and were largely used on the major passenger trains. The next batch were built for the Phosphate Hill mineral traffic, but were later used in general traffic. Locomotive 1550 was experimentally modified as the first of a program to allow driver-only operation, and was initially given the suffix letter 'S', signifying a single control station. Units 1551 – 1570 were thus modified from 1990 until 1992, gaining the letter 'D' as a suffix to the number. Units 1571 – 1576 were similarly altered, but retained bi-directional controls, and received suffix letters 'H' to their numbers. All of these locomotives have been rebuilt to 2250 or 2300 class locomotives.

2410 on a work train at Yukan, September 2002. (Peter Clark)

2400 – 2423, 2450 – 2467

Type	GL 22C-2	**Wheel Arrangement**	Co'Co'
Engine	EMD 645E	**Length**	17.04 m
Cylinders	V-12	**Width**	2.77 m
Power	1120 kW	**Height**	3.85 m
Alternator	EMD AR10	**Weight**	91.5 t
Motors	EMD D-29	**Axle Load**	150 kN
Builder	Clyde Qld	**Tractive Effort**	225 kN
Introduced	1977	**Maximum Speed**	100 km/h
Number Built	42	**Gauge**	1067 mm

The 2400 class were basically a continuation of the 1550 class, but since insufficient free running numbers existed following the 1550 class without renumbering the English Electric branch line units in the 1600 series, the opportunity was taken to use the next free group of numbers. The 2400 class

did introduce the Dash-2 modular electrical equipment to the 12-cylinder series, but the locomotives were otherwise very similar to the 1550 class. The 2400 – 2423 group of locomotives was ordered for general traffic on main lines. The 2450 – 2467 group were ordered for the German Creek coal traffic to Gladstone, and, relieved of these duties when that line was electrified, they became available for main line freight traffic. Units 2400 – 2423 were all equipped with the modified cab and air-conditioning for the driver-only operation program between 1989 and 1992. 2467 was destroyed in an accident at Mitakoodi in August 1989. All but six of these units have been rebuilt to the 2300 class.

2484H at Mackay, September 2002. This view shows the modifications for driver-only operation (Peter Clark)

2470 – 2507

Type	GL 22C-2	Wheel Arrangement	Co'Co'
Engine	EMD 645E	Length	17.04 m
Cylinders	V-12	Width	2.77 m
Power	1120 kW	Height	3.85 m
Alternator	EMD AR6	Weight	91.5 t
Motors	EMD D-29	Axle Load	150 kN
Builder	Clyde Qld	Tractive Effort	225 kN
Introduced	1980	Maximum Speed	100 km/h
Number Built	38	Gauge	1067 mm

The 2470 class proved to be the final version of the 12-cylinder main line unit, and had some further weight-saving features, including the lighter body structure and the smaller AR6 alternator. The unit now numbered 2501 was originally built for the Townsville sugar terminal and was numbered ST5 and painted an overall yellow scheme. It lacked dynamic brakes as built, but these were fitted in 1988 when it was taken over by the QR, and it is now a standard member of the class. It was initially numbered 2507 but was renumbered when the original 2501 was rebuilt as a 2300 class. No buffers were fitted to units numbered from 2496 to 2506. These locomotives were originally ordered for use on export mineral traffic, but many are now used for general main line traffic as a result of the electrification program. Many were rebuilt as 2300 class and all remaining units now have the modified cab for single-person operation.

A 60 – A 85

Type	AAT 22C-2R	**Wheel Arrangement**	Co'Co'
Engine	EMD 645E3B	**Length**	18.08 m
Cylinders	V-12	**Width**	2.97 m
Power	1678 kW	**Height**	4.26 m
Alternator	EMD AR-10	**Weight**	118 t
Motors	EMD D-57	**Axle Load**	193 kN
Builder	Clyde SA	**Tractive Effort**	212 kN
Introduced	1984	**Maximum Speed**	133 km/h
Number Built	11	**Gauge**	1600 mm

This class was a complete rebuild of the B class, the first mainline diesel locomotive in Victoria. The original 567B engine, D 12 generator and the entire electrical and radiator systems were removed and replaced by current designs, resulting in a higher tractive effort and nearly a 50% increase in locomotive power output. This was all achieved with a relatively small change in the appearance of the locomotive, largely confined to the ventilation openings and a modified roofline and cooling fan arrangement. The cost of the rebuild was high, and the rebuilt locomotive did not meet modern standards of accessibility for maintenance. As a result the program was stopped after 11 units, and the remaining 15 B class remained in their original form until withdrawal, many years later in some cases. N 461 – N 475 were built in lieu of the proposed rebuilding of the remaining 15 units of the B class, and as a result had the earlier EMD 645E3B engine and lower builders numbers than the first 10 units. Some members of the A class carry names, one of a former commissioner (Sir Harold Clapp) and five of AFL footballers, recipients of the Brownlow Medal. The A class were at first almost exclusively used on passenger services in Victoria, but see more freight service following the introduction of the Sprinter Railcars. The locomotive numbers are 60, 62, 66, 70, 71, 73, 77, 78, 79, 81, 85. A 73 was the first conversion and A 79 was the last. A 66 carried two special liveries, for the Australian Bicentennial and an Olympic Games bid for Melbourne.

N 461 in Southern Cross Station, January 2009. (Peter Clark)

N 451 – N 475

Type	JT 22HC-2	**Wheel Arrangement**	Co'Co'
Engine	EMD 645E3C	**Length**	18.87 m
Cylinders	V-12	**Width**	2.97 m
Power	1678 kW	**Height**	4.26 m
Alternator	EMD AR-10	**Weight**	118 t
Motors	EMD D-43	**Axle Load**	193 kN
Builder	Clyde Victoria	**Tractive Effort**	260 kN
Introduced	1985	**Maximum Speed**	115 km/h
Number Built	25	**Gauge**	1600 mm

This class was the design selected by V/Line for an improved country passenger service which involved the biggest change in services for many years. They were equipped with a separate GM Detroit 8V-92T diesel alternator set of 240 kW for train power, allowing the full locomotive power to be used for traction. A full carbody design was originally proposed, but a double ended hood design,

as developed for Ireland, was used. Conventional Hi-Ad trucks were used, with the D-43 narrow-gauge traction motor, which reduces the unsprung weight, an advantage for high speed operation. Several units have been rebuilt with D78 motors. The locomotives were built in two groups, the first group of 10 being equipped as indicated above, and described by V/Line diagram N-1. The second group, N 461 – N 475, were built in lieu of the proposed rebuilding of the remaining 15 units of the B class, and as a result had the earlier EMD 645E3B engine. The whole class carries names of cities and towns served by V/Line passenger services. The N class were almost exclusively used on passenger services in Victoria and on the Melbourne to Adelaide Overland service until conversion of the line to standard gauge. They are now all allocated to V/Line Passenger with some units converted to standard gauge for the Albury service.

2301 – 2392

2330D at Fisherman Islands, November 2011. (Peter Clark)

Type	GTL 22C-AC	**Wheel Arrangement**	Co'Co'	
Engine	EMD 645E3	**Length**	17.04 m	
Cylinders	V-12	**Width**	2.77 m	
Power	1680 kW	**Height**	3.85 m	
Alternator	EMD AR10	**Weight**	94.5 t	
Motors	EMD D-29	**Axle Load**	155 kN	
Builder	Clyde Qld	**Tractive Effort**	225 kN	
Introduced	1997	**Maximum Speed**	100 km/h	
Number Built		**Gauge**	1067 mm	

scavenged 16-cylinder locomotives, while only slightly increasing the weight. 2301 was equipped with the enlarged cab allowing for two-man operation. These units were converted from all groups of 12-cylinder units of this type and groups of numbers were used to indicate technical differences inherited from the original units. These are now the main 'general purpose' units on QR, being light enough to run on most main lines.

The 1550 class were a lighter version of the 2100 series for use on the main lines, since the 2100 could not operate with full fuel tanks except on the Special class mineral lines. They originally had the smaller 12-cylinder engine and a lower power rating. In 1997, locomotive 1564 was rebuilt with a turbocharged engine and enlarged cooling systems, becoming No. 2301, a number that had remained unused in the QR lists. This made it more powerful than the blower

2301 – 2320	ex	1550 class
2330 – 2339	ex	2400 class
2346 – 2353	ex	2400 class
2355 – 2366	ex	2450 class
2370 – 2374	ex	2450 class
2387 – 2392	ex	2470 class

DFZ 2404 at Forrestfield, June 2008. (Peter Clark)

DFZ 2401 – DFZ 2407

Type	GTL 22C-AC	**Wheel Arrangement**	Co'Co'
Engine	EMD 645E3	**Length**	17.04 m
Cylinders	V-12	**Width**	2.77 m
Power	1680 kW	**Height**	3.85 m
Alternator	EMD AR10	**Weight**	94.5 t
Motors	EMD D-29	**Axle Load**	155 kN
Builder	Clyde Qld	**Tractive Effort**	225 kN
Introduced	1997	**Maximum Speed**	100 km/h
Number Built	7	**Gauge**	1067 mm

The first step in transferring QR locomotives to their ARG subsidiary occurred during 2007 when locomotive 2370 was transferred to Western Australia. It received an overhaul at ARG Forrestfield and was placed in traffic, mainly as a trailing unit. It retained the QR maroon and yellow livery but had the left-hand illuminated number on each end altered to 2300 to indicate its class. After a short period of service, including service on the Geraldton iron ore traffic, it returned to Forrestfield where it was fitted with a toilet at the long hood end, was fitted with new handrails and repainted in the ARG colours, with the number DFZ 2404. The class 'D' isn't quite correct since all other D series have 16-645E engines while the DFZ has a 12-645E3 which is slightly more powerful. There were no other locomotives in WA with the turbocharged 12-645E3 engine at the time. Surprisingly, the DFZ class retain the QR right-hand driving location, while the AC and DD classes have had the controls moved to the standard WA left-side layout.

2251 – 2275

Type	GT 22C-AC	**Wheel Arrangement**	Co'Co'
Engine	EMD 645E3	**Length**	17.04 m
Cylinders	V-12	**Width**	2.77 m
Power	1680 kW	**Height**	3.85 m
Alternator	EMD AR10	**Weight**	110 t
Motors	EMD D-29	**Axle Load**	180 kN
Builder	Clyde Qld	**Tractive Effort**	225 kN
Introduced	2005	**Maximum Speed**	100 km/h
Number Built	25	**Gauge**	1067 mm

After the success of the multi-purpose 2300 class, it was decided to build a heavier version for use on lines available for heavier locomotives to supplement the 2100 and 2200 classes. Although the power increase from 2000 HP to 2250 HP is minimal, the specific fuel consumption of the turbocharged engine was better, particularly at full power, and it is this aspect that has determined the rebuilding. The locomotives are ballasted up to 110 tonnes to suit them to heavy haul duties. They are converted from the alternator fitted 16-cylinder locomotives and the remaining 12-cylinder locomotives but are numbered only in the sequence of conversion, without reference to the original type. In 2014, twenty units were sold to Transnet in South Africa, leaving only 2260–2262, 2269 and 2275 in service in Queensland. The older 2300 class, with a wider route availability, were retained.

DL 36 – DL 50

Type	AT 42C	**Wheel Arrangement**	Co'Co'
Engine	EMD 710G3A	**Length**	18.51 m
Cylinders	V-12	**Width**	2.96 m
Power	2259 kW	**Height**	4.26 m
Alternator	EMD AR-11	**Weight**	122 t
Motors	EMD D-87	**Axle Load**	199 kN
Builder	Clyde NSW	**Tractive Effort**	317 kN
Introduced	1988	**Maximum Speed**	153 km/h
Number Built	15	**Gauge**	1435 mm

Like the preceding NSW 81 class, the DL used the modular body comprising removable cowls permitting accessibility for maintenance but included a number of engine room doors similar to those on a hood unit. The appearance was quite distinctive, with a covered heavy plate girder forming the frame and four reinforcing ribs running the length of the body. The cab with a nose design similar to contemporary US locomotives suffered aesthetically from the reduction in overall height, and has not been used on any other design. This was the first use of the 710G3A engine in Australia, but the electrical equipment was similar to the second and later series of V/Line G class. After overcoming some early difficulties, the DL class has proved both reliable and economical compared to the earlier 16-cylinder locomotives of similar power. They are all on the standard gauge and operate mostly on freight services, since the later EL class and the CLP rebuilds are preferred for passenger services. They do not normally operate on NSW or Westrail tracks. One unit was destroyed in an accident while operating in WA on lease to NR.

AN AUSTRALIAN LOCOMOTIVE GUIDE

GML 10

GML 10 at Goulburn Workshops, August 2011. (Peter Clark)

Type	JT 42C	**Wheel Arrangement**	Co'Co'
Engine	EMD 710G3A	**Length**	18.87 m
Cylinders	V-12	**Width**	2.97 m
Power	2259 kW	**Height**	4.26 m
Alternator	EMD AR-11	**Weight**	129 t
Motors	EMD D-87	**Axle Load**	211 kN
Builder	Clyde NSW	**Tractive Effort**	399 kN
Introduced	1990	**Maximum Speed**	113 km/h
Number Built	1	**Gauge**	1435 mm

For a Goldsworthy Mining single unit order a double-ended hood design, based on the V/Line N class body, as originally developed for Ireland was used, but with the longer stroke 710G series engine. The conventional Hi-Ad trucks of the N class were not used, but the Trimount design of the AN DL class

was substituted. To cope with the higher power, larger radiators were fitted, and a much larger dynamic brake unit replaced the head end power alternator installation. This was the first Australian-built hood unit with the EMD free flow blower duct. As delivered, the locomotive carried the V/Line orange and grey livery, with Goldsworthy badges on the cab side and the number GML 10. It now carries QUBE yellow and silver.

The locomotive originally operated on the former Mount Goldsworthy line from Finucane Island to Mount Goldsworthy, Shay Gap and Nimingarra, in iron ore export traffic. After the merger with the former Mount Newman Railroad, the unit was transferred to Weipa as R 1004, replacing the GT 26 C 1002. As GML 10 this locomotive operated on trial in NSW, and served as the prototype for the very similar 82 class. It is now operated by QUBE on the national network and has reverted to its original number.

8229 at Morandoo Sidings, May 2007. (Peter Clark)

8201 – 8258

Type	JT 42C	**Wheel Arrangement**	Co'Co'
Engine	EMD 710G3A	**Length**	20.83 m
Cylinders	V-12	**Width**	2.93 m
Power	2260 kW	**Height**	4.27 m
Alternator	EMD AR-11	**Weight**	132 t
Motors	EMD D-87	**Axle Load**	216 kN
Builder	Clyde NSW	**Tractive Effort**	413 kN
Introduced	1994	**Maximum Speed**	121 km/h
Number Built	58	**Gauge**	1435 mm

The 82 class was the first of two classes of locomotives leased by Freight Rail from Clyde Engineering on a 'Ready Power' contract. Clyde are responsible for maintenance of the locomotives, which is carried out at a new facility on Kooragang Island, near Newcastle. Unlike the imported 90 class, these locomotives were built locally in a factory at Braemar, near Mittagong. The design is based on the single prototype JT 42C supplied to BHP Iron Ore, but now operating with Comalco at Weipa in Queensland. The 82 class were modified with a larger fuel capacity and with the new design of cab similar to that on Pilbara locomotives. The cab is flexibly mounted to the frame to reduce the effect of noise and vibration on the crew. Although generally similar in overall appearance to the 90 class, apart from the dual cabs, many other details are different, including the locally designed Trimount trucks. The dynamic brake equipment is mounted above the air filtration system, which is just above floor level behind the No. 1 end cab. The space above the engine (often used for dynamic brakes in other EMD locos) is used for a large additional muffler so that the exhaust is at the rear of the engine instead of the front. Unlike the 90 class, the 82 class was designed for state-wide use in general freight traffic, and is not restricted to a specific area. The first four units were handed over for use on 23 March 1994. The builder's numbers are 94-1308 to 94-1340 and 95-1341 to 95-1365.

S 2101 – S 2111, later S 3301 – S3311

S 2109 at Kwinana Provisioning Depot, June 2008. (Peter Clark)

Type	JT 42C	**Wheel Arrangement**	Co'Co'
Engine	EMD 710G3B-ES	**Length**	20.79 m
Cylinders	V-12	**Width**	2.86 m
Power	2260 kW	**Height**	3.99 m
Alternator	EMD AR-8SBEH	**Weight**	118 t
Motors	EMD D-43TR	**Axle Load**	194 kN
Builder	Clyde WA	**Tractive Effort**	332 kN
Introduced	1998	**Maximum Speed**	100 km/h
Number Built	11	**Gauge**	1067 mm

These were the first EMD narrow-gauge turbocharged units built for use in Australia. The units brought the power rating of WA narrow-gauge units up to that of the standard-gauge units in general use on the government systems. They are intended for single-person operation, and are double ended to allow use as single units on lines without locomotive turning facilities. They share with the standard-gauge Q class the feature of radial steering bogies which reduce wheel and rail wear and improve adhesion. Because of their weight, they are limited to operating in the South West between Kwinana and Bunbury, where they are used mainly in bauxite, alumina and coal traffic.

4027 approaching Clinton Point, Gladstone, July 2010. (Peter Clark)

4001 – 4049

Type	JT 42CU-AC	**Wheel Arrangement**	Co'Co'
Engine	EMD 710G3B-ES	**Length**	20.80 m
Cylinders	V-12	**Width**	2.85 m
Power	2260 kW	**Height**	3.87 m
Alternator	EMD TA12-8CA	**Weight**	120 t
Motors	EMD 1TB2622	**Axle Load**	197 kN
Builder	Clyde EDI Qld	**Tractive Effort**	460 kN
Introduced	1999	**Maximum Speed**	100 km/h
Number Built	49	**Gauge**	1067 mm

These are only the second narrow-gauge turbocharged units with an EMD engine for use in Australia, but the first with alternating current traction motors. These are the most powerful narrow-gauge units and are equal to that of standard-gauge units in general use on the government systems. Their main advantage is the high tractive effort, which allows replacement of four conventional units with two 4000 class, particularly in diesel operated export coal traffic. The AC motors require variable frequency power from two converters, one supplying each bogie. The converters are placed one forward and one behind the engine compartment. The 4000 class have dual control stations in the single cab. They share with the S class and standard-gauge Q class the Clyde design of radial steering bogies which reduce wheel and rail wear and improve adhesion. The wheels, at 1030 mm, are slightly larger than the standard 1016 mm. The 'tunnel motor' radiator arrangement has a pair of 1321 mm fans mounted under the radiators rather than the familiar three 1220 mm fans above the radiators. This contributes to the reduced height of the 4000 class, which are about 115 mm lower than the S class. The isolated cab is suspended at floor level, like the S class, rather than at waist height like all current standard-gauge Clyde and Downer locomotives with this type of cab.

PN007on a container train near Aldoga, September 2009. (Peter Clark)

PN 001 – PN 013

Type	JT 42CU-AC	**Wheel Arrangement**	Co'Co'
Engine	EMD 710G3B-ES	**Length**	20.80 m
Cylinders	V-12	**Width**	2.85 m
Power	2260 kW	**Height**	3.87 m
Alternator	EMD TA12-8CA	**Weight**	120 t
Motors	EMD 1TB2622	**Axle Load**	197 kN
Builder	Clyde EDI Qld	**Tractive Effort**	460 kN
Introduced	2004	**Maximum Speed**	100 km/h
Number Built	13	**Gauge**	1067 mm

The PN class are very similar to the QR 4000 class and were built by EDI at Maryborough at the same time as the second batch of this class. There are minor differences, particularly in respect of radio equipment, and the fitting of ATP equipment to the PN class. The locomotives are externally identical, although the striking yellow, white and blue livery in the form of the Australian flag is unlikely to allow a PN to be confused with any other locomotive. These locomotives were purchased for commencement of the PN Queensland container service, largely on behalf of then part owner Toll, between Brisbane, Mackay and Cairns.

8334 is seen at Abbott Point on an empty coal train on 24 June 2014. (Peter Clark)

4101 – 4175, 8301 – 8352, GWN 001 – GWN 005

Type	JT 42CU-ACe	**Wheel Arrangement**	Co'Co'
Engine	EMD 710G3B-ES	**Length**	20.80 m
Cylinders	V-12	**Width**	2.85 m
Power	2260 kW	**Height**	3.87 m
Alternator	EMD TA12-8CA	**Weight**	120 t
Motors	EMD A2619-8	**Axle Load**	197 kN
Builder	Clyde EDI Qld	**Tractive Effort**	460 kN
Introduced	2007	**Maximum Speed**	100 km/h
Number Built	132	**Gauge**	1067 mm

These locomotives are generally similar to the earlier QR 4000 class locomotives, but are fitted with Mitsubishi power inverters rather than the Siemens design used in earlier units, as a result of EMD changing its supplier for this equipment. They are used for export coal traffic by both operators in Queensland including operating on the electrified Blackwater system. A number of the 4100 class (4141–4152, 4168–4175) have been transferred to Western Australia where they operate as class ACN both in the South West and in iron ore traffic in the Geraldton area. Genesee and Wyoming Australia obtained five units, class GWN, for the Whyalla narrow-gauge iron ore traffic.

AN AUSTRALIAN LOCOMOTIVE GUIDE

Above: ACN 4172 is seen at Picton Junction on 17 November 2013. (Peter Clark)

Below: GWN 003 leads an empty train out of Whyalla on 3 September 2013 (Peter Clark)

R 1005 – R 1006

Type	JT 42C	**Wheel Arrangement**	Co'Co'
Engine	EMD 710G3B-ES	**Length**	20.79 m
Cylinders	V-12	**Width**	2.86 m
Power	2260 kW	**Height**	4.07 m
Alternator	EMD AR-11	**Weight**	128 t
Motors	EMD D-87BTR	**Axle Load**	209 kN
Builder	EDI Port Augusta	**Tractive Effort**	413 kN
Introduced	2009	**Maximum Speed**	115 km/h
Number Built	2	**Gauge**	1435 mm

Both locomotives can be considered an updated version of the 1067 mm gauge Westrail S Class, although obviously modified for standard-gauge service, and outfitted with more recent electronics. Built in Port Augusta, the two locomotives were transferred to the Rio Tinto Aluminium (former Comalco) operation in Weipa on Queensland's Cape York. In some ways these two units are also an update of the similarly powered 1990-built JT 42C unit R 1004, which was acquired second-hand by Comalco from BHP Iron Ore in 1994. Aside from a number of technological upgrades (revised engine firing order, electronic fuel injection, later electronic controls), the two units are slightly lighter (at 128 tonnes) and also a little longer than R 1004.

GM 10 at Fyshwick, ACT in July 2004. (Peter Clark)

GM 1 – GM 11

Type	ML-1	**Wheel Arrangement**	A1A'A1A'
Engine	EMD 567B	**Length**	17.88 m
Cylinders	V-16	**Width**	2.97 m
Power	1120 kW	**Height**	4.27 m
Generator	EMD D-12	**Weight**	111 t
Motors	EMD D-27	**Axle Load**	185 kN
Builder	Clyde NSW	**Tractive Effort**	132 kN
Introduced	1951	**Maximum Speed**	143 km/h
Number Built	11	**Gauge**	1435 mm

These were the first mainline diesel-electric locomotives built in Australia. The power equipment in these locomotives was similar to that in contemporary US F-7 model freight locomotives. The carbody was of usual EMD cab unit style, with streamlined nose. The Flexicoil bogies are of cast construction and US manufacture. The engine compartment is pressurised to exclude dust, and there were only small radiator grilles centrally placed above the engine room door. Another smaller grille was fitted behind the cab doors after construction to supply a second pressurising fan. The engine room side panels carry three portholes each side. Only a single set of controls is fitted. Four cooling fans are arranged in a group above the radiator grille. A single fan is mounted behind these for pressurising the carbody. GM 1 is named 'Robert Gordon Menzies' (after the then prime minister). It completed two million miles in service on 24 March 1965, becoming the first Australian diesel locomotive to do so. It is now preserved. The GM 1 type locomotives (sometimes known as the F-type, from the four motors) were used on the Trans-Australian railway on both passenger and freight trains, often in pairs. They were eventually reduced to shunting duties. GM 1 was restored to original colours. GM 10 is operated by Southern Shorthaul, GM 2 is in the NRM and GM 3, also restored to original colours, is owned by EDI.

B74 at Albury on the Seventieth Anniversary *Spirit of Progress*, November 2007. (Peter Clark)

B 60 – B 85

Type	ML-2	**Wheel Arrangement**	Co'Co'
Engine	EMD 567B	**Length**	18.08 m
Cylinders	V-16	**Width**	2.97 m
Power	1120 kW	**Height**	4.27 m
Generator	EMD D-12	**Weight**	113.2 t
Motors	EMD D-27	**Axle Load**	188 kN
Builder	Clyde NSW	**Tractive Effort**	179 kN
Introduced	1952	**Maximum Speed**	134 km/h
Number Built	26	**Gauge**	1600 mm

The distinctive feature of this class of locomotive was the double-cab body, streamlined at each end. Full controls are fitted at each end. The locomotives had four of the traditional EMD porthole windows on each side of the engine room. Above these, ventilation grilles ran the full distance between the cab doors on each side. Two horns were mounted above each cab. A single dynamic brake fan was mounted on the centreline of the roof, either side of the central radiator group of four. The Flexicoil bogies were of local construction and were originally of a fabricated type, although cast bogies are were later fitted.

The B class locomotives were used on all main lines on the V/Line 1600 mm gauge system, including some weekend working on the electrified Gippsland line. In VR days they were rarely used on 1435 mm gauge lines. B60 was named 'Harold W. Clapp' after a former VR commissioner. Eleven units, including B60, were converted to A class, and the remainder were withdrawn by V/Line, although a number continued in service with private operators.

5450 – 5451

Type	F-7	**Wheel Arrangement**	Bo'Bo'
Engine	EMD 567B	**Length**	15.44 m
Cylinders	V-16	**Width**	3.00 m
Power	1120 kW	**Height**	4.57 m
Generator	EMD D-12	**Weight**	104 t
Motors	EMD D-27	**Axle Load**	260 kN
Builder	EMD	**Tractive Effort**	179 kN
Introduced	1968	**Maximum Speed**	143 km/h
Number Built	2	**Gauge**	1435 mm

These two units were representatives of the most numerous class of diesel locomotive in the Western world. They were originally used by the Western Pacific Railroad in the USA, but being considered obsolescent, were sold. Mount Newman used them initially for hauling construction trains. The F-7s were later used only for shunting at Port Hedland.

These units were delivered by sea to Dampier and hauled up the Hamersley Iron line to mile post 117, where they were transferred to road vehicles for the journey to Port Hedland. This complicated route was required as the old wharf at Port Hedland could not safely take the load. 5450 was preserved in Mount Newman colours by the PRHS, and the shell of 5451 is on display in Port Hedland.

GM 41 is seen at Stirling North on 25 April 1978 (Peter Clark)

GM 12 – GM 47

Type	A-7	**Wheel Arrangement**	Co'Co'
Engine	EMD 567C	**Length**	17.88 m
Cylinders	V-16	**Width**	2.97 m
Power	1340 kW	**Height**	4.27 m
Generator	EMD D-12	**Weight**	116 t
Motors	EMD D-27	**Axle Load**	193 kN
Builder	Clyde NSW	**Tractive Effort**	255 kN
Introduced	1955	**Maximum Speed**	134 km/h
Number Built	36	**Gauge**	1435 mm

The CR GM-12 class was very similar in appearance to the GM-1 class but could be distinguished by the four portholes on each side of the engine room. Like the GM-1 class, they have only a single streamlined cab, with no controls in the flat rear end. All the GM-12s have nose-mounted multiple-chime air horns. The cast Flexicoil bogies were rather plain in appearance. One alteration to the last group was the introduction of dynamic brakes, resulting in small humps on the roofs over the rear pressurising fan, and small air intakes towards the rear of the locomotives concerned. AN later provided similar shields over the forward fan to a number of units. Originally purchased for the Leigh Creek–Port Augusta coal traffic, the GM-12 class later worked freight and passenger trains on both the Central Australian and Trans-Australian routes, and were later used on the former SAR 1600 mm gauge lines. As built, these locomotives also had varying traction motor types owing to the extended production period, as follows:

GM 12-21, D 37 motors	GM 30-39, D 67 motors
GM 22-26, D 47 motors	GM 40-47, D 77 motors
GM 27-29, D 57 motors	

G&WA retain several of the later GM class in service. GM 22 and GM 27 are owned by CFCLA and carry the Southern Shorthaul livery. GM 36, nominally preserved, has seen extensive use on grain traffic in Victoria.

4204 at Moss Vale on a wagon transfer, April 2012. (Peter Clark)

4201 – 4206

Type	A-7	**Wheel Arrangement**	Co'Co'
Engine	EMD 567C	**Length**	17.88 m
Cylinders	V-16	**Width**	2.97 m
Power	1300 kW	**Height**	4.27 m
Generator	EMD D-12	**Weight**	122 t
Motors	EMD D-37	**Axle Load**	203 kN
Builder	Clyde NSW	**Tractive Effort**	273 kN
Introduced	1955	**Maximum Speed**	114 km/h
Number Built	6	**Gauge**	1435 mm

The NSWR 42 class had cabs in the flat ends of the locomotives but with limited controls usually only used when the locomotives were running as 'light engines', without a train. The 42 class also had the older Flexicoil bogies of rather plain appearance, and had faired in fuel tanks. Large oval buffers were fitted at the front and rear, and a five-chime air horn was mounted on the nose. On the sides, the ventilation grilles ran for about three-quarters of the length, and there were four portholes each side. During the early 1960s, the 42 class were downrated to 1600 HP, but the original rating was later restored. The class were based at Enfield (Sydney) and were mainly used on freight and passenger traffic on the main Southern line to Albury. 4201 was repainted green and yellow, lined red in 1980 for the 125th anniversary of railways in NSW, but all units were withdrawn about that time. A number of units are preserved, including 4201 in green and 4204 in maroon, both in working order.

S303 at South Dynon, June 2011. (Peter Clark)

S 300 – S 317

Type	A-7	**Wheel Arrangement**	Co'Co'	
Engine	EMD 567C	**Length**	17.88 m	
Cylinders	V-16	**Width**	2.97 m	
Power	1300 kW	**Height**	4.27 m	
Generator	EMD D-12	**Weight**	116 t	
Motors	EMD D-37	**Axle Load**	193 kN	
Builder	Clyde NSW	**Tractive Effort**	239 kN	
Introduced	1959	**Maximum Speed**	134 km/h	
Number Built	18	**Gauge**	1600 mm	

The VR S class generally resembled the NSWR 42 class, but had no buffers, and originally had only pairs of air horns mounted on the cab roof, although some units later received five-chime horns on the nose. The later units had the later style of Flexicoil bogies. The S class was permitted to haul trains with the flat cab leading, but only at 60 km/h. The first group, S300 to S309, were originally rated at 1300 kW but were later uprated to 1340 kW. The second group, S310 to S317, was purchased for standard-gauge working. S316 and S317 were the first locomotives to run through from the builders in NSW to Victoria, on the just-completed standard-gauge line. S314 and S316 were destroyed in a collision near Violet Town in 1965. They were mainly used on the North Eastern standard-gauge line, the North Eastern broad-gauge, and the Western line to Adelaide. Several S class have been withdrawn and a number were sold to the West Coast Railway and then to CFCLA, except for S302 which went to V/Line Passenger and then El Zorro. S317 is operated by Southern Shorthaul. S308 was modified for use as a training aid for maintainers.

42103 at Broadmeadow Locomotive Depot, April 2005. (Peter Clark)

42101 – 42110

Type	AJ-16C	**Wheel Arrangement**	Co'Co'
Engine	EMD 567C	**Length**	17.63 m
Cylinders	V-16	**Width**	2.95 m
Power	1340 kW	**Height**	4.22 m
Generator	EMD D-32	**Weight**	110 t
Motors	EMD D-37	**Axle Load**	183 kN
Builder	Clyde NSW	**Tractive Effort**	316 kN
Introduced	1965	**Maximum Speed**	113 km/h
Number Built	10	**Gauge**	1435 mm

These were the only locomotives of their type in Australia. They were modified type J 16 cab units with streamlined GM cabs on the No. 1 end, and centre doorways cut in the No. 2 end cabs. A single dynamic brake fan was mounted forward, immediately behind the streamlined cab. Four portholes and ventilation grilles were installed on each side. The radiator air intake was on the left side only. NSWR buffing plates were fitted at each end. Pairs of horns were mounted above each cab, and dual sealed-beam headlights are installed at each end. Bogies were of the EMD Flexicoil GLC type, with a shorter wheelbase than those used on the A-7 type. No fairing was fitted over the fuel tank.

The class were based at Enfield (Sydney) and were mainly used on passenger and freight trains on the main Southern and Illawarra lines, after a short period of use to Broken Hill. Most of the class, including all odd numbered units, has been retained, with many of these sold to the Northern Rivers Railroad, based in Casino. These in turn passed to QR National, who still operate some of them.

X41 at South Dynon, May 2008. (Peter Clark)

X 31 – X 44

Type	G 16C	**Wheel Arrangement**	Co'Co'
Engine	EMD 567E	**Length**	17.37 m
Cylinders	V-16	**Width**	2.87 m
Power	1340 kW	**Height**	4.27 m
Generator	EMD D-32	**Weight**	114 t
Motors	EMD D-77	**Axle Load**	188 kN
Builder	Clyde NSW	**Tractive Effort**	239 kN
Introduced	1966	**Maximum Speed**	134 km/h
Number Built	14		

The X class has a mansard-roofed cab and a low profile short hood. To improve forward vision with the long hoods leading, the long hoods taper downward, from a point just ahead of the dynamic brake unit. This provided two rearward-facing cab windows. The air horns are mounted on the long hood near the dynamic brake cooling fan. The X class controls are arranged facing along the long hood. Locomotives numbered from X 37 were equipped with 645E engines rated at 1490 kW, and had slightly deeper radiator air intakes. They were model G 26C. Bogies are of the later Flexicoil pattern. They were initially used on the North Eastern standard-gauge line and on the Western broad-gauge line to Adelaide, but are now used for general freight work within Victoria and NSW. X 33 was badly damaged in an accident at Broadford in January 1967, and was rebuilt by Clyde by June 1967. X 37 and X 38 were built as replacements for S 314 and S 316 destroyed in a collision at Violet Town in February 1969. Certain salvaged components were used, but new 16-cylinder 645E engines were used. Several of the earlier units were rebuilt as 3000 HP XR class locomotives.

DC 2205 stands at Forrestfield on 16 November 2013 (Peter Clark)

42201 – 42220, 2201 – 2216, HL 203

Type	J-26C	**Wheel Arrangement**	Co'Co'
Engine	EMD 645E	**Length**	17.17 m
Cylinders	V-16	**Width**	2.97 m
Power	1490 kW	**Height**	4.24 m
Generator	EMD D-32	**Weight**	110 t
Motors	EMD D-77	**Axle Load**	183 kN
Builder	Clyde NSW	**Tractive Effort**	317 kN
Introduced	1969	**Maximum Speed**	114 km/h
Number Built	20	**Gauge**	1435 mm

The 422 class may be distinguished from the earlier 421 class by the noseless cabs at each end, being the first Australian diesel locomotives with this feature. They use Hi-Ad bogies intended to increase adhesion and reduce weight transfer on starting. This involves placing all the traction motors on the side of the axle nearer the centre of the locomotive. The side panels carry three portholes, and the roof carries a single fan over the dynamic braking resistors on one end and a pair of fans over the engine radiator at the other. Standard NSWR buffing plates were originally fitted. The 422 class were originally based at Enfield (Sydney) and were used on Southern line goods and passenger trains, also working into Port Kembla with through steel traffic. They were later extensively used by National Rail on through services to Melbourne. 42203 and 42220 went to CountryLink and later to CFCLA, 42202 and 42206 went to Northern Rivers, and then Aurizon. The 16 others were sold to ARG and became 2201 to 2216 (except 44209 and 44211). Of these, 2207, 2210, 2212, 2214 and 2216 went to G&WA. 2201, 2203, 42211 and DC2215 were sold to Africa and the others became class DC.

42220, FL 220

Type	J-26C	**Wheel Arrangement**	Co'Co'
Engine	EMD 645E	**Length**	17.17 m
Cylinders	V-16	**Width**	2.97 m
Power	1490 kW	**Height**	4.24 m
Generator	EMD AR-16	**Weight**	110 t
Motors	EMD D-77	**Axle Load**	183 kN
Builder	Clyde NSW	**Tractive Effort**	337 kN
Introduced	1969	**Maximum Speed**	114 km/h
Number Built	1	**Gauge**	1435 mm

In 1980, 42220 was rebuilt by Clyde Engineering in Adelaide as a demonstration locomotive for the improved Super Series wheel slip control system. It was fitted with an AR-16 alternator and an entirely new electrical system. New central air intakes were placed on the left side behind the No. 1 end cab. A modified version of the original colour scheme was applied, with distinctive yellow pilot beams, which it carried until sale. 42203 and 42220 were transferred to CountryLink to operate the Griffith and Broken Hill trains, and were fitted with cab air-conditioning. These two were sold to CFCLA, becoming HL 203 and FL 220.

X48 on Kooragang Island, December 2010. (Peter Clark)

X 45 – X 54

Type	G 26C-AC	**Wheel Arrangement**	Co'Co'
Engine	EMD 645E	**Length**	17.37 m
Cylinders	V-16	**Width**	2.87 m
Power	1490 kW	**Height**	4.27 m
Alternator	EMD AR-10	**Weight**	114 t
Motors	EMD D-77	**Axle Load**	188 kN
Builder	Clyde SA	**Tractive Effort**	239 kN
Introduced	1975	**Maximum Speed**	134 km/h
Number Built	10	**Gauge**	1600 mm

The third group of X class were mechanically the same as their predecessors but used the AR-10 alternator as a replacement for the D-32 generator. A much more visible change was the cab and low nose which were redesigned for improved visibility. The cab doors were moved to the back, and two large windows replaced the smaller four of previous units. The short hood was cut away to improve visibility. The colour schemes and utilisation were much the same as the earlier locomotives. Some were rebuilt by Freight Australia with toilets at the end of the long hood, and some also had the cab and low nose modified to permit driver-only operation.

D 1561 at North Fremantle, August 1975. (Peter Clark)

D 1561 – D 1565

Type	G 26C	**Wheel Arrangement**	Co'Co'
Engine	EMD 645E	**Length**	17.20 m
Cylinders	V-16	**Width**	2.79 m
Power	1490 kW	**Height**	4.01 m
Generator	EMD D-32	**Weight**	107.5 t
Motors	EMD D-29	**Axle Load**	180 kN
Builder	Clyde NSW	**Tractive Effort**	245 kN
Introduced	1971	**Maximum Speed**	100 km/h
Number Built	5	**Gauge**	1067 mm

These locomotives are noticeably larger and more massive in appearance than the preceding A series 12-cylinder locomotives, but are similar in general appearance. While closely related to the QR 2100 series, the high short hood carrying the dynamic brake unit gives a very different appearance. The D class were originally used on the Jarrahdale bauxite line. The total weight of 107.5 tonnes limits the use of this class to the heaviest narrow-gauge main lines, and resulted in the introduction of the lighter DA class. D 1563 was sold to the Antofagasta and Bolivia Railway in Chile, where it was rebuilt with a low nose and is in regular service. D 1564 and D 1565 were sold to Tranz Rail and were rebuilt in NZ for service in Tasmania. D 1562 was rebuilt by Goninan with modified engine air intakes and remained in service until 2014 when it was sold for use in Africa, while D 1561 has been scrapped.

2020 – 2021

Type	G 26C	**Wheel Arrangement**	Co'Co'
Engine	EMD 645E	**Length**	17.20 m
Cylinders	V-16	**Width**	2.79 m
Power	1490 kW	**Height**	4.01 m
Generator	EMD D-32	**Weight**	107.5 t
Motors	EE 548	**Axle Load**	180 kN
Builder	Clyde NSW	**Tractive Effort**	245 kN
Introduced	1971	**Maximum Speed**	100 km/h
Number Built	2	**Gauge**	1067 mm

These two units, D 1564 and D 1565, were sold to Tranz Rail and shipped to Wellington, NZ, where they were rebuilt with an NZR design of cab suitable for driver-only operation by the Hutt workshops. This cab design had been used on NZR DXR 8007, a rebuilt GE U26C locomotive. They were shipped to Tasmania and fitted with English Electric traction motors removed from surplus ZC class locomotives at the East Tamar workshops. They re-entered service in 2001 in this greatly modified form in the Wisconsin Central maroon and yellow colour scheme, barely recognisable as their former identities.

1907 leads a loaded train into Whyalla on 9 January 2010. (Peter Clark)

DA 1571 – DA 1577,
later DAZ 1901 – DAZ 1906, 1907

Type	G 26C	**Wheel Arrangement**	Co'Co'
Engine	EMD 645E	**Length**	17.20 m
Cylinders	V-16	**Width**	2.79 m
Power	1490 kW	**Height**	4.01 m
Generator	EMD D-32	**Weight**	96.7 t
Motors	EMD D-29	**Axle Load**	160 kN
Builder	Clyde NSW	**Tractive Effort**	245 kN
Introduced	1972	**Maximum Speed**	100 km/h
Number Built	7	**Gauge**	1067 mm

The DA class were intended for general traffic on the WAGR narrow-gauge main lines. These lighter Westrail locomotives are as heavy as the heavier version of the Queensland locomotives, which were originally limited to export coal and mineral lines. The DA class lack the dynamic brakes fitted to the D class, which provides the best means of distinguishing the two classes.

The DA class were painted originally in polyurethane enamel, and retained their larch green and red scheme longer than most other classes. They were later all repainted in the standard orange and blue livery but many gained the yellow and black livery after major overhauls. They are progressively getting the G&W orange and black. DA 1577 was the last locomotive built at the Granville works of Clyde Engineering. This locomotive was rebuilt with a low nose, but other locomotives only had a modified air intake fitted. They have been renumbered into the ARG horsepower based numbering system. 1907 has been transferred to operate on the Whyalla iron ore lines. The locomotives that remained in WA received letter codes back, including the suffix 'Z' for ZTR power control electronics. DAZ 1902 – DAZ 1906 were sold for use in Africa in 2014.

2100 – 2123

Type	GL-26C	**Wheel Arrangement**	Co'Co'
Engine	EMD 645E	**Length**	17.04 m
Cylinders	V-16	**Width**	2.77 m
Power	1490 kW	**Height**	3.85 m
Generator	EMD D-32	**Weight**	97.5 t
Motors	EMD D-29	**Axle Load**	160 kN
Builder	Clyde Qld	**Tractive Effort**	245 kN
Introduced	1971	**Maximum Speed**	100 km/h
Number Built	24	**Gauge**	1067 mm

Clyde Engineering used Commonwealth Engineering as a major subcontractor for these and most other Queensland-built locomotives, and the latter built and painted the locomotive carbody. These were the first Queensland locomotives with a low profile front hood. The 2100 and 2200 classes could originally only operate at maximum weight on the Moura, Goonyella and Greenvale mineral lines. They could operate on all main lines (known as A-class lines) suitable for 150 kN axle loads with part of the fuel tank blanked off to reduce the

maximum weight. The 2100 class and other 1490 kW classes have two 1.22 m fans above the radiators, whereas the 1120 kW locomotives have one large and one small fan in this location. Originally the 2100 class were all based at Jilalan (near Mackay) on the Goonyella line in the Central division, but following electrification of this line they have been used in general freight traffic.

All of this class were modified to operate on normal main lines, known as A class lines, and gained the suffix 'A' to their numbers. Later the units from 2105 were converted to single-person operation, getting the suffix 'D'. Units from 2119 also received enlarged fuel tanks, getting the suffix 'F'. Meanwhile the early units were converted to bidirectional single-person operation, gaining the suffix 'H'. This is the only class with members having carried the full range of these suffixes. Ten of these DC generator-equipped locomotives have been sold to Chile.

DD2355 near Benger, May 2009. (Peter Clark)

DD 2355 – DD 2359

Type	GL-26C	**Wheel Arrangement**	Co'Co'
Engine	EMD 645E	**Length**	17.04 m
Cylinders	V-16	**Width**	2.77 m
Power	1490 kW	**Height**	3.85 m
Generator	EMD D-32	**Weight**	97.5 t
Motors	EMD D-29	**Axle Load**	160 kN
Builder	Clyde Qld	**Tractive Effort**	245 kN
Introduced	1971	**Maximum Speed**	100 km/h
Number Built	5	**Gauge**	1067 mm

These units are the most extensively modified of the QR locomotives transferred to WA, and this transfer leaves only a few of these pioneer 'heavy' locomotives in Queensland, since many had been sold to the FCAB in Chile. These were the last QR Clyde locomotives built with a DC generator. The locomotives were rebuilt by EDI at Port Lincoln. The cab was rebuilt without front entry doors and the steps and handrails were altered to match WA standards. A toilet compartment was added at the end of the long hood, and the locomotive could be considered as a narrow-gauge equivalent of the modified PN X class. These locomotives are equivalent to the DA class, and are available for lighter tracks than the D and DB classes. They are suitable for driver-only operation and have dynamic brakes, both features that are lacking on the DA and DAZ classes. So far they have not been fitted with ZTR electronic control. They were used in grain service on the lighter lines and the Albany woodchip service. All these units were sold for use in Africa in 2014.

DD class conversions

2355	2101
2356	2105
2357	2109
2358	2117
2359	2120

2130 – 2148

Type	GL 26C-AC	**Wheel Arrangement**	Co'Co'
Engine	EMD 645E	**Length**	17.04 m
Cylinders	V-16	**Width**	2.77 m
Power	1490 kW	**Height**	3.85 m
Alternator	EMD AR10	**Weight**	97.5 t
Motors	EMD D-29	**Axle Load**	160 kN
Builder	Clyde Qld	**Tractive Effort**	245 kN
Introduced	1973	**Maximum Speed**	100 km/h
Number Built	19	**Gauge**	1067 mm

The first of this group, originally 2200 – 2207, later 2141 – 2148, were used on the now closed Greenvale line, near Townsville in the Northern division.

They were renumbered in 1982 when it was realised that many more of this type of locomotive would be needed. They were originally used for nickel ore traffic. A second group of this class was ordered for the Saraji extension of the Goonyella line. The numbers of this group were 2130 – 2140. They mainly differed from the original 2100 class in having an alternator in place of the 2100 class generator. These locomotives are now in general freight traffic. Most of these units have been rebuilt with 12-645E3 turbocharged engines and ballasted to 110 tonnes as a new 2250 class.

2205D departing Clinton Point, December 2006. (Peter Clark)

2150 – 2163, 2170 – 2214, 2051 – 2054

Type	GL 26C-2	**Wheel Arrangement**	Co'Co'
Engine	EMD 645E	**Length**	17.04 m
Cylinders	V-16	**Width**	2.77 m
Power	1490 kW	**Height**	3.85 m
Alternator	EMD AR10/AR6	**Weight**	97.5 t
Motors	EMD D-29	**Axle Load**	160 kN
Builder	Clyde Qld	**Tractive Effort**	245 kN
Introduced	1978/1982	**Maximum Speed**	100 km/h
Number Built	14/45	**Gauge**	1067 mm

These were the last two groups in the 2100 series with the Dash-2 modular electrical equipment, the second having the smaller and lighter AR6 alternator. These locomotives were equipped with air-conditioning when new. They had a lighter body structure, and were built without buffers with the result that many weighed less than the nominal weight, often as low as 93.5 tonnes. This was used to advantage when, after conversion to driver-only operation, this higher weight was accepted on some main lines. These locomotives were originally used for export coal traffic on the lines from Hay Point, which have since been electrified, and they are now used in general freight traffic on main lines. Unit 2175 was destroyed in the Mitakoodi accident in 1989, but the remaining units have all been modified for single-person operation with enlarged fuel tanks. Locomotives 2150, 2151, 2153 and 2154 were sold to Tasrail in 2012 as numbers 2051 to 2054. In 2014, fourteen 2170 class units were sold to Transnet in South Africa.

DBZ 2305 near Benger, May 2009. (Peter Clark)

DB 1581 – DB 1593, later DBZ 2301 – 2313

Type	G 26CW-2	**Wheel Arrangement**	Co'Co'
Engine	EMD 645E	**Length**	18.01 m
Cylinders	V-16	**Width**	2.79 m
Power	1490 kW	**Height**	4.06 m
Alternator	EMD AR6	**Weight**	110 t
Motors	EMD D-29	**Axle Load**	181 kN
Builder	Clyde SA	**Tractive Effort**	245 kN
Introduced	1982	**Maximum Speed**	100 km/h
Number Built	13	**Gauge**	1067 mm

The DB class, which followed the earlier D and DA classes by 10 years, were equipped with the more modern Dash-2 modular electrical equipment, and the AR6 alternator in place of the previous generator. A modification was the introduction of dynamic air filter elements and a centralised air system. The dynamic brakes were moved to above the air system, allowing a low, wide nose to be used, improving forward view, and the cab was air-conditioned. Like the earlier D class, the DB class are limited to the higher capacity narrow-gauge tracks, and are largely used in export mineral and woodchip traffic, and were initially used mainly in the south-west of the state. The 'Z' indicates the fitting of ZTR traction and power control.

3080 shunting at Nelson Point, July 2006. (Peter Clark)

3078 – 3080, 3086 – 3097

Type	SD40	**Wheel Arrangement**	Co'Co'
Engine	EMD 645E3	**Length**	18.75 m
Cylinders	V-16	**Width**	3.12 m
Power	2240 kW	**Height**	4.47 m
Alternator	EMD AR-10	**Weight**	178.8 t
Motors	EMD D-77	**Axle Load**	293 kN
Builder	EMD La Grange	**Tractive Effort**	357 kN
Introduced	1966	**Maximum Speed**	114 km/h
Number in Service 15		**Gauge**	1435 mm

BHP Billiton decided that it needed locomotives urgently. GE offered ex Southern Pacific SD40s that IC&E didn't want, and the offer was accepted. The first two locomotives, now 3078 and 3079, arrived on the heavy lift ship *BBC Frisia* on 9 November 2003. One more blue and yellow SD40, 3080, was unloaded from the *BBC China* over the New Year period of 2003/04. These three units were fitted with air-conditioners and were used as yard shunters at Port Hedland. The second batch, which GE at San Luis Potosi had time to properly repaint in the full BHP Billiton livery (locally known as the 'Bubble' scheme) was of six locomotives, numbered 3086 to 3091, which arrived on 8 June 2004. These locomotives were very well finished in high quality paint, and showed little sign of their many years of service in the USA. The third and final batch, 3092 to 3097, arrived on the *BBC Sealand* on 6 August 2004. Within two days, these locomotives were given a few initial test runs and entered service as trailing units. As new SD70ACe units arrived, these units were stored and in 2014 were scrapped.

3078	7861-13	SP7302/SP8422
3079	7861-52	SP7308/SP8461
3080	7083-4	SP7377/SP8482
3086	7861-1	SP7354/SP8410
3087	7861-29	SP7321/SP8438
3088	*7861*-23	SP7312/SP8432
3089	7861-22	SP7331/SP8431
3090	7083-10	SP7374/SP8488
3091	7861-6	SP7322/SP8415
3092	7861-8	SP7334/SP8417
3093	7083-9	SP7349/SP8487
3094	7861-25	SP7306/SP8434
3095	7083-7	SP7327/SP8485
3096	7861-20	SP7309/SP8429
3097	7875-10	SP7345/SP8409

DIESEL LOCOMOTIVES WITH EMD ENGINES

L 251 – L 275

Type	GT 26C	**Wheel Arrangement**	Co'Co'
Engine	EMD 645E3	**Length**	19.35 m
Cylinders	V-16	**Width**	2.95 m
Power	2240 kW	**Height**	4.23 m
Alternator	EMD AR-10	**Weight**	137 t
Motors	EMD D-77	**Axle Load**	225 kN
Builder	Clyde NSW	**Tractive Effort**	270 kN
Introduced	1967	**Maximum Speed**	134 km/h
Number Built	25	**Gauge**	1435 mm

This class was the first Australian use of the turbocharged EMD 2-cycle engine. In appearance, as well as in equipment, this locomotive resembles the contemporary North American EMD model SD40. The Australian locomotive is lower in overall height owing to the more limited loading gauge, and has been lengthened to accommodate the same equipment. The dynamic braking resistors are mounted above the prime mover, and are cooled by air drawn in by two roof-mounted fans. A 13350 litre fuel tank is hung between the two Hi-Ad bogies. The radiators are below three 1220 mm fans at the rear of the long hood. The air intake for the engine room with a pressurising fan lies behind the main electrical cabinet, itself immediately behind the cab. In locomotives L 274 and L 275, built in Queensland after the closing of the Granville plant, the US standard central air intake, with Farr Dynavane filters was substituted for the pressurisation system. The major change since construction was air-conditioning of the cab, with the compressor unit being mounted on the battery box below the driver's window. The former Comalco unit R 1002 was leased by Westrail, and operated in its Comalco orange livery numbered as 276. These locomotives formed the greater portion of the WAGR standard-gauge fleet, and operated between Kalgoorlie, Perth and Kwinana on freight and passenger traffic.

1.001 – 1.002

Type	GT 26C	**Wheel Arrangement**	Co'Co'
Engine	EMD 645E3	**Length**	19.35 m
Cylinders	V-16	**Width**	2.95 m
Power	2240 kW	**Height**	4.23 m
Alternator	EMD AR-10	**Weight**	148 t
Motors	EMD D-77	**Axle Load**	240 kN
Builder	Clyde NSW	**Tractive Effort**	270 kN
Introduced	1967	**Maximum Speed**	134 km/h
Number Built	2	**Gauge**	1435 mm

1.001, renumbered L277, at South Dynon, January 2012. (Peter Clark)

Comalco obtained two heavier versions of the Westrail L class locomotives to perform line haul at Weipa. Since the entire line had very few gradients, the dynamic braking option was not taken. The only other change was the adoption of the US standard central air intake with Farr Dynavane air filters, the first use of the standard arrangement in Australia. They thus look very similar to US SD40 type locomotives, but are lower in overall height. One minor alteration was the fitting of a double roof to the cab to reduce the internal heat. The two locomotives operated at Weipa, between the open cut mine and the ore stockpile at the port. They haul bauxite in enclosed aluminium hoppers. They usually operated as single units. The numbers were revised to R 1001 – R 1002. In 1994, R 1001 was rebuilt at Clyde's plant at Kelso, NSW, and repainted in yellow with red lining. R 1002 was replaced by the former Goldsworthy JT 42C and sold to Westrail as 276. In 2011 R1001 was sold to Australian Loco Leasing and was renumbered L277 for operation in NSW and Victoria.

LQ 3121 at Forrestfield, February 2010. (Peter Clark)

LZ 3101 – LZ 3107, LZ 3111, LZ 3117, LZ 3119 – LZ 3120, LQ 3121 – LQ 3122

Type	GT 26C-3	**Wheel Arrangement**	Co'Co'
Engine	EMD 645E3	**Length**	19.35 m
Cylinders	V-16	**Width**	2.95 m
Power	2240 kW	**Height**	4.23 m
Alternator	EMD AR-10	**Weight**	137 t
Motors	EMD D-77	**Axle Load**	225 kN
Rebuilder	EDI SA and WA	**Tractive Effort**	270 kN
Introduced	2002	**Maximum Speed**	134 km/h
Number Built	16	**Gauge**	1435 mm

ARG rebuilt four L class as construction locomotives for the Darwin line and they introduced a new all numeric classification, becoming 3101 – 3104. These units included digital ZTR wheelslip and electrical control equipment, which proved successful. As other L class were overhauled, they also received ZTR equipment and were numbered in the 3100 series, but now in numerical order of the old number. When QRN took over the Western section of ARG, letter codes were reintroduced while retaining the horsepower based numbering, and a 'Z' suffix added to the classification of ZTR fitted units. Six units were

sold to ATN in 2000 for standard-gauge grain service in NSW and Victoria and of these 251, 254, 265 and 270 were overhauled and entered service for ATN. The others passed to RTS, who also took over 265 as a lease unit. This passed to Interail, and was joined by 271. The three remaining ATN units, and the two Interail units, were rebuilt by RTS using Q-Tron wheelslip and electrical controls, becoming equivalent to the LQ type. The three ATN units went to PN, but 254 was withdrawn following a fire.

L 252	LZ 3101	L 264	L 3112
L 257	LZ 3102	L 266	L 3113
L 259	LZ 3103	L 267	L 3114
L 273	LZ 3104	L 268	L 3115
L 255	LZ 3105	L 272	L 3116
L 256	LZ 3106	L 274	LZ 3117 (WMC)
L 258	LZ 3107	L 275	L 3118 (WMC)
L 260	L 3108	L 253	LZ 3119
L 261	L 3109	276	LZ 3120 (1.002)
L 262	L 3110	L265	LQ3121
L 263	LZ 3111	L271	LQ3122

CL 10 at Port Pirie, April 1978. (Peter Clark)

CL 1 – CL 17

Type	AT-26C	**Wheel Arrangement**	Co'Co'
Engine	EMD 645E3	**Length**	19.63 m
Cylinders	V-16	**Width**	2.96 m
Power	2240 kW	**Height**	4.09 m
Alternator	EMD AR-10	**Weight**	128 t
Motors	EMD D-77	**Axle Load**	210 kN
Builder	Clyde NSW	**Tractive Effort**	270 kN
Introduced	1970	**Maximum Speed**	154 km/h
Number Built	17	**Gauge**	1435 mm

This class resembled the GM class in the shape of the cab, but the car body behind the cab resembled the centre section of a J 26C complete to the mansard roof, which carried an arrangement of fans similar to those of the GT 26C. Hi-Ad bogies were used, and as was usual for CR locomotives, the CL class was single ended. The sides carried the traditional portholes, but the air intakes and the radiators were incorporated in the angled roofs, unlike the earlier Clyde-GM cab units. CL 1 was the first CR diesel to be delivered entirely under its own power, and was the leading locomotive between Port Pirie and Kalgoorlie on the inaugural *Indian Pacific*, the first through Sydney–Perth passenger train, in February 1970. The CL class were used on the Trans-Australian and Central Australian lines, replacing double-headed GM class locomotives. These locomotives were rebuilt by Morrison Knudsen in 1993 into the CLF and CLP classes

3081 – 3085

3084 at the North West Coastal Highway crossing, July 2006. (Peter Clark)

Type	SD40-2	**Wheel Arrangement**	Co'Co'
Engine	EMD 645E3	**Length**	19.71 m
Cylinders	V-16	**Width**	3.12 m
Power	2240 kW	**Height**	4.47 m
Alternator	EMD AR-10	**Weight**	186 t
Motors	EMD D-77	**Axle Load**	305 kN
Builder	EMD La Grange	**Tractive Effort**	357 kN
Introduced	1972	**Maximum Speed**	114 km/h
Number in Service	5	**Gauge**	1435 mm

numbers. While this resulted in a fairly shabby looking group of locomotives, their original identities were fairly easily found. The five grey SD40-2s which became BHPB 3081 to 3085 were unloaded from the *BBC China* over the New Year period of 2003/04. These units were used as trailing units on ore trains. As new SD70ACe units arrived, these units were stored and in 2014 were scrapped.

To meet BHP Billiton's requested delivery times, as well as three locomotives already rebuilt for IC&E, including the rejected unit 6401, five former UP SD40-2 locomotives in the process of being rebuilt for IC&E were shipped to Port Hedland. The SD40-2s arrived in grey undercoat with their former UP

3081	786170-75	UP 3573	All painted grey
3082	786263-31	UP 3639	
3083	786170-2	UP 3500	
3084	786263-35	UP 3643	
3085	786170-25	UP 3523	

AL 22 at Morrison Knudsen Australia for conversion in 1994. (Peter Clark)

AL 18 – AL 25

Type	JT 26C	**Wheel Arrangement**	Co'Co'
Engine	EMD 645E3	**Length**	19.82 m
Cylinders	V-16	**Width**	2.97 m
Power	2240 kW	**Height**	4.24 m
Alternator	EMD AR-10	**Weight**	129 t
Motors	EMD D-77	**Axle Load**	210 kN
Builder	Clyde SA	**Tractive Effort**	270 kN
Introduced	1976	**Maximum Speed**	155 km/h
Number Built	8	**Gauge**	1435 mm

Clyde Engineering had only just moved the locomotive building function from its Granville plant to Rosewater in South Australia, when an order was won to build eight units of similar power to the CL class. The ALs were built with a flat fronted cab (based on the design used for the NSW 422 and the narrow-gauge NJ class) at each end, thus avoiding the need to turn the unit. When first introduced there was a problem with overall locomotive weight

and axle loading and some ALs were returned from Port Augusta to the Clyde workshops at Rosewater for modification to reduce the total weight. After this operation, and some rewiring resulting from the inexperience of the new factory, they were delivered back to Port Augusta. The AL class originally worked over the whole of the Northern Region, and later the AL class interworked with the Comeng Alco 80 class, basically between Port Pirie and Lithgow, where electric traction took over for the steep mountain grades. AL 18, named 'Malcolm Fraser', after the then prime minister, hauled the first official train into Alice Springs. AL 24 was named 'Peter Nixon' after the then Federal minister for transport. Their builder's numbers were 76/834 to 76/838 and 77/839 to 77/841. All were rebuilt by Morrison Knudsen into single ended ALF class units.

C508 is seen in Junee yard, 6 January 2013. (Peter Clark)

C 501 – C 510

Type	GT 26CW	**Wheel Arrangement**	Co'Co'
Engine	EMD 645E3	**Length**	19.35 m
Cylinders	V-16	**Width**	2.97 m
Power	2240 kW	**Height**	4.25 m
Alternator	EMD AR-10	**Weight**	135 t
Motors	EMD D-77	**Axle Load**	225 kN
Builder	Clyde SA	**Tractive Effort**	289 kN
Introduced	1977	**Maximum Speed**	133 km/h
Number Built	10	**Gauge**	1435 mm

This locomotive resembles the North American EMD model SD40-2, but is lower in overall height owing to the more limited loading gauge, and has been lengthened to accommodate similar equipment. The C class has conventional rather than modular control equipment, and is not a Dash-2 model. The dynamic braking equipment is mounted above the prime mover, and is cooled by two roof-mounted fans. A 10 130 litre fuel tank is hung between the two Hi-Ad bogies. The radiators are mounted in a vee arrangement below three 1220 mm fans at the rear of the long hood. The air intake follows the US standard central air intake layout, with Farr Dynavane filters. The major visible modifications to this class were the addition of a small platform around the nose, and the addition of retained multiple unit cables. These locomotives were originally split evenly between the VR broad and standard-gauge fleets, but the arrival of the G 2 class returned all of them to broad gauge. All were converted to standard gauge in 1995, following conversion of the Adelaide–Melbourne line to standard gauge. C 501 is preserved, C 502, 503 and 508 are with CFCLA and the remainder with Greentrains.

AN AUSTRALIAN LOCOMOTIVE GUIDE

CLF 5 leads a loaded grain train at Tailem Bend on 11 January 2015. (Peter Clark)

CLF 1 – CLF 7

Type	AT 26C-2M	**Wheel Arrangement**	Co'Co'
Engine	EMD 645E3C	**Length**	19.63 m
Cylinders	V-16	**Width**	2.96 m
Power	2460 kW	**Height**	4.09 m
Alternator	EMD AR-10	**Weight**	128 t
Motors	EMD/MK D-78	**Axle Load**	210 kN
Builder	MKA	**Tractive Effort**	270 kN
Introduced	1993	**Maximum Speed**	130 km/h
Number Built	7	**Gauge**	1435 mm

The original CL class locomotives were built by Clyde Engineering in Granville from 1970 as their model AT26C, and were the last new locomotives built with the GM nose dating back to 1939. They were all in service until withdrawn for rebuilding. Australian National entered an arrangement for the remanufacture of 25 locomotives from its fleet. The Morrison Knudsen Corporation of Australia Limited purchased 17 CL class and 8 AL class locomotives from Australian National, remanufactured and upgraded them at its facility in Whyalla, South Australia, and then leased them back to AN on a fully maintained basis. The traditional GM nose of the CL was retained, but with the horns relocated beneath the underframe near the coupler. Common changes to all units were new control arrangement with a desk top and T-bar control handle, MK microprocessor engine control, retention toilets, single brakes with high friction non-metallic blocks and flange lubricators. The CLF class are used on standard-gauge freight traffic interchangeably with other units of similar power.

3010, later renumbered to CLP 10, at Dry Creek, July 2004. (Peter Clark)

CLP 8 – CLP 17

Type	AT 26HC-2M	**Wheel Arrangement**	Co'Co'	
Engine	EMD 645E3C	**Length**	19.63 m	
Cylinders	V-16	**Width**	2.96 m	
Power	2460 kW	**Height**	4.09 m	
Alternator	EMD AR-10	**Weight**	140 t	
Motors	EMD/MK D-78	**Axle Load**	230 kN	
Builder	MKA	**Tractive Effort**	270 kN	
Introduced	1993	**Maximum Speed**	140 km/h	
Number Built	10	**Gauge**	1435 mm	

'City of Port Augusta', CLP 8, was the first AN Passenger locomotive to emerge from Morrison Knudsen Corporation's plant at Whyalla as part of a 'power by the hour' contract. It was the first locomotive repainted in the AN Passenger & Travel livery of green, yellow and silver. The other CLP class units are all named after Aboriginal tribal areas across the Australian Outback: 'Mirning', 'Barngarla', 'Nukunu', 'Ngadjuri', 'Wiljakali', 'Kaurna', 'Arabana', 'Kokatha' and 'Murunitja'. The CLP units were equipped with a pair of Cummins/Onan 140 DFDG self contained generating sets each of 125 kW, and were capable of heading an Indian Pacific or Ghan providing head end power. They could also be used on high-speed freight trains that required HEP for refrigerated containers. Now divided between G&WA and QR National, they are used on freight traffic and the HEP equipment has been removed.

ALF 18 – ALF 25, ALZ 3208

Type	JT 26C-2M	**Wheel Arrangement**	Co'Co'
Engine	EMD 645E3C	**Length**	19.82 m
Cylinders	V-16	**Width**	2.97 m
Power	2460 kW	**Height**	4.24 m
Alternator	EMD AR-10	**Weight**	129 t
Motors	EMD/MK D-78	**Axle Load**	210 kN
Builder	MKA	**Tractive Effort**	270 kN
Introduced	1994	**Maximum Speed**	130 km/h
Number Built	8	**Gauge**	1435 mm

The whole of the AL class were purchased by Morrison Knudsen and rebuilt from late 1993 with upgraded engine and electrical equipment. The number two end cab was removed, and the locomotive batteries were relocated in that position. The ALF class are now effectively the same as the CLF class, and are used on AN standard-gauge freight traffic. The locomotives were renumbered in the order of their rebuilding. The first rebuild was named 'City of Port Pirie', the third of the Iron Triangle cities to be commemorated. They were modified for operating with BU class slug units rebuilt from 600 class. This allowed each of a pair of ALFs to drive eight traction motors rather than the six on each unit. This program was not really successful and ALFs operated as normal units and the BU units were scrapped. Seven remain with G&WA, but ALF 25 was renumbered ALZ 3208 and operated for QR National until withdrawn.

8101 – 8184

Type	JT 26C-2SS	**Wheel Arrangement**	Co'Co'
Engine	EMD 645E3B	**Length**	19.67 m
Cylinders	V-16	**Width**	2.93 m
Power	2240 kW	**Height**	4.26 m
Alternator	EMD AR-16	**Weight**	129 t
Motors	EMD D-77	**Axle Load**	210 kN
Builder	Clyde NSW	**Tractive Effort**	337 kN
Introduced	1982	**Maximum Speed**	114 km/h
Number Built	84	**Gauge**	1435 mm

8101, when built, carried the new SRA corporate image colour scheme and was the second Australian production locomotive type with the Super Series radar Doppler wheel slip control system. A new feature was the adoption of a true cowl type structure rather than the load-bearing carbody design. The modular body comprising removable cowls improved accessibility for maintenance. The appearance was quite distinctive, with a heavy plate girder forming the frame and four reinforcing ribs running the length of the body. The 81 used the 1967 Hi-Ad pattern bogie rather than the Trimount design

on the other JT 26C-2SS units. The hydraulic handbrakes, with four small hand wheels on each side of the locomotive, were distinctive. An early problem was exhaust recirculation. The solution adopted was to move the air intake ducts downward to the top of the side panels. Also, to improve cooling for normal running maintenance, additional doors and cooling louvres were added. Four complete spare sets of equipment were originally ordered for use as spares, but it was later decided to complete these as additional locomotives. Rebuilt D-67 traction motors from withdrawn 421 class locomotives were used. The first 20 locomotives were allocated to Broadmeadow for export coal traffic in the Hunter Valley, and the remainder were mainly used on the Southern line, including operation through to Melbourne on the standard-gauge. They saw some use on the Western line. They are used widely on freight since the 90 class took over Hunter Valley coal traffic, and are extensively used on Port Kembla grain traffic.

BL 26 – BL 35

BL 27 at Morandoo Sidings, May 2007. (Peter Clark)

Type	JT 26C-2SS	**Wheel Arrangement**	Co'Co'
Engine	EMD 645E3B	**Length**	19.82 m
Cylinders	V-16	**Width**	2.97 m
Power	2240 kW	**Height**	4.27 m
Alternator	EMD AR-16	**Weight**	130 t
Motors	EMD D-77	**Axle Load**	210 kN
Builder	Clyde SA	**Tractive Effort**	337 kN
Introduced	1983	**Maximum Speed**	114 km/h
Number Built	10	**Gauge**	1435 mm

The third of the ANR series of 2240 kW locomotives was classified BL more to fill the 'gap' between AL and CL than to convey any encrypted meaning. These units were also built at Rosewater, incorporating lessons learned with the AL class and a series of technical improvements resulting from work carried out by EMD in the United States. The updates resulted in a change in model designation from JT 26C to JT 26C 2SS. The BL class appeared in two groups delivered concurrently. BL 27 to BL 30 were allocated to the standard gauge and entered service between August 1983 and December 1984. BL 31 to BL 35 appeared on the broad gauge between November 1983 and July 1984, and BL 26, named 'Bob Hawke' after the then prime minister, commenced operation on the broad gauge in March 1984. They carry Clyde builder's numbers 83/1010 – 83/1016 and 84/1017 – 84/1019 in numerical order. In appearance the BL differed from the AL in the shape of the cab roof, the simpler flat roof providing more room for an air-conditioning unit. The BL was the first AN class to have air-conditioned cabs on all units. The removal of the No. 2 end body pressurising fan was the only external change to this class. These locomotives are now mainly employed on the standard gauge in NSW and on the broad-gauge steel traffic in Victoria.

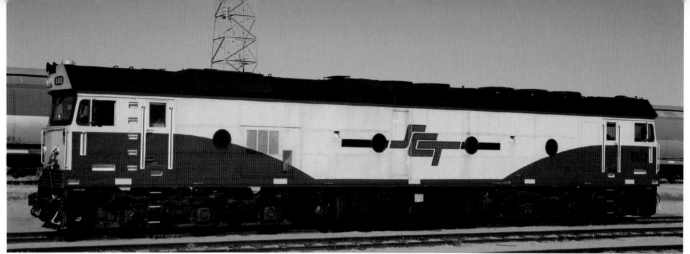

G 512 at Merriden, June 2008. (Peter Clark)

G 511 – G 515

Type	JT 26C-2SS	**Wheel Arrangement**	Co'Co'
Engine	EMD 645E3B	**Length**	19.82 m
Cylinders	V-16	**Width**	2.97 m
Power	2240 kW	**Height**	4.27 m
Alternator	EMD AR-16	**Weight**	127 t
Motors	EMD D-77	**Axle Load**	210 kN
Builder	Clyde SA	**Tractive Effort**	337 kN
Introduced	1984	**Maximum Speed**	114 km/h
Number Built	5	**Gauge**	1600 mm

The first G class were ordered from Clyde Engineering in August 1983, but by April 1984, before any deliveries on the first order were received, V/Line asked for the then current production run for the ANR BL class to be extended by five units, becoming G 511 to G 515 with builder's numbers 84/1239 to 84/1243. They were only slightly different from the BL class, and conformed to the first generation of Super Series units with the AR-16 alternator and D77 motors, and were fitted with Trimount bogies. These bogies give better adhesion than the conventional Hi-Ad type fitted to the N class and the C class locomotives. G 511 to G 515 are described by V/Line diagram G 1. These numerical suffixes have spread to more general usage to describe the various subgroups of locomotives. The G 1 group were initially used on the broad gauge, but they were converted to standard gauge when sold to SCT. They are now operated by CFCLA or Southern Shorthaul.

200   **AN AUSTRALIAN LOCOMOTIVE GUIDE**

G 516 – G 525

Type	JT 26C-2SS	**Wheel Arrangement**	Co'Co'
Engine	EMD 645E3B	**Length**	19.82 m
Cylinders	V-16	**Width**	2.97 m
Power	2240 kW	**Height**	4.27 m
Alternator	EMD AR-11	**Weight**	127 t
Motors	EMD D-77	**Axle Load**	210 kN
Builder	Clyde SA	**Tractive Effort**	337 kN
Introduced	1985	**Maximum Speed**	114 km/h
Number Built	10	**Gauge**	1435/1600 mm

Delivery of the first order of G class followed the second with units numbered G 516 to G 525, and with lower builder's numbers 85/1229–1235 and 86/1236–1238. It was originally intended that these be built at Somerton in Victoria, but they were actually built in Rosewater following the first batch.

This group mainly differed in having AR-11 alternators with internal series-parallel switching. They were most easily recognised by their roof-mounted cab air-conditioning units rather than the body side-mounted units used in the earlier locos. The NSW pattern ditch lights at coupler level were first fitted to this group for standard-gauge use, but are now on other locomotives. G 516 to G 525 were described by V/Line diagram G 2, and are often generally known by this title. Most of the G 2s were initially used on the standard-gauge Sydney–Melbourne line. One unit was sold to QR National.

G 526 – G 543

G 540 at Dry Creek, July 2006. (Peter Clark)

Type	JT 26C-2SS	**Wheel Arrangement**	Co'Co'
Engine	EMD 645E3C	**Length**	19.82 m
Cylinders	V-16	**Width**	2.97 m
Power	2240 kW	**Height**	4.27 m
Alternator	EMD AR-11	**Weight**	127 t
Motors	EMD D-87	**Axle Load**	210 kN
Builder	Clyde Victoria	**Tractive Effort**	337 kN
Introduced	1988	**Maximum Speed**	114 km/h
Number Built	18	**Gauge**	1435/1600 mm

V/Line were obviously happy with the G Class, and a third batch were ordered. These were known as the G 3 group. They were also equipped as the second generation of Super Series units with AR11 alternators with internal series-parallel switching and the new D87 traction motors. Externally they are most easily distinguished from the G 2 type by the double engine room doors (rather than single) on the body sides. The G 3s are numbered G 526 to G 536 and have builder's numbers 88/1256–1265 and 89/1266. A fourth batch, known as the G 4s followed, numbered G 537 to G 543. They are essentially identical to the G 3s, with minor internal changes. However, the last unit has desk type control consoles, similar to those on the ANR DL class, which have the same electrical equipment. The G class was the largest class of non-steam mainline locomotives in Victoria. They took a major share of broad-gauge freight traffic, including grain haulage, but only two units remain on broad gauge with Pacific National, the remainder being used on standard gauge.

XR 550 – XR 555, XR557 – XR 559

XR 555 at South Dynon, January 2006. (Peter Clark)

Type	GT 26C-3	**Wheel Arrangement**	Co'Co'
Engine	EMD 645E3C	**Length**	17.37 m
Cylinders	V-16	**Width**	2.96 m
Power	2240 kW	**Height**	4.36 m
Alternator	EMD AR10	**Weight**	124 t
Motors	EMD D78	**Axle Load**	203 kN
Builder	FA Dynon	**Tractive Effort**	344 kN
Introduced	2001	**Maximum Speed**	115 km/h
Number Built	9	**Gauge**	1435 mm

The work of upgrading the XR class started in early 2000 with the G class locomotive upgrade (the replacement of the 16-645E3C engines with 16-645F3B engines) followed by the X class upgrade (replacement of the 16-645E blower engines by 16-645E3C turbocharged engines). What makes this upgrade program unusual is the decision to build three new members of the XR class to be assembled from spare parts from other similar locomotives, but with completely new frames. The XRs have all been equipped for driver-only operation. The gear ratio has been changed from 59:18 to 61:16. The wheel slip detection system relies on the Wabtech Q-Tron system using a microprocessor to detect wheel slip through differences in current flow. XR 555 and the new build locomotives are fitted with large sound baffles around the radiator inlets and a large muffler forming the hood top. New radiators, similar to those in A class locomotives, have been fitted resulting in flared radiator air intakes.

Old and new identities are as follows:

X 38	XR 550
X 35	XR 551
X 40	XR 552
X 33	XR 553
X 34	XR 554
X 32	XR 555

XRB 560 at Port Adelaide Flat, January 2009. (Peter Clark)

XRB 560 – XRB 562

Type	GT 26C-3B	**Wheel Arrangement**	Co'Co'
Engine	EMD 645E3C	**Length**	17.37 m
Cylinders	V-16	**Width**	2.96 m
Power	2240 kW	**Height**	4.36 m
Alternator	EMD AR10	**Weight**	124t
Motors	EMD D78	**Axle Load**	203 kN
Builder	PN Dynon	**Tractive Effort**	344 kN
Introduced	2005	**Maximum Speed**	115 km/h
Number Built	3	**Gauge**	1435 mm

The last three new XR locomotives were completed as cabless locomotives. These locomotives can only operate coupled to and controlled from another conventional locomotive. This allowed the fitting of a larger radiator (expanding to occupy the toilet compartment) and a much larger dynamic brake of the radial pattern occupying the space of the cab. Otherwise the locomotives are very similar to the XR class. The XRB did introduce a new livery, with broad white and yellow diagonal lines in the centre of the hood, and with the Southern Cross on the radiator baffles (later removed), a simpler form of the PN livery used in Queensland.

VL 356 at South Dynon, May 2008. (Peter Clark)

VL 351 – VL 362, BRM 001 – BRM 002

Type	GT 26C-3	**Wheel Arrangement**	Co'Co'
Engine	EMD 645E3C	**Length**	17.37 m
Cylinders	V-16	**Width**	2.96 m
Power	2240 kW	**Height**	4.36 m
Alternator	EMD AR10	**Weight**	124 t
Motors	EMD D78	**Axle Load**	203 kN
Builder	Avteq, SSR	**Tractive Effort**	344 kN
Introduced	2001	**Maximum Speed**	115 km/h
Number Built	14	**Gauge**	1435 mm

The VL class were a modification of the XR class built new for CFCLA by Avteq, a company previously involved in aviation, in a workshop in Sunshine, Victoria. While they followed the same basic design as the XR, the design of the hood and the nose were altered, the batteries being moved to the nose to allow for a larger fuel tank.

SSR have built two generally similar locomotives at their Bendigo workshops during 2012–2013 which are known as class BRM. Some aspects of that design more closely resemble the XR class, but the wide nose, although more rounded, increases the resemblance to the VL design.

1107 is seen in Goulburn yard on 2 August 2014 (Peter Clark)

1101 – 1108

Type	E-3000E3B (GT 26C-3)	**Wheel Arrangement**	Co'Co'
Engine	EMD 645E3B	**Length**	19.50 m
Cylinders	V-16	**Width**	2.85 m
Power	2240 kW	**Height**	4.24 m
Alternator	EMD AR-10/CA5	**Weight**	132 t
Motors	EMD D-78	**Axle Load**	215 kN
Builder	NREC	**Tractive Effort**	
Introduced	2011	**Maximum Speed**	115 km/h
Number Built	8	**Gauge**	1435 mm

These locomotives are the first new design of locomotive from the USA to operate on the ARTC Network and NSW Country lines for quite some time (but not the last, with two other companies delivering new designs for WA and Tasmania in the near future). The National Railway Equipment Corporation (NREC) are thus the first of a number of US locomotive builders to enter the Australian locomotive market. The first two locomotives, 1101 and 1103, were landed in Newcastle on 19 November 2011 and commenced testing soon afterwards.

The 1100 class are roughly equivalent to the Clyde designed and built WAGR L class of 1967, modernised to meet current regulations, being about the same size but a little lighter to allow unrestricted operation at 115 km/h on main lines.

6064 at Seven Mile Yard, April 1994. (Peter Clark)

6060 – 6064

Type	SD50S	**Wheel Arrangement**	Co'Co'
Engine	EMD 645F3	**Length**	19.70 m
Cylinders	V-16	**Width**	3.13 m
Power	2830 kW	**Height**	4.67 m
Alternator	EMD AR-16	**Weight**	190 t
Motors	EMD D-87	**Axle Load**	310 kN
Builder	Clyde SA	**Tractive Effort**	414 kN
Introduced	1983	**Maximum Speed**	105 km/h
Number Built	5	**Gauge**	1435 mm

The SD50S was the first modern EMD locomotive design on any of the Pilbara iron ore railways, which had previously relied almost exclusively on Alco designs. The Hamersley SD50S were amongst the first built, and later US locomotives had a longer frame. This resulted in the earlier locomotives gaining an 'S' suffix, for 'short'. These units had the only EMD 645F engines installed in new locomotives in Australia. The only visible modification from the US original was the lowering of both radiator vents to provide a better air flow path to the radiators as a concession to the high operating temperatures in the Pilbara. The equipment layout prevented the forward vent from being as large as the rear vent. Following delivery of the GE Dash-9 locomotives, these locomotives were sold to NREC, who shipped them to the USA and sold them all to the Utah Railway where they are still in service with the same road numbers.

G 523, G 526, G 529, G 530, G 531, G 536, G 541 and G 543

G 543 approaching Kalamunda Road on an SCT service, July 2006. (Peter Clark)

Type	JT 36C	**Wheel Arrangement**	Co'Co'
Engine	EMD 645F3B	**Length**	19.82 m
Cylinders	V-16	**Width**	2.97 m
Power	2600 kW	**Height**	4.27 m
Alternator	EMD AR-11	**Weight**	127 t
Motors	EMD D-87	**Axle Load**	210 kN
Builder	Clyde Victoria	**Tractive Effort**	337 kN
Introduced	2000	**Maximum Speed**	114 km/h
Number Built	8	**Gauge**	1435 mm

A number of G class locomotives were fitted with rebuilt EMD 645F3B engines of increased power to improve their performance on the large SCT trains between Melbourne and Perth. The 645F3B engine runs at a higher speed of 950 rpm, compared to 900 rpm for the previous E series engine, but the engines are otherwise of the same displacement. While this modification increased the power and the speed of the trains, it did not increase the haulage power of the locomotives, and only a small number were converted.

RL 304 at Spencer Junction, January 2009. (Peter Clark)

RL 301 – RL 310

Type	AT 36C	**Wheel Arrangement**	Co'Co'
Engine	EMD 645F3B	**Length**	19.1 m
Cylinders	V-16	**Width**	2.96 m
Power	2610 kW	**Height**	4.32 m
Alternator	EMD AR10	**Weight**	132 t
Motors	GE 752	**Axle Load**	216 kN
Builder	NREC/RTS SA	**Tractive Effort**	313 kN
Introduced	2005	**Maximum Speed**	130 km/h
Number Built	10	**Gauge**	1435 mm

The RL class have had a Lazarus-like revival from frames and components left when Morrison Knudsen Australia ceased operations at Whyalla in the mid-1990s. The RL class were to use the outer frames, bogies and traction motors of Alco DL500G type locomotives, in conjunction with new central frame sections adapted to take EMD 16-645 engines and EMD alternators.

Following a finite element analysis of the existing frame design new frame ends were designed and built and fitted to the new frame centre sections. The bogie pivot castings from the DL500G and the MLW/Dofasco bogies, and the GE 752 traction motors were retained. The body design used a cab shape as used on the MKA class in conjunction with a full width body. This new body is about 2 m shorter than the similar AN class. The RL uses the older pattern of EMD dynamic brakes located above the engine, with two 48 inch cooling fans, rather than the radial grid arrangement on the AN class. The muffler is mounted forward of the engine. The Wabtech Q-Tron QES-3 system is fitted to the RL but it does not have the suspended isolated cab of the AN class. The overall similarity in appearance to the AN is still quite striking. RL 308 was not built due to damage to the frame incurred in the move from Whyalla. The RL class are divided between Greentrains and QUBE.

AN 1 – AN 11

Type	AT 46C	**Wheel Arrangement**	Co'Co'
Engine	EMD 710G3A	**Length**	20.89 m
Cylinders	V-16	**Width**	2.96 m
Power	2860 kW	**Height**	4.26 m
Alternator	EMD AR-11	**Weight**	130 t
Motors	EMD D-87	**Axle Load**	213 kN
Builder	Clyde Victoria	**Tractive Effort**	323 kN
Introduced	1992	**Maximum Speed**	152 km/h
Number Built	11	**Gauge**	1435 mm

The AN class has an interesting combination of features used on previous classes, combining the complete electrical system of the DL class with a 16-cylinder version of the 710G3 engine, not previously used in Australia, and the self-supporting truss carbody of the BL and previous classes. The multiple engine room doors of the DL were used for the first time with this form of structure. A flexibly mounted cab, with an external design similar to the Goninan-built EL class and the largest possible fuel tank completed the then most powerful locomotive on a government system. The AN class are all on the standard gauge, and were used mainly in the Trans Australian fast freight traffic, when operating for AN and National Rail. One unit was destroyed in an accident in Western Australia. They are now used as trailing units on PN intermodal and steel services, and on the Sydney-Tarago garbage train. AN3 is painted for *The Ghan*, where it is used as a trailing unit with an NR when required.

9034 on Kooragang Island, December 2005. (Peter Clark)

9001 – 9035

Type	GT 46CW	**Wheel Arrangement**	Co'Co'
Engine	EMD 710G3A	**Length**	20.75 m
Cylinders	V-16	**Width**	2.93 m
Power	2860 kW	**Height**	4.26 m
Alternator	EMD AR-11	**Weight**	165 t
Motors	EMD D-87	**Axle Load**	270 kN
Builder	GMDD Canada	**Tractive Effort**	437 kN
Introduced	1994	**Maximum Speed**	115 km/h
Number Built	35	**Gauge**	1435 mm

The 90 class was the first of two classes of locomotives leased by Freight Rail from Clyde Engineering on a 'power per kilometre' contract. Clyde was responsible for maintenance of the locomotives, which was carried out at a purpose-built facility on Kooragang Island. These were the first new locomotives of EMD design to have been imported complete from North America, which was done to meet the short timescale required. Many details of these locomotives differ from those of locally built locomotives, the most noticeable being the longer wheelbase and heavier construction of the trucks, which are of the standard North American domestic design. The main differences from the SD60 design are the lower overall height, the local cab design and the location of the dynamic brake unit at the rear end, instead of between the engine and the cab. These locomotives were specifically designed for use in the Hunter Valley export coal traffic, where the track has been upgraded with concrete sleepers and 60 kg/m rail, and they are too heavy for general use elsewhere, although they meet standard clearance restrictions. After entering service, they were fitted with sound screens beside the dynamic brakes. These locomotives were all sold to PN at the end of the Ready Power contract. Four additional locomotives were assembled largely from imported components but with a locally built frame at EDI Cardiff in late 2005.

Q 4013 at Forrestfield on 16 November 2013 (Peter Clark)

Q 301 – Q 319, later Q 4001 – Q 4019

Type	GT 46C	**Wheel Arrangement**	Co'Co'
Engine	EMD 710G3B ES	**Length**	20.84 m
Cylinders	V-16	**Width**	2.96 m
Power	2860 kW	**Height**	4.26 m
Alternator	EMD AR-11	**Weight**	133.5 t
Motors	EMD D-87	**Axle Load**	219 kN
Builder	Clyde	**Tractive Effort**	408 kN
Introduced	1997	**Maximum Speed**	115 km/h
Number Built	19	**Gauge**	1435 mm

These were the first new standard-gauge locomotives for Westrail since the L class, the first of which were delivered in 1967. Just as the L class introduced the turbocharged 645E3 engine to Australia, the Q class are the first Australian locomotives with a locally designed equivalent of the EMD radial steering truck. This design should greatly reduce locomotive flange wear and improve adhesion, while reducing track damage caused by the long wheelbase of locomotive bogies. This bogie is a fabricated design, in order to keep the weight within acceptable limits. It is interesting to compare this locomotive with the Pacific National NR class, since they are effectively equivalent units from the local associates of the two major US suppliers. Also generally similar to the imported NSW 90 class, the Q class differ in many details, as well as being of lighter construction using a trussed hood structure. The Q class make use of microprocessors in engine control and fuel injection and in the Super Series adhesion control but the technology is most visible in the Integrated Cab Electronics displays which replace conventional instruments.

FQ 02 in Spencer Junction Yard, 3 September 2013 (Peter Clark)

V 544, FQ 01 – FQ 04

Type	GT 46C	**Wheel Arrangement**	Co'Co'
Engine	EMD 710G3B ES	**Length**	20.84 m
Cylinders	V-16	**Width**	2.96 m
Power	2860 kW	**Height**	4.26 m
Alternator	EMD AR-11	**Weight**	133.5 t
Motors	EMD D-87	**Axle Load**	219 kN
Builder	EDI Rail Victoria	**Tractive Effort**	408 kN
Introduced	2002-2003	**Maximum Speed**	115 km/h
Number Built	5	**Gauge**	1435 mm

V 544 is an insurance replacement for G 517 and G 518, damaged in a collision at Ararat in 1999. It is painted in Freight Australia livery relettered for Pacific National. It was used extensively on Leigh Creek coal trains.

FreightLink operated the Alice Springs–Darwin railway and these units were used with G&WA locomotives on the freight services to Alice Springs and Darwin from Adelaide. These four locomotives were assembled at the EDI

Rail Port Augusta workshops. These locomotives are basically similar to the earlier Q class, but have a later generation of electronic control equipment, particularly in the cab. They were painted in a distinctive colour of orange-red, quite different to the G&WA shade. They have names with connections to the area, and two units have Indigenous designs on the hood side, as well as the 'archer' FreightLink symbol. These locomotives were absorbed by G&WA when they took over the operation of the Darwin service.

The names of these units are as follows:

V 544 'Tim Fischer'

FQ 01 'Kurra Kurraka'   FQ 03 'Wagiman'

FQ 02 'Purnu'   FQ 04 'Aboriginal Stockman'

4319 approaching Nelson Point, September 2007.

4301 – 4323, 4334 – 4346, 4356 – 4487, 701 – 721

Type	SD70ACe/lci	**Wheel Arrangement**	Co'Co'
Engine	EMD 710G3C-T2	**Length**	21.36 m
Cylinders	V-16	**Width**	3.12 m
Power	3200 kW	**Height**	4.79 m
Alternator	EMD TA-17/CA8	**Weight**	195 t
Motors	EMD A3432	**Axle Load**	320 kN
Builder	EMD Canada	**Tractive Effort**	700 kN
Introduced	2005	**Maximum Speed**	115 km/h
Number Built	189	**Gauge**	1435 mm

While BHP Billiton Iron Ore ordered 13 locomotives from EDI and EMD, an additional locomotive, 4300, was provided as a source of spare parts. This locomotive was used by EMD for software and integration development testing. These units lacked isolated cabs and have been returned to the USA for sale and re-use. These units represent a break with previous EMD locomotives in this category. The frame is a different design, gaining additional strength and rigidity from deeper beam sections. The location of the traction inverter units behind the cab on the left-hand side was new, as was the separation of power cabling and air piping to the left and right sides respectively, under the walkways on each side. EMD still use two inverters, one providing power for each truck. The cab design is also a striking change from the previous EMD 'M' cabs, which followed styling adopted for the FP45 cowl units of the late 1960s. The new design has a raised centre section to allow for a taller entry door and is much simpler in overall design. Units from 4314 onward had isolated cabs, becoming model SD70ACe/lci. Fortescue Metals have purchased 21 SD 70ACe/lci locomotives for their current expansion program, which are numbered 701 to 721.

SCT 001 – SCT 015, LDP 001 – LDP 009, WH 001 – WH 003, TT 01 – TT 08, TT 101 – TT 132, GWA 001 – GWA 010

Type	GT 46C-ACe	**Wheel Arrangement**	Co'Co'
Engine	EMD 710G3C-T2	**Length**	20.84 m
Cylinders	V-16	**Width**	2.96 m
Power	3200 kW	**Height**	4.26 m
Alternator	EMD TA-17/CA8	**Weight**	133.5 t
Motors	Siemens 1TB2622	**Axle Load**	219 kN
Builder	EDI Rail	**Tractive Effort**	700 kN
Introduced	2007	**Maximum Speed**	115 km/h
Number Built	73	**Gauge**	1435 mm

SCT placed an order with EDI in late 2005 for 11 locomotives of its own. These were intended to haul the SCT trains from Melbourne to Perth. SCT have used Freight Australia locomotives since the inception of this train, but the takeover of FA by Pacific National meant that the locomotives were controlled by Toll, a half owner of PN and a direct competitor to SCT. These were the most powerful locomotives to operate generally on the ARTC system, and with AC traction motors are able to haul greater loads than the locomotives previously used on this service. QR National leased the next nine units for their East Coast intermodal services, and Pacific National and Whitehaven Coal obtained units for Hunter Valley and North West coal traffic. Genesee and Wyoming purchased their units for the Darwin services, having taken these over from FreightLink.

Above: GWA 010 in Spencer Junction Yard, 26 April 2014 (Peter Clark)

Below: TT 04 at Sandgate, January 2011. (Peter Clark)

4329 at Nelson Point, July 2008. (Peter Clark)

4324 – 4333, 4347 – 4355

Type	SD70ACe	**Wheel Arrangement**	Co'Co'
Engine	EMD 710G3C-T2	**Length**	21.36 m
Cylinders	V-16	**Width**	3.12 m
Power	3200 kW	**Height**	4.90 m
Alternator	EMD TA-17/CA8	**Weight**	195 t
Motors	EMD A3432	**Axle Load**	320 kN
Builder	EMD Canada	**Tractive Effort**	700 kN
Introduced	2008	**Maximum Speed**	115 km/h
Number Built	19	**Gauge**	1435 mm

To meet the increasing demand for iron ore, 19 standard SD70ACe units not immediately required owing to the economic downturn were made available to BHP Billiton. The first 10 were from a BNSF order and were almost complete when transferred to BHP Billiton and painted in the BNSF base colour of orange with silver trucks. The remaining nine were completed to BHP Billiton specifications and were indistinguishable from the earlier units. These units all have isolated cabs. The first 10 units were limited to trailing units until modified to BHP Billiton standards, but so far they retain the orange colour scheme.

GT46C-ACe Gen II 180 Tonne with 12,000 L Fuel Tank, SD70ACe (HTSC) Bogies, and #2 End Platform

GT46C-ACe Generation II

A diagram of the heavier GT46C-ACe generation II locomotive. It is understood that the units being built will be of the lighter version, similar in appearance apart from the bogie design. (EMD)

Type	GT 46C-ACe gen II	Wheel Arrangement	Co'Co'
Engine	MTU 20V4000R43	Length	22.0 m
Cylinders	V-20	Width	2.85 m
Power	2550kW	Height	3.87 m
Alternator	ABB	Weight	120 t
Motors	ABB	Axle Load	197 kN
Builder	EMD	Tractive Effort	450 kN
Introduced	2016	Maximum Speed	100 km/h
Number Built	3	Gauge	1067 mm

EMD are building in the USA three updated GT46C-ACe locomotives. The new design has a desktop style controller offset to the right with a brake controller on the left side.

A visible feature of the new units is a small end platform at the rear. The space for this was obtained by the use of new inverters, one for each traction motor, which are all located in a section forward of the engine and alternator, rather than the older arrangement on existing GT46C ACe units with one inverter cabinet forward of the engine and one behind, each serving the three motors on the nearest bogie.

An entirely new version offered is a 180 tonne locomotive, effectively an SD70 ACe fitted to the restricted Australian loading gauge. This type has a similar body arrangement to the lighter locomotive but uses the bogies and A3432 traction motors of the US domestic locomotive.

1428 at Botany Yard, April 2007. (Peter Clark)

1427 – 1429, 1431 – 1435, 1437, 1438, 1440, 1443, 1445, 1446

Type	JT 30C	**Wheel Arrangement**	Co'Co'
Engine	EMD 645E3	**Length**	20 m
Cylinders	V-20	**Width**	2.96 m
Power	2680 kW	**Height**	4.20 m
Alternator	EMD AR10	**Weight**	121.2 t
Motors	EMD D77	**Axle Load**	199 kN
Builder	Nohab, Sweden	**Tractive Effort**	270 kN
Introduced	1972	**Maximum Speed**	165 km/h
Number Built	16	**Gauge**	1435 mm

These locomotives represent an interesting development, the importation of American (EMD) design locomotives which had been built under licence by Nydquist & Holm AB (Nohab) in Sweden. Because the European loading gauge and axle loadings are similar to those in Australia, these locomotives are more suitable than locomotives from the USA.

These units, known as MZ III in Denmark, were fitted with a 20-cylinder EMD 645E3 engine in order to provide additional power for electric train heating. This power is of course available for traction when not needed for train power, and these were the first locomotives with the 20-cylinder EMD engine to operate in Australia. Sixteen of the 20 locomotives were purchased by LVRF, and are their first large mainline locomotives. Two units were damaged in transit and their equipment was used as spares and the bodies were scrapped.

1427 was built in 1972 as builder's number 2858
1428 to 1442 were built in 1973 with builder's numbers 2859 to 2873
1443 to 1446 were built in 1974 with builder's numbers 2874 to 2877

901 – 917

Type	SD90MAC-H Phase II	**Wheel Arrangement**	Co'Co'
Engine	EMD 265H	**Length**	24.43 m
Cylinders	V-16	**Width**	3.12 m
Power	4474 kW	**Height**	4.79 m
Alternator	EMD TA-22/CA8	**Weight**	190 t
Motors	Siemens 1TB2830	**Axle Load**	310 kN
Builder	EMD Canada	**Tractive Effort**	734 kN
Introduced	2000	**Maximum Speed**	128 km/h
Number Built	17	**Gauge**	1435 mm

903 at the Rollingstock Yard, Boodarie, June 2011. (Toad Montgomery)

Forty locomotives of a modified SD90MAC design, recognisable by a new cab design with a very angular nose, were built by EMD and leased to Union Pacific in 2000, carrying numbers 8522 to 8561. These carried the four-stroke 16-cylinder 265H engine, which has not been very successful in railway use. Union Pacific terminated their lease in 2008, and returned these locomotives to EMD. Five SD90MAC-H units – EMD-owned former Union Pacific units – were sold to Fortescue Metals Group and were to be converted to 4300 HP with an EMD 16-710G3B-ES engine by NS Juniata workshops at Altoona,

Pennsylvania, prior to delivery. Two of the locomotives at Juniata in the best condition, were refurbished with their original engine and shipped to Port Hedland. Two additional locomotives were repainted into Fortescue colours at Mid America Car and shipped with the two from Altoona. These locomotives were renumbered 901 to 904 in the order of their UP numbers. Two more units were obtained and sent to Altoona to replace the two refurbished locomotives in the rebuild program. In 2014, eight more locomotives with the 265H engine were obtained to allow rapid expansion of iron ore shipments. It is intended that the 265H engine units will be rebuilt with the 710G3 in due course as were 901-904.

Locomotive Numbers with known former UP identity:

901 8522	905 8527	909 8554	913 8557	917 8547
902 8529	906 8530	910 8538	914 8525	
903 8539	907 8531	911 8548	915 8553	
904 8549	908 8541	912 8550	916 8543	

ADF 491 – ADF 496

ADF 492 on a farewell ARHS tour near Mundijong, 1975. (Peter Clark)

Type		Wheel Arrangement	A1A'A1A'
Engine	EE 6HT	**Length**	18.89 m
Cylinders	2 x Inline 6	**Width**	2.69 m
Power	2 x 165 kW	**Height**	3.40 m
Generator	EE	**Weight**	58.5 t
Motors	EE	**Axle Load**	95 kN
Builder	WAGR Midland	**Tractive Effort**	25 kN
Introduced	1949	**Maximum Speed**	81 km/h
Number Built	6	**Gauge**	1067 mm

These units were used with two ADU class 64-seat coaches which took their power from the ADF. Multiple sets of two ADF units, either end of four ADU cars, could be operated. The ADF contained a central baggage compartment, between the two engines. Four ADU class trailers were upgraded in May 1964 and formed the Perth–Bunbury 'The Shopper' and 'Bunbury Belle' with two of the ADF units. After the ADU trailers were withdrawn, AYU class cars, themselves rebuilt from ADU cars, were used until the ADFs were withdrawn. The final colour scheme was green and white, with a red waistband. They were named after wildflowers native to Western Australia.

Unit names:

491 'Boronia'	494 'Hovea'
492 'Crowea'	495 'Leschenaultia'
493 'Grevillea'	496 'Banksia'

519 shunting at Tailem Bend, 1978. (Peter Clark)

500 – 533

Type		Wheel Arrangement	Bo'Bo'
Engine	EE 4SRKT	**Length**	11.73 m
Cylinders	Inline 4	**Width**	2.84 m
Power	375 kW	**Height**	4.05 m
Generator	EE 827/4c	**Weight**	56.9 t
Motors	EE 548/2a	**Axle Load**	140 kN
Builder	SAR Islington	**Tractive Effort**	133 kN
Introduced	1964	**Maximum Speed**	64 km/h
Number Built	34		

This type was the only application of a four-cylinder medium speed engine for railway traction in Australia. It is interesting to compare this class with the 1949-built 350 class which developed only 260 kW from naturally aspirated six-cylinder engines of the same bore and stroke. The appearance was that of a conventional end-cab hood unit, but with an overhanging cab roof resembling that of a steam locomotive. A warning bell was mounted above the hood, and since the height was measured, a square-section exhaust stack has been added; the bogies were welded, outside equalised and coil sprung.

AN also renumbered 500 to 534 to clear the 'class number', as was done for other classes.

500 class locomotives were used in major yards throughout South Australia, and in addition worked employees' trains in the Adelaide suburban area. Survivors now shunt at Islington and at ARG Forrestfield locomotive workshops.

350 – 351

Type		**Wheel Arrangement**	Bo'Bo'	
Engine	EE 6KT	**Length**	10.67 m	
Cylinders	Inline 6	**Width**	2.88 m	
Power	260 kW	**Height**	4.05 m	
Generator	EE 801	**Weight**	50.3 t	
Motors	EE 505D	**Axle Load**	124 kN	
Builder	SAR Islington	**Tractive Effort**	22 kN	
Introduced	1949	**Maximum Speed**	72 km/h	
Number Built	2	**Gauge**	1600 mm	

These were the first diesel-electric locomotives built in Australia. They were high-hood end-cab units, with outside equalised trucks. End platforms and shunter's steps are provided. These units have a rather slab-sided appearance with simple lines and rounded hood ends.

They were painted black below the running board and tangerine (deep orange) lined regal red on the hood and cab roofs, with a regal red waistband.

They were mainly used for shunting work at Islington Workshops (Adelaide). One unit was leased to ICI for a period. Both units are preserved.

F 208 at Newport Workshops, 1992. (Peter Clark)

F 201 – F 216

Type		Wheel Arrangement	C
Engine	EE 6KT	Length	7.85 m
Cylinders	Inline 6	Width	2.78 m
Power	260 kW	Height	3.80 m
Generator	EE 801	Weight	50.2 t
Motors	EE 506	Axle Load	167 kN
Builder	EE Dick Kerr	Tractive Effort	49 kN
Introduced	1951	Maximum Speed	32 km/h
Number Built	16	Gauge	1600 mm

These were standard London, Midland and Scottish Railway shunting locomotives, modified for 1600 mm gauge and air brakes. The Australian locomotives also had coupling rod protection, shunters' footboards, automatic couplers, steel pilots and electric headlights. The short length, high hood and

end cab made these locomotives very distinctive. The first 10 locomotives were bought new by VR and numbered F 310 – F 319. The State Electricity Commission of Victoria loaned their Numbers 4 to 6 to the VR from April 1953, and the VR bought SECV No. 3 in June 1957. In 1958 the VR locomotives were given their current numbers, and this was extended to the former SECV locomotives in 1959. The F class were allocated to Dynon (Melbourne) and Geelong and were used for shunting in larger goods yards. F 209 and 210 were equipped with dual automatic and screw couplers, and modified buffers for shunting at Spencer Street terminal station. SECV locomotives Nos 1 and 2 were taken over by the VR during 1971 and were renumbered F 215 and F 216.

AN AUSTRALIAN LOCOMOTIVE GUIDE

D 9 – D 15, D 20 – D 25

Type		**Wheel Arrangement**	B'B'
Engine	EE 6KT	**Length**	10.6/ m
Cylinders	Inline 6	**Width**	2.82 m
Power	260 kW	**Height**	4.23 m
Generator	EE 801	**Weight**	60.9 t
Motors	EE 506	**Axle Load**	150 kN
Builder	Comeng Qld	**Tractive Effort**	49 kN
Introduced	1956	**Maximum Speed**	28 km/h
Number Built	13	**Gauge**	1435 mm

This type generally resembles the 565 kW Bo'Bo' of AIS but can be recognised by the radiator fan visible at the end of the long hood, and by the outside coupling rods on the equalised bogies. These provide power from the motored axle to the adjacent axle. The original livery was the orange and black colour scheme, but a number of other schemes have been used, including yellow. They were used for lighter shunting duties around the Port Kembla Steelworks system, and one unit was transferred to John Lysaght at Cringila. A number have been preserved.

X 1 – X 32

X 4 as preserved at the Don River Railway, November 1998. (Peter Clark)

Type		**Wheel Arrangement**	Bo'Bo'
Engine	EE 6SRKT	**Length**	10.37 m
Cylinders	Inline 6	**Width**	2.70 m
Power	450 kW	**Height**	3.86 m
Generator	EE 801	**Weight**	58 t
Motors	EE 521A	**Axle Load**	142 kN
Builder	Vulcan Foundry	**Tractive Effort**	57 kN
Introduced	1950	**Maximum Speed**	81 km/h
Number Built	32	**Gauge**	1067 mm

The X and XA class are end-cab high-hood units. The long wheel base bogies have no equalisation. The X class was the first diesel-electric mainline type to enter service in Australia. The first 20 units were built at Vulcan Foundry, Newton Le Willows, but the last 12 were erected at the Dick Kerr works in Preston. They can be distinguished from the later Y class by the three large windows in the cab front, the horizontal bar type pilot, and the lack of a platform at the cab end. The traction motors of five units, X 9, X 12, X 14, X 22, and X 28 were rewound to permit lower speed operation. These units were renumbered XA 1 to XA 5. With the Y class, the X and XA classes operated all freight and passenger traffic on the TGR main lines until the arrival of the Z class and their successors. All are now withdrawn.

800 – 809

Type		**Wheel Arrangement**	Bo'Bo'
Engine	EE 6SRKT	**Length**	12.80 m
Cylinders	Inline 6	**Width**	2.90 m
Power	490 kW	**Height**	4.19 m
Generator	EE 827	**Weight**	73 t
Motors	EE 526	**Axle Load**	180 kN
Builder	EE Rocklea,	**Tractive Effort**	102 kN
Introduced	1956	**Maximum Speed**	97 km/h
Number Built	10	**Gauge**	1600 mm

This was the only English Electric locomotive class on the former SAR not built in Islington shops. The rounded-end hood configuration resembled that of other six-cylinder EE hood units, but the cab was higher and wider, although of similar design to those of narrow-gauge types also built at Rocklea. The 800 class was used for heavy shunting work, and transfer duties particularly around Adelaide, and was on occasion used for passenger work, for example, employees' trains to Islington. All are now withdrawn from service.

F 40 at Bellevue, June 2008. (Peter Clark)

F 40 – F 46

Type		Wheel Arrangement	A1A'A1A'
Engine	EE 6SRKT	Length	12.80 m
Cylinders	Inline 6	Width	2.71 m
Power	520 kW	Height	3.82 m
Generator	EE 827	Weight	64.8 t
Motors	EE 525	Axle Load	107 kN
Builder	EE Rocklea,	Tractive Effort	100 kN
Introduced	1958	Maximum Speed	81 km/h
Number Built	7	Gauge	1067 mm

These locomotives were purchased to enable dieselisation of the lightly-tracked Midland Railway of Western Australia, then a private railway company. They were typical EE end-cab hood units. They had two-motor bogies, with underhung equalising beams, to keep the axle load below 107 kN, and could thus be distinguished from the similar G class. The numbers, classification, maroon and cream colour scheme and brass MRWA number plates were retained after absorption into the WAGR. After the takeover, F class worked the narrow-gauge branches from Kalgoorlie until standardisation, and other minor duties until withdrawal.

Y 1 – Y 8, later 2150 and 2151

Type		Wheel Arrangement	Bo'Bo'
Engine	EE 6SRKT	Length	12.65 m
Cylinders	Inline 6	Width	2.71 m
Power	595 kW	Height	3.71 m
Generator	EE 827	Weight	58 t
Motors	EE 537	Axle Load	145 kN
Builder	TGR	Tractive Effort	151 kN
Introduced	1961	Maximum Speed	72 km/h
Number Built	8	Gauge	1067 mm

The Y class were a development of the X class, utilising the same type of engines, but at a higher rating, and more powerful motors. The Y class were longer and had a generally more rounded appearance than the X class. The cab doors were on the front and rear walls, rather than the side, resulting in a different cab window arrangement.

Y 4 was named 'Lord Rowallan' and Y 5 'Sir Charles Gairdner' after former Tasmanian governors, and they were placed in service in 1965. The Y class worked the heaviest goods traffic on the TGR main lines, until the introduction of the larger Z and ZA types. The survivors are restricted to secondary duties.

1612 at Mayne Junction, 1982. (Peter Clark)

1600 – 1617

Type		Wheel Arrangement	Co'Co'
Engine	EE 6CSRKT	Length	12.42 m
Cylinders	Inline 6	Width	2.75 m
Power	625 kW	Height	3.85 m
Generator	EE 827	Weight	62.5 t
Motors	EE 540	Axle Load	105 kN
Builder	EE Rocklea	Tractive Effort	134 kN
Introduced	1963	Maximum Speed	81 km/h
Number Built	18	Gauge	1067 mm

These were the first QR locomotives to be fitted with an intercooler, which increases the density of the air charge to the cylinders, and increases power output per cylinder. The body was the usual EE end-cab hood unit design. Modifications for Queensland involved dual sealed-beam headlights and number indicators at each end, and dual controls. A 1600 class could operate in multiple with 1620, 1250, 1270 1300 and 2350 classes as well as with other 1600 class members. The 1600 class was designed for operation on light track in the western areas of Queensland, the class being initially based at Alpha, but they were in wide use, not being limited to the Central line. All are now withdrawn from service, but one unit has been retained for preservation.

H 1 – H 5

Type		**Wheel Arrangement**	Bo'Bo'	
Engine	EE 6CSRKT	**Length**	12.95 m	
Cylinders	Inline 6	**Width**	2.90 m	
Power	640 kW	**Height**	4.17 m	
Generator	EE 819	**Weight**	72.4 t	
Motors	EE 538	**Axle Load**	177 kN	
Builder	EE Rocklea	**Tractive Effort**	168 kN	
Introduced	1965	**Maximum Speed**	105 km/h	
Number Built	5	**Gauge**	1435 mm	

These were the first standard-gauge locomotive class for the then WAGR. They had four-wheel trucks with underslung equalisers, a slightly squared-off hood preceded by a raised pressurising compartment, cab and higher short hood, giving the type a distinctive profile. The WAGR initially used these units for construction work. The H class was later used for transfer duties around the Perth metropolitan area.

1 – 2

Goldsworthy Mining No. 1 at Six Mile PRHS Museum, September 2007. (Peter Clark)

Type		**Wheel Arrangement**	Bo'Bo'	
Engine	EE 6CSRKT	**Length**	12.95 m	
Cylinders	Inline 6	**Width**	2.90 m	
Power	640 kW	**Height**	4.17 m	
Generator	EE 819	**Weight**	81.3 t	
Motors	EE 538	**Axle Load**	200 kN	
Builder	EE Rocklea	**Tractive Effort**	168 kN	
Introduced	1965	**Maximum Speed**	105 km/h	
Number Built	2	**Gauge**	1435 mm	

Mount Goldsworthy initially used these units for construction work. The two locomotives hauled iron ore traffic between the mine and Port Hedland, often in multiple, until No. 1 was written off after a head-on collision with a 1340 kW unit in mid-1968. A new unit was built at Rocklea, and fitted with the rebuilt engine and generator, and the number, from No. 1. It was placed in traffic in 1971. Both units were later used on track maintenance and freight trains until withdrawal. After the combination with BHP Iron Ore, the locomotives were renumbered 21 and 22, but retained the orange and white colours. One unit has been preserved at Dampier and the other in Port Hedland.

1620 – 1653

1650 at Redbank, July 2010. (Peter Clark)

Type	EE 6CSRKT	Wheel Arrangement	Co'Co'
Engine	EE 6CSRKT	**Length**	12.80 m
Cylinders	Inline 6	**Width**	2.79 m
Power	642 kW	**Height**	3.66 m
Generator	EE 827	**Weight**	63 t
Motors	EE 540	**Axle Load**	105 kN
Builder	EE Rocklea	**Tractive Effort**	135 kN
Introduced	1967	**Maximum Speed**	81 km/h
Number Built	34	**Gauge**	1067 mm

This class differed from all previous EE 'branch line' units in Australia in having a short hood. The design was based on that of five similar but more powerful locomotives built for the NZR. The bogies were of the underslung equaliser type, and the bodywork resembled that of the 1300 class, but was shorter by six feet. Apart from the higher rating, the same equipment as in the 1600 class was used. Multiple unit operation was possible with all other EE units so equipped. The 1620 class was mainly used on lighter track, particularly in Northern districts, and was based at Brisbane, Alpha, Townsville and Cairns.

D 35 – D 45

Type		Wheel Arrangement	Bo'Bo'
Engine	EE 6CSRKT	**Length**	12.81 m
Cylinders	Inline 6	**Width**	2.90 m
Power	698 kW	**Height**	4.25 m
Generator	EE 819	**Weight**	89.5 t
Motors	EE 538	**Axle Load**	220 kN
Builder	EE Rocklea	**Tractive Effort**	178 kN
Introduced	1971	**Maximum Speed**	50 km/h
Number Built	11	**Gauge**	1435 mm

Although these last AIS EE shunters have only a six-cylinder engine, the turbocharger and intercooler make them more powerful than the eight-cylinder engines fitted in the earlier D1 series locomotives. These locomotives are used for general shunting duties around the Port Kembla Steelworks and replaced the last steam locomotives in use there.

D 7 and the smaller D 24 at Port Kembla, 1995. (Peter Clark)

D 1 – D 8

Type		**Wheel Arrangement**	Bo'Bo'
Engine	EE 8SRKT	**Length**	12.50 m
Cylinders	Inline 8	**Width**	2.82 m
Power	565 kW	**Height**	4.27 m
Generator	EE 819	**Weight**	86.3 t
Motors	EE 506	**Axle Load**	213 kN
Builder	Comeng NSW	**Tractive Effort**	111 kN
Introduced	1950	**Maximum Speed**	34 km/h
Number Built	8	**Gauge**	1435 mm

These locomotives are of the normal US switcher design, with an end cab, low hood, end platforms and shunters' steps. The bogies use coil springs and overhung equalising beams. The in line engine has two widely spaced exhaust stacks mounted above two Napier turbochargers. Large chromium plated numbers were carried on the cabside.

This type were used for heavy shunting and transfer work around the former AIS Port Kembla Steelworks, and for hauling coal from the collieries to the steelworks.

DIESEL LOCOMOTIVES WITH ENGLISH ELECTRIC ENGINES

D 16 – D 19, D 26 – D 33

D 19 at Port Kembla, 1995. (Peter Clark)

Type		Wheel Arrangement	Bo'Bo'
Engine	EE 8SRKT Mk II	Length	12.50 m
Cylinders	Inline 8	Width	2.82 m
Power	645 kW	Height	4.27 m
Generator	EE 819	Weight	93.4 t
Motors	EE 506	Axle Load	230 kN
Builder	EE Rocklea	Tractive Effort	133 kN
Introduced	1959	Maximum Speed	34 km/h
Number Built	12	Gauge	1435 mm

Although they generally resembled the preceding Comeng-built units, many of the standard details of English EE designs were worked into these two batches. Use and colour scheme were much the same as the earlier units, but these units have also carried the later blue and yellow colour schemes. This type is still in service

G 50 at Pinjarra in faded Midland colours, July 2006. (Peter Clark)

G 50 – G 51

Type		**Wheel Arrangement**	Co'Co'
Engine	EE 8SVT	**Length**	12.50 m
Cylinders	V-8	**Width**	2.72 m
Power	710 kW	**Height**	3.85 m
Generator	EE	**Weight**	76 t
Motors	EE 548A	**Axle Load**	125 kN
Builder	EE Rocklea,	**Tractive Effort**	191 kN
Introduced	1963	**Maximum Speed**	97 km/h
Number Built	2	**Gauge**	1067 mm

These are conventional end-cab hood units. They are similar in size to the six-cylinder F class but can be recognised by their heavy bogies with overhung equalisers. These two locomotives are powered by the only EE V-8 type engines in locomotives in Australia. These locomotives were taken over from the Midland Railway of Western Australia, with the other company assets, on 1 August 1964. In 1968 the locomotives still retained the maroon and cream MRWA livery and the cast number plates with the company lettering. The G class were used in the Perth suburban area as well as on the former Midland line but have now been withdrawn.

1200 – 1209

1208 at Mayne Junction, 1982. (Peter Clark)

Type		Wheel Arrangement	Co'Co'
Engine	EE12SVT Mk II	Length	15.70 m
Cylinders	V-12	Width	2.84 m
Power	960 kW	Height	3.78 m
Generator	EE 828	Weight	89.5 t
Motors	EE 525	Axle Load	145 kN
Builder	Vulcan Foundry	Tractive Effort	134 kN
Introduced	1953	Maximum Speed	81 km/h
Number Built	10	Gauge	1067 mm

These were the first and only cab units on the QR system. They have controls only at the streamlined end and had no provision for multiple unit operation, and thus the usual nose and rear end doors were missing on this class. Further features to note were the large radiator-grilles above the rear bogie, and the traction motor blower vents on the body rear end and either side of the nose. The bogies were of the conventional pattern with outside equalisers and prominent sandboxes mounted on the bogie frames. A pressed steel non-streamlined pilot was mounted beneath the oval buffers at the cab end, but no illuminated number boards are fitted. During 1965 the 1200 and the early 1250 class locos were fitted with sun visors, as were fitted initially to later 1250 class locomotives. Painted in the standard QR blue, grey and white colour scheme, the 1200s were introduced on the Sunlander service but were later widely used on 150 kN axle load track. They were all allocated to Mayne (Brisbane). All are now withdrawn. 1208 was rebuilt as 1225, and 1200 is held for preservation.

AN AUSTRALIAN LOCOMOTIVE GUIDE

1225

1225 in storage at Redbank, July 2010. (Peter Clark)

Type		**Wheel Arrangement**	Co'Co'
Engine	EE12SVT Mk II	**Length**	15.70 m
Cylinders	V-12	**Width**	2.84 m
Power	960 kW	**Height**	3.78 m
Generator	EE 828	**Weight**	89.5 t
Motors	EE 525	**Axle Load**	145 kN
Builder	Vulcan Foundry	**Tractive Effort**	134 kN
Introduced	1953	**Maximum Speed**	81 km/h
Number Built	1	**Gauge**	1067 mm

This unit, formerly 1208, was rebuilt as a cab hood type to extend its usefulness as a secondary locomotive in 1982 at a time of locomotive shortage in Queensland. It was rebuilt at Redbank workshops. The age of this unit counted against it and it had a short life in its modified form. It is held for preservation, however.

1250 – 1266

1260 at Mayne Junction, 1982. (Peter Clark)

Type		Wheel Arrangement	Co'Co'
Engine	EE12SVT Mk II	**Length**	15.09 m
Cylinders	V-12	**Width**	2.81 m
Power	1040 kW	**Height**	3.79 m
Generator	EE 822	**Weight**	87 t
Motors	EE 525	**Axle Load**	145 kN
Builder	EE Rocklea	**Tractive Effort**	179 kN
Introduced	1959	**Maximum Speed**	81 km/h
Number Built	17	**Gauge**	1067 mm

The 1250 class resembled the 1200 class, except for a more square profile, as far as the back of the cab. Behind the cab back plate, the prime mover was enclosed in a rounded canted side hood, of a style common to most early EE hood units. Nos 1250 – 1254 were rated at 960 kW when built, and weighed 89.5 t. Nos 1255 onward were built with the higher power rating and were fitted for multiple unit operation. The bogies of the 1250 class were equalised and of cast construction, but had more prominent external secondary springing than those on the 1200 class locomotives. All had illuminated number boards and sun visors, the latter being fitted to 1255 onward when built, as they were obtained for the reconstructed Mount Isa line. Originally fitted with single conventional headlights, twin sealed beams were substituted by the early 1980s. The 1250 class carried the standard QR blue, grey and white colour scheme and were extensively used on both freight and passenger trains where the track standard permitted. They were based at Mayne (Brisbane), Rockhampton and Townsville.

AN AUSTRALIAN LOCOMOTIVE GUIDE

C 1702 at Forrestfield, April 1994. (Peter Clark)

C 1701 – C 1703

Type		**Wheel Arrangement**	Co'Co'
Engine	EE12SVT Mk II	**Length**	15.09 m
Cylinders	V-12	**Width**	2.75 m
Power	1040 kW	**Height**	3.94 m
Generator	EE 822	**Weight**	90.4 t
Motors	EE 548	**Axle Load**	148 kN
Builder	EE Rocklea	**Tractive Effort**	203 kN
Introduced	1962	**Maximum Speed**	97 km/h
Number Built	3	**Gauge**	1067 mm

The C class was a modification of the QR 1250 class for the then WAGR. Apart from altered brakes, couplings and driving position, 1015 mm wheels and heavier duty motors were used. Additionally a short hood with sloping front, rounded corners and prominent single headlight, in the earlier EE tradition, was substituted for the nosed cab of the 1250 class.

These locomotives were ordered early in the second wave of WAGR dieselisation, but proved less suitable than the Clyde G 12C (A class) and were not re-ordered.

The C class were modified by the addition of handrails beside the long hood, US style, as were other Westrail locos. The livery was the standard larch green lined red and cream. They could operate in multiple within the class and also with the R and RA classes which used the same type of traction motor. They were relegated from passenger to freight duties only, on the Eastern and Southern lines. All were withdrawn from service, but C 1702 and C 1703 have been preserved.

1295 at Mayne Junction, 1982.
(Peter Clark)

1270 – 1299

Type	-	Wheel Arrangement	Co'Co'
Engine	EE12SVT Mk II	Length	15.09 m
Cylinders	V-12	Width	2.81 m
Power	1040 kW	Height	3.79 m
Generator	EE 822	Weight	90.4 t
Motors	EE 525	Axle Load	148 kN
Builder	EE Rocklea	Tractive Effort	185 kN
Introduced	1964	Maximum Speed	81 km/h
Number Built	30	Gauge	1067 mm

The 1270 class was a direct development of the 1250 class, retaining most of the latter's equipment, but housing it in a new body of conventional hood type, with a squarer appearance than any previous EE hood unit. The cab was fitted with dual controls for bidirectional operation, and provision was made for multiple operation with other EE types so equipped. They were painted in the standard QR blue, grey and white livery. 1281 was named 'Century', in connection with the 1965 QR Centenary celebrations, and is painted gold on areas usually painted blue. The 1270 class were in wide use for freight and passenger trains where track conditions permitted their use, particularly in the coalfields area around Rockhampton and Gladstone, where triple heading of coal trains by 1270 and 1300 classes was common. They were also used on the main line from Brisbane to Wallangarra and Roma, and were allocated to Mayne (Brisbane), Rockhampton and Gladstone depots. All were withdrawn in 1988 and 1989.

K 208 still operates as a shunter at SCT Forrestfield, seen here on 24 May 2009. (Peter Clark)

K 201 – K 210

Type		**Wheel Arrangement**	Co'Co'
Engine	EE 12 CSVT	**Length**	16.76 m
Cylinders	V-12	**Width**	2.90 m
Power	1340 kW	**Height**	4.17 m
Generator	EE 822	**Weight**	109.8 t
Motors	EE 538	**Axle Load**	180 kN
Builder	EE Rocklea	**Tractive Effort**	198 kN
Introduced	1966	**Maximum Speed**	129 km/h
Number Built	10	**Gauge**	1435 mm

These were the first standard-gauge mainline type to be built by English Electric. The heavy duty underframe resulted in a higher than usual engine mounting, and a taller locomotive. The cab is placed further forward than is usual, resulting in a very short forward hood. Initially used on construction work, the K class hauled the first revenue trains of wheat from Merredin to Fremantle. Four K class were used on 8000-ton ore trains from Koolyanobbing to Kwinana but this practice was discontinued with the introduction of the L class, and they were later used on interstate freight and passenger trains, and some local and branch line operation. K 202 was purchased from WAGR by Mount Goldsworthy Mining and a new locomotive, K 210, was delivered to WAGR to replace it. Later, K 206 was sold to Mount Goldsworthy Mining without replacement. The two former WAGR units became GML Nos 6 and 9. Greentrains scrapped their units in 2014, but K 208 still operates as a shunter for SCT at Forrestfield.

D 49 shunting at Bellevue, June 2008. (Peter Clark)

3 – 8, later D 46 – D 51

Type		**Wheel Arrangement**	Co'Co'
Engine	EE 12 CSVT	**Length**	16.76 m
Cylinders	V-12	**Width**	2.90 m
Power	1340 kW	**Height**	4.17 m
Generator	EE 822	**Weight**	109.8 t
Motors	EE 538	**Axle Load**	180 kN
Builder	EE Rocklea	**Tractive Effort**	198 kN
Introduced	1966	**Maximum Speed**	129 km/h
Number Built	7	**Gauge**	1435 mm

They were originally Mount Goldsworthy Nos 3 to 9. K 202 was purchased from WAGR following an accident becoming No 6. A new locomotive, K 210, was delivered to WAGR to replace K 202. K 203 was also added to the Goldsworthy fleet in 1986 as No 9. Goldsworthy No. 4 was not repaired after an accident in 1990. They originally operated between Port Hedland and Mount Goldsworthy, and later Shay Gap, on iron ore trains. Six of these units were transferred to Port Kembla from Port Hedland after the combination of the former Mount Goldsworthy Mining railway with the former Mount Newman operation as BHP Iron Ore. They were mostly used between BHP collieries and the Port Kembla Steelworks on coal trains. These units were sold to South Spur and then Greentrains. They were scrapped in 2014. The old and new numbers were:

No 3	D46	No 8		D49
No 5	D47	No 6	K202	D50
No 7	D48	No 9	K203	D51

2145 at East Tamar, November 1998. (Peter Clark)

1300 – 1344, later ZC 1 – ZC 45, 2141 – 2145

Type		**Wheel Arrangement**	Co'Co'
Engine	EE 12CSVT	**Length**	14.63 m
Cylinders	V-12	**Width**	2.82 m
Power	1340 kW	**Height**	3.78 m
Generator	EE 822	**Weight**	89.5 t
Motors	EE 548	**Axle Load**	147 kN
Builder	EE Rocklea	**Tractive Effort**	216 kN
Introduced	1967	**Maximum Speed**	81 km/h
Number Built	45	**Gauge**	1067 mm

These units, built as the QR 1300 class, differed only slightly in appearance from the earlier 1270 class, but had an intercooler which raised the power to that of contemporary standard-gauge locomotives. The bogies were of a later design and used underhung equalising beams, and other details differed, but the easiest way of identifying a 1300 class from a 1270 class was the different cab side window arrangement. No. 1300 (now ZC 1) carried a plate on the cab side indicating that its engine was the 2000th English Electric 'V' type. The QR colour scheme was the standard blue, grey and white. The 1300 class were based at Mayne (Brisbane), Rockhampton and Gladstone and worked freight and passenger trains as well as operating in multiples of three on the heavy trains conveying export coal to Gladstone for shipment to Japan. In 1990, these units were sold as a group to AN for use in Tasmania, and were renumbered from 1300 to 1344 to ZC 1 to ZC 45 in the same order. Not all were placed in service, and some were only used briefly. A number were retained and repainted. These units were used on main line freight work on the AN Tasrail system. Eight units were sold to Morrison Knudsen for rebuilding as the MKA type, and others were scrapped.

R 1902 at Brunswick Junction, May 2009. (Peter Clark)

R 1901 – R 1905

Type		Wheel Arrangement	Co'Co'
Engine	EE 12CSVT	Length	15.24 m
Cylinders	V-12	Width	2.84 m
Power	1340 kW	Height	3.96 m
Generator	EE 822	Weight	89.6 t
Motors	EE 548	Axle Load	160 kN
Builder	EE Rocklea	Tractive Effort	227 kN
Introduced	1968	Maximum Speed	96 km/h
Number Built	5	Gauge	1067 mm

The WAGR R class differed from the ZC (1300) class mainly in the type of bogie. The WAGR locomotives had special high adhesion bogies with leaf springs and with all motors on the side nearest the centre of the locomotive. Special conical rubber pivots were used, at a lower level than usual, causing an uneven wheel spacing. They had dual air and vacuum braking systems and knuckle couplers, and a larger 1615 kW dynamic braking system. The larch green and red colour scheme was originally used, but later the Westrail orange and blue was applied. R 1901 and R 1902 were used on mainline freight and passenger working, particularly wheat and mineral trains. R 1903 to R 1905 were initially used for Jarrahdale bauxite trains and were ballasted to 94 tonnes to increase adhesion for this work, hauling 4500-tonne trains, then amongst the heaviest on 1067 mm gauge in Australia. Later all were used on narrow-gauge main line traffic, and R 1901 and R 1902 were also ballasted up to 96 tonnes. They were withdrawn in late 1990 and in 1991, but R 1902 was restored to service by Greentrains.

RA 1915 at Forrestfield, 1978. (Peter Clark)

RA 1906 – RA 1918

Type		Wheel Arrangement	Co'Co'
Engine	EE 12CSVT	Length	15.85 m
Cylinders	V-12	Width	2.84 m
Power	1340 kW	Height	3.96 m
Generator	EE 822	Weight	96.0 t
Motors	EE 548	Axle Load	155 kN
Builder	EE Rocklea	Tractive Effort	227 kN
Introduced	1969	Maximum Speed	96 km/h
Number Built	13	Gauge	1067 mm

A later variation on the R class, the RA class also had dual air and vacuum braking systems and knuckle couplers. Ballast replaced the dynamic braking system. Minor differences included the longer frame with the larger front walkway on the RA class and the differing headlights: horizontal pairs on the RA class and vertical pairs on the R class. The larch green and red colour scheme was originally used, and later the Westrail orange and blue was applied. RA 1908 was one of the first in the Westrail scheme, and lacked the white separating lines. RA 1917 and 1918 were originally purchased by Lefroy Salt for use on their traffic, and after standardisation these and RA 1914 were converted to standard gauge. RA 1918 was later returned to narrow gauge and is now preserved. Used generally on narrow-gauge main lines, all are now withdrawn.

D 34

Type		Wheel Arrangement	Co'Co'
Engine	EE 12CSVT	**Length**	16.50 m
Cylinders	V-12	**Width**	2.90 m
Power	1340 kW	**Height**	4.25 m
Generator	EE 822	**Weight**	132 t
Motors	EE 548	**Axle Load**	215 kN
Builder	EE Rocklea	**Tractive Effort**	254 kN
Introduced	1969	**Maximum Speed**	49 km/h
Number Built	1	**Gauge**	1435 mm

This was a considerably larger locomotive than the others operated by AIS at Port Kembla, and remained so for many years. It incorporates the hood and engine layout of a Westrail R class on a heavier frame with an end cab. D 34 is used in the coal traffic to the steelworks from Mount Kembla colliery and is fitted with a 1615 kW dynamic brake unit. Since construction, large mufflers have been applied to the hood top at the cab end. The standard orange and black colour scheme of AIS was initially applied to D 34, but the BHP corporate blue was later used. A 1750 kW version of D 34 was ordered, but it was never built.

Z 1 – Z 4, later 2110 – 2113

Type		**Wheel Arrangement**	Co'Co'
Engine	EE 12CSVT	**Length**	15.85 m
Cylinders	V-12	**Width**	2.84 m
Power	1340 kW	**Height**	3.77 m
Generator	EE 822	**Weight**	97.4 t
Motors	EE 558	**Axle Load**	160 kN
Builder	EE Rocklea	**Tractive Effort**	240 kN
Introduced	1972	**Maximum Speed**	81 km/h
Number Built	4	**Gauge**	1067 mm

The TGR Z class were direct copies of the WAGR RA class altered only in the coupling arrangements, and by the rearrangement required for a low profile short hood. The cab front windows are exceptionally large, providing improved visibility.

The Z class were obtained as a stopgap measure as the more powerful ZA class could not be obtained sufficiently early for the opening of the Bell Bay line, and the Z class followed the WAGR RA class design to speed production. The Z class first carried a yellow livery with black warning stripes on the locomotive ends, but later AN standard green and yellow and more recently yellow and green were used. They were initially used in log traffic to the Bell Bay wood chip plant, but later were used on main line traffic.

KA 212 at Forrestfield, 1975. (Peter Clark)

KA 211 – KA 213

Type		Wheel Arrangement	Co'Co'
Engine	EE 12CSVT	Length	15.85 m
Cylinders	V-12	Width	2.84 m
Power	1340 kW	Height	3.96 m
Generator	EE 822	Weight	94.5 t
Motors	EE 548	Axle Load	155 kN
Builder	EE Rocklea	Tractive Effort	227 kN
Introduced	1974	Maximum Speed	96 km/h
Number Built	3	Gauge	1435 mm

After the conversion of the branch lines from Kalgoorlie, RA 1914, 1917 and 1918 were converted to standard gauge to provide additional locomotives of the appropriate gauge. New bogies, looking more like an EMD design than the RA class design, were cast at Midland Workshops. The original traction motors were retained, fitted to new axles. The second version of the standard-gauge colour scheme, light and dark blue with yellow lining, was applied. Later, the Westrail orange and blue, and in one case the orange with blue lettering scheme, was used. The KAs were not confined to specific traffic. At one stage, when a shortage of standard-gauge wheat hoppers existed, a KA operated a train of vacuum-braked narrow-gauge hoppers fitted with standard-gauge bogies. KA 213 was converted back to RA 1918, and 212 was converted back to RA but kept its later number.

MKA 1 – MKA 8, later 2131 – 2134, 2137 – 2138

Type		Wheel Arrangement	Co'Co'
Engine	EE 12CSVT	Length	14.63 m
Cylinders	V-12	Width	2.82 m
Power	1340 kW	Height	3.78 m
Generator	EE 822	Weight	89.5 t
Motors	EE 548	Axle Load	147 kN
Builder	EE Rocklea	Tractive Effort	216 kN
Introduced	1995	Maximum Speed	81 km/h
Number Built	8	Gauge	1000 mm

These units were purchased from Tasmania, and rebuilt in Whyalla with a new MKLOC microprocessor control system replacing the former load regulator control. This provided a standard eight notch control system in place of the previous stepless system, and allowed a new desktop console to be fitted. The modification also allowed these locomotives to operate in multiple with EMD and GE locomotives, not previously possible. A modified cab based on the AN EL class was also fitted. The first of these units worked trials on the BHP main line from Whyalla. The first four of these units were initially leased to the privatised railway workshop organisation in Malaysia. They were used by the metre-gauge KTM in Malaysia, to cover for locomotives undergoing repairs and overhauls. They were often used on express passenger trains. MKA 1 to 3 were used by Pacific National for setting up their Queensland operation. MKA 4, 7 and 8 were taken over by Pacific National for use in Tasmania, and the other three followed, renumbered as 2131 – 2134, 2137 and 2138. The other two were sold for use in Africa.

The new and original numbers are as follows:

MKA 1	1332	MKA 5	1340
MKA 2	1329	MKA 6	1321
MKA 3	1325	MKA 7	1326
MKA 4	1320	MKA 8	1330

2350 – 2361, 2370 – 2373, later ZB 1 – ZB 16, 2120 – 2129

Type		**Wheel Arrangement**	Co'Co'
Engine	EE 12 RK3CT	**Length**	15.85 m
Cylinders	V-12	**Width**	2.82 m
Power	1750 kW	**Height**	3.82 m
Alternator	Toyo Denki	**Weight**	91.5 t
Motors	EE 548	**Axle Load**	150 kN
Builder	EE Rocklea	**Tractive Effort**	216 kN
Introduced	1973	**Maximum Speed**	97 km/h
Number Built	16	**Gauge**	1067 mm

These units, originally the QR 2350 (2350 to 2361) and 2370 (2370 to 2373) classes, were the last QR units in the series of 12-cylinder locomotives developed from the 1200 class of 1953. The input power to the generator has almost doubled in the 20 years although the basic engine dimensions are unaltered. A minor difference between the two groups was the rounded corners on the low nose. The 2350 and 2370 class locomotives were used for Central division coal traffic, between Blackwater or Moura and Gladstone. The standard QR blue grey and white colour scheme was applied to the 2350 and 2370 classes. On transfer to Tasmania, they were renumbered ZB 1 to ZB 16 in the order of their original numbers. Most units were repainted in the AN green and yellow scheme. They operated on Tasmanian main lines. One unit, ZB 9, was rebuilt with a new control system at Port Augusta and renumbered as ZR 1 (later ZP 1) and a second, ZB 6, was rebuilt as ZR 2. Three units, 2120, 2125 and 2129, were sold to Greentrains for use in WA.

ZA 1 – ZA 6, later 2114 – 2118

Type		**Wheel Arrangement**	Co'Co'
Engine	EE 12 RK3CT	**Length**	16.10 m
Cylinders	V-12	**Width**	2.82 m
Power	1750 kW	**Height**	3.84 m
Alternator	Toyo Denki	**Weight**	97.5 t
Motors	EE 558	**Axle Load**	160 kN
Builder	EE Rocklea	**Tractive Effort**	240 kN
Introduced	1973	**Maximum Speed**	97 km/h
Number Built	6	**Gauge**	1067 mm

The ZA class were a development of the Z class, which have a similar but slower running engine. The Z class were obtained only because the ZA class could not be delivered sufficiently early. They use the high adhesion bogie of the Z class but otherwise differ only in detail from the QR 2350 class. The second group of two units shared the rounded short hood edge modification of the 2370 class. The ZA class were painted yellow with black warning stripes, but later appeared in AN green and yellow. The ZA class were first used on the Bell Bay log traffic, but were later used on all main lines.

ZP 1, ZR 2, later 2100, 2101

2101 and 2100 at East Tamar, November 1998. (Peter Clark)

Type		**Wheel Arrangement**	Co'Co'
Engine	EE 12 RK3CT	**Length**	15.85 m
Cylinders	V-12	**Width**	2.82 m
Power	1750 kW	**Height**	3.82 m
Alternator	Toyo Denki	**Weight**	98 t
Motors	EE 548	**Axle Load**	160 kN
Builder	EE Rocklea	**Tractive Effort**	216 kN
Introduced	1995	**Maximum Speed**	97 km/h
Number Built	2	**Gauge**	1067 mm

The first unit was rebuilt at Port Augusta from ZB 9 after damage from

a fire in 1994. It incorporated a microprocessor control system which replaced the original load regulator control and stepless 'power lever' control pedestal. A new American pattern control desk with eight notch control is fitted, which will probably restrict this unit to multiple operation with EMD locomotives and the MKA class. A modified cab similar to the EL class was fitted, and a yellow and green livery was applied. The unit was ballasted with lead to increase the weight to that of a ZA class. A second unit, ZB 6, was rebuilt in Tasmania but with a cab more like the DL class, which became ZR 2.

900 – 909

900 arriving in Port Pirie on the morning train from Adelaide, January 1970. (Peter Clark)

Type		**Wheel Arrangement**	A1A'A1A'
Engine	EE 16SVT	**Length**	19.30 m
Cylinders	V-16	**Width**	2.97 m
Power	1190 kW	**Height**	4.19 m
Generator	EE 822	**Weight**	128 t
Motors	EE 523	**Axle Load**	210 kN
Builder	SAR Islington	**Tractive Effort**	151 kN
Introduced	1951	**Maximum Speed**	119 km/h
Number Built	10	**Gauge**	1600 mm

No. 900 was the first Australian-built diesel-electric mainline locomotive to enter service and was named 'Lady Norrie'. This class was easily identified by the long square nose and high arched roof. The cast bogies have no outside equalising beams and have transverse leaf spring secondary suspension. The class was painted in the standard SAR colour scheme of regal red and silver, with a stainless steel band on the side panels. The class were used on both passenger and freight trains on all former SAR main lines but tended to work mainly on the Port Pirie line. The 900 class were unable to operate in multiple unit with 930 class and other Alco engined SAR locomotives, but could operate in multiple within the class. Examples have been preserved.

Goninan-GE 35 Ton

Type	35 Ton	**Wheel Arrangement**	Bo
Engine	Cummins NS743	**Length**	5.49 m
Cylinders	Inline 6	**Width**	2.90 m
Power	201 kW	**Height**	m
Generator	GE GT 558	**Weight**	32.5 t
Motors	GE 763	**Axle Load**	159 kN
Builder	Goninan NSW	**Tractive Effort**	51 kN
Introduced	1972	**Maximum Speed**	56 km/h
Number Built	1	**Gauge**	1435 mm

This unit is effectively half of a 70 Ton model, but with a rigid frame rather than the bogies of the larger locomotive. It replaced a steam shunting locomotive that had previously been used at the Waratah plant. It is the only example in Australia of a standard type relatively common in industrial use in the United States. It was delivered in a metallic blue colour scheme.

DIESEL LOCOMOTIVES OF GENERAL ELECTRIC DESIGN

The preserved 7921, previously DE 90, at Sydney Station, 1995. (Peter Clark)

7920 – 7923

Type	44 Ton	Wheel Arrangement	Bo'Bo'
Engine	Cat D17000	Length	9.09 m
Cylinders	2 x V-8	Width	2.90 m
Power	2 x 130 kW	Height	4.09 m
Generators	2 x GE GT 555A	Weight	39.8 t
Motors	GE 733	Axle Load	98 kN
Builder	GE	Tractive Effort	58 kN
Introduced	1944	Maximum Speed	56 km/h
Number Built	4	Gauge	1435 mm

Four of this type were obtained under Lend Lease conditions for use at St Mary's Munitions Factory, and carried the numbers 7920 – 7923 allocated by the US Army. Only one was used, until the end of the war, at the factory. Nos 7921 and 7922 were transferred to Woomera (South Australia) in April 1948, and Nos 7920 and 7923 were purchased by NSWR in September 1948. 7921 – 7922 passed to the CR and were renumbered DE 90 and DE 91 respectively.

These are standard US branch line and shunting units, of rather square appearance. NSWR units had buffers and knuckle couplers, and lacked the end shunters' steps; CR units had knuckle couplers and steps. 7920 and 7923 were coaching shunters at Sydney Terminal. DE 90 and DE 91 shunted at Port Augusta and Port Pirie. The two NSW locomotives were transferred to Christmas Island and the former CR units were preserved, DE 90 at the NSWRTM as 7921.

Lysaghts locomotive 'Ann' at the Rolling Mills at Cringila. (Leon Oberg)

JL 1 – JL 3

Type	45 Ton	**Wheel Arrangement**	B'B'
Engine	Cummins H6-B1	**Length**	8.33 m
Cylinders	2 x Inline 6	**Width**	2.90 m
Power	2 x 97 kW	**Height**	3.73 m
Generators	2 x GE GT 1503	**Weight**	45.6 t
Motors	GE 733	**Axle Load**	113 kN
Builder	Goninan	**Tractive Effort**	kN
Introduced	1955	**Maximum Speed**	32 km/h
Number Built	3	**Gauge**	1435 mm

These locomotives were the industrial version of the GE 44-ton locomotive. Although very similar in appearance, they differ in having only one traction motor per bogie, with chain drive to the other axle.

The bogies are of the equalised type with fabricated frames. These three locomotives are fitted for multiple unit operation. They were used for shunting at the company's Springhill works and occasionally worked over the NSWR to the former Commonwealth Rolling Mills (now owned by Lysaght) at Port Kembla North. These locomotives were supplanted by an English Electric unit transferred from BHP.

Locomotive names were:

No. 1 'Ann'   No. 2 'Primrose'

No. 3 'Helen Mary'

These locomotives were named after the daughters of Mr D.R. Lysaght.

The two ex BHP locomotives at Junee Workshops, March 2006. (Peter Clark)

37 – 58

Type	80 Ton	**Wheel Arrangement**	Bo'Bo'
Engine	Cummins NHS	**Length**	10.33 m
Cylinders	2 x Inline 6	**Width**	2.97 m
Power	2 x 202 kW	**Height**	4.15 m
Generator	2 x GE GT 558	**Weight**	73 l
Motors	GE 763	**Axle Load**	180 kN
Builder	Goninan	**Tractive Effort**	91 kN
Introduced	1960	**Maximum Speed**	km/h
Number Built	22	**Gauge**	1435 mm

This varied group formed most of the non-government output of the Goninan plant, until work recommenced on large GE locomotives. These units were all similar in appearance, generally resembling the US-built 44-ton locomotives. BHP Nos 37 – 52 and 56 were built to a narrow profile for use on the Newcastle Steelworks 0.915 m gauge line as well as on the standard gauge. Most were rebuilt to the normal standard-gauge profile, but 37 – 41 and 56 remained to the narrow profile. Units 48 to 53 were built with two Rolls-Royce C6TFL engines of 194 kW each. Units 55 to 58 were built with Cummins NT855 engines of 202 kW each, and units 48 to 51 and 53 have also had these engines fitted. Air-conditioning has been fitted to these units. The similar Sulphide Corporation locomotive (RR C6TFL engines) was based at the company's plant at Cockle Creek, near Newcastle. The John Lysaght locomotive JL 4 (Cummins NT 335 engines) was used on private and government lines at Port Kembla. Australian Portland Cement's two locomotives, D 1 and D 2 (Cummins NT 380 engines), were used at their Berrima cement works and Medway quarry.

32 – 36

Type	70 Ton	**Wheel Arrangement**	Bo'Bo'
Engine	C-B FWL	**Length**	11.84 m
Cylinders	Inline 6	**Width**	2.97 m
Power	490 kW	**Height**	4.24 m
Generator	GE GT 571	**Weight**	71.5 t
Motors	GE 747	**Axle Load**	176 kN
Builder	Goninan	**Tractive Effort**	89 kN
Introduced	1954	**Maximum Speed**	40 km/h
Number Built	5	**Gauge**	1435 mm

These Australian versions of the GE 70-ton industrial switcher were used in and around the BHP Newcastle Steelworks. They differed from their American counterparts in having a rounded cab roof and were fitted with large buffers as well as automatic couplers. They were used for shunting on standard-gauge tracks within the BHP Newcastle Steelworks.

1170 – 1181

Type	(U6A)	**Wheel Arrangement**	A1A'A1A'
Engine	C-B FWL	**Length**	11.58 m
Cylinders	Inline 6	**Width**	2.74 m
Power	485 kW	**Height**	3.84 m
Generator	GE GT 571	**Weight**	61 t
Motors	GE 756	**Axle Load**	100 kN
Builder	Walkers	**Tractive Effort**	88 kN
Introduced	1956	**Maximum Speed**	80 km/h
Number Built	12	**Gauge**	1067 mm

This was the original 60-ton branch line diesel-electric locomotive for QR. It was an end-cab hood unit, carried on two equalised four motor six axle bogies, which took all draw gear stresses through an articulated joint. The class were fitted for multiple unit operation, but were single ended, with pilots only on the hood ends. The wheels are of the SCOA-P pattern, 915 mm in diameter. Much of the equipment on this type was similar to that on the larger 1150 class. The colour scheme was the usual blue, grey and white.

When this class were first introduced they were spread out over many country depots to work main passenger and some through goods trains over light country lines. As other 60-tonne locomotives were introduced the class were gradually allocated to the Northern division and they were last based at Cairns and Townsville. These locomotives were originally numbered 1270 – 1281, and later 1500 – 1511.

U 201

Type	UM 20C	**Wheel Arrangement**	Co'Co'
Engine	7FDL 8	**Length**	14.14 m
Cylinders	V-8	**Width**	2.74 m
Power	1395 kW	**Height**	3.67 m
Generator	GE GT 581	**Weight**	88.9 t
Motors	GE 761	**Axle Load**	145 kN
Builder	GE PT Lokindo	**Tractive Effort**	109 kN
Introduced	1996	**Maximum Speed**	103 km/h
Number Built	1	**Gauge**	1067 mm

This locomotive had been used by International Container Terminal Services in Manila until the rail service was replaced by road trucks. This unit is similar to locomotives used in Indonesia, and the cab design was developed by Goninan for GE. The locomotive and container wagons were purchased by South Spur in 2007, but the intended traffic did not eventuate. This locomotive is very small compared to former WAGR locomotives of similar power. The locomotive has been overhauled and repainted but was used rarely by Greentrains. It was sold to TransPerth for use transferring electric train sets between depots and workshops.

1150 stored at Townsville, November 1998. (Peter Clark)

1150 – 1162

Type	(U11C)	**Wheel Arrangement**	Co'Co'
Engine	C-B FVBL	**Length**	16.00 m
Cylinders	V-12	**Width**	2.74 m
Power	820 kW	**Height**	3.85 m
Generator	GE GT 581	**Weight**	89.5 t
Motors	GE 756	**Axle Load**	151 kN
Builder	GE, Goninan	**Tractive Effort**	138 kN
Introduced	1952	**Maximum Speed**	80 km/h
Number Built	13	**Gauge**	1067 mm

These were the first diesel-electric locomotives on the Queensland Railways. The first 10 units were built by GE at their Erie works, but the later three units were built under licence by Goninan at Broadmeadow. They are conventional hood units, with rounded hood ends and a plain appearance. The outside equalised bogies carry not only the pilot, but also buffers and couplers: they are not, however, articulated. A single set of controls is installed. Dual sealed-beam headlights are fitted, but illuminated number indicators are not. The standard livery of blue, grey and white was applied. The 1150 class mainly operated in the northern area of Queensland, allocated to Townsville, and worked on lines available for 90-tonne locomotives, mainly the Mount Isa and Collinsville lines.

These locomotives were originally numbered 1210 – 1222 and later 1300 – 1312, the later numbers being changed to permit the continuous numbering of English Electric 90-tonne locomotives. The sole remaining unit, 1150, has been preserved and is to be restored to working order.

2603 at Pring, September 1994. (Peter Clark)

2600 – 2612

Type	U22C	**Wheel Arrangement**	Co'Co'
Engine	GE 7FDL	**Length**	17.92 m
Cylinders	V-12	**Width**	2.72 m
Power	1640 kW	**Height**	3.84 m
Alternator	GE 5GTA 28A	**Weight**	97.6 t
Motors	GE 761A20	**Axle Load**	163 kN
Builder	Goninan Qld	**Tractive Effort**	225 kN
Introduced	1983	**Maximum Speed**	80 km/h
Number Built	13	**Gauge**	1067 mm

After nearly 30 years, an order was placed by QR with Goninan for further General Electric mainline locomotives. Goninan had built the last three 1150 class and all of the 1170 class branch line locomotives in the 1950s. A new assembly plant was set up in Townsville, and these 13 locomotives were produced there. No further orders were obtained until the recent order for CM30-8 was placed. Although based on the standard GE export type locomotive, as exemplified by the New Zealand Dx class, also originally numbered in the 2600 series, the underframe, bogies and short hood were extensively modified to suit Queensland requirements. The bogies, in particular, were longer in the wheelbase to meet QR bridge loading limits, and this resulted in a much more balanced appearance than the standard export locomotive. The nose was modified to take the standard air-conditioning unit fitted to Clyde locomotives, and the underframe was altered to meet the clearance diagram and to reduce the weight. The cab and the long hood were very similar to the standard design. These are not described as Dash-7 units, although they incorporate some of the improvements of that design. These locomotives have always worked in the Northern division, being originally used exclusively on the coal traffic from Newlands and Collinsville to Abbot Point (near Bowen). They were based at Pring Locomotive Depot and operated in three groups of four, with one unit spare.

2600 – 2612

Type	C22-7Mmi	**Wheel Arrangement**	Co'Co'
Engine	GE 7FDL	**Length**	17.92 m
Cylinders	V-12	**Width**	2.72 m
Power	1640 kW	**Height**	3.84 m
Alternator	GE 5GTA 28A	**Weight**	109.7 t
Motors	GE 761A20	**Axle Load**	kN
Builder	Goninan Qld	**Tractive Effort**	253 kN
Introduced	2001	**Maximum Speed**	80 km/h
Number Built	13	**Gauge**	1067 mm

During 1999–2001 new standard cabs suitable for driver-only operation were fitted, changing the appearance quite dramatically. As rebuilt, the 2600 class were considered as microprocessor equipped units, and were ballasted to increase their adhesion. However, the modified cabs resulted in inconvenient step arrangements at the cab end, and these units were initially used as second units on the Mount Isa line, an unfortunate result from a major cab upgrade. Steps are now provided only in diagonally opposite corners of the locomotive, giving an odd aspect to the appearance of the unit. The cab itself resembles the large replacement cab used on Clyde locomotives, and incorporates the improved roll over protection built into those cabs. It does make the 2600 look much more like the more common Clyde locomotives, losing the distinctive profile of the original GE cab. The engine hood retains most of its original appearance, but the short hood has been lowered and extended beyond the front headstock, resulting in a greater length of 19.3 m over coupling points. The rebuilt locomotives operated initially on the Mount Isa line but later returned to Pring for Newlands service. The whole class was sold and now operates in Africa.

EL 59 at Kalgoorlie, April 1994. (Peter Clark)

EL 51 – EL 64

Type	CM30-8	**Wheel Arrangement**	Co'Co'
Engine	GE 7 FDL	**Length**	20.50 m
Cylinders	V-12	**Width**	2.91 m
Power	2380 kW	**Height**	4.19 m
Alternator	GE GMG192	**Weight**	112.7 t
Motors	GE 761ANR1	**Axle Load**	190 kN
Builder	Goninan NSW	**Tractive Effort**	197 kN
Introduced	1990	**Maximum Speed**	140 km/h
Number Built	14	**Gauge**	1435 mm

The EL class was the first GE cowl type locomotive type in Australia, the first GE locomotive class purchased new by AN or its predecessors, and introduced the sharply sloped flat nose, since the class was intended for use on passenger and fast light freight trains. The cowl body has a number of engine room doors on each side of the body, to permit access for maintenance and to aid cooling for inspection. The bogie frame castings were to a design associated with the Montreal Locomotive Works, and were imported from Canada, where they were manufactured by Dofasco. These units had lightweight traction motors suitable for metre gauge. The EL class were used extensively on AN standard-gauge passenger services until replaced by the HEP equipped CLP class. They were also frequently used on intermodal Roadrailer trains, and National Rail freight trains. After the sale of Australian National, these locomotives were overhauled in Perth and sold to Chicago Freight Car Leasing Australia, who lease them to private operators in NSW and Victoria. They have been repainted into CFCLA blue and silver.

P2517 at the Kwinana grain loop, 8 November 2014. (Peter Clark)

P 2001 – P 2017, later P 2501 – P 2517

Type	CM25-8	**Wheel Arrangement**	Co'Co'
Engine	GE 7 FDL	**Length**	18.90 m
Cylinders	V-12	**Width**	2.85 m
Power	1830 kW	**Height**	4.01 m
Alternator	GE GMG191	**Weight**	98.5 t
Motors	GE 761F1	**Axle Load**	161 kN
Builder	Goninan WA	**Tractive Effort**	286 kN
Introduced	1990	**Maximum Speed**	90 km/h
Number Built	17	**Gauge**	1067 mm

The P class were the first GE type on Westrail, and the first narrow-gauge Dash-8 type anywhere. The small wide nose is vaguely reminiscent of that on the huge US U 50 types, but on a much smaller scale. The bogies, like those of the Queensland 2600 class, are of a Trimount design, and longer in the wheelbase than the standard GE export design. The sharp edged body design is quite distinct from the rounded design used since the 1950s for other GE narrow-gauge designs, and reflects the parallel change to US domestic designs. The cab is air-conditioned and isolated from sound and vibration. This was the first Westrail locomotive with illuminated numbers, a feature deleted from many previous designs. The class all carry names of shires. The axle load allows wide use over WA main and secondary lines.

2801 – 2850, PA 2819, 3209, 3215, 3221

3209 at Carrington, 23 December 2013. The roof mounted mufflers are only on the standard gauge units, but the lower cab roof is being applied to all units. (Peter Clark)

Type	CM30-8	**Wheel Arrangement**	Co'Co'
Engine	GE 7 FDL	**Length**	20.48 m
Cylinders	V-12	**Width**	2.87 m
Power	2380 kW	**Height**	3.68 m
Alternator	GE GMG191H1	**Weight**	116 t
Motors	GE 761ANR1	**Axle Load**	191 kN
Builder	Goninan Qld	**Tractive Effort**	266 kN
Introduced	1995	**Maximum Speed**	110 km/h
Number Built	50	**Gauge**	1067 mm

The 2800 class were the fourth GE type on QR, and the second narrow-gauge Dash-8 type in Australia. This is the only double cab GE design in Australia. The bogies are a fabricated version of the US domestic Dash-9 type, with prominent external primary coil springs. The sharp edged hood design is quite distinct from the rounded design used on earlier units, and is similar to the Australian Railroad Group P class.

The radiator and air intakes are flanked by large sound-absorbing plates which serve to reduce noise transmission. Both cabs are isolated from sound and vibration, with the air-conditioning unit mounted vertically behind the cab on the walkway. The axle load is significantly higher than any previous QR diesel locomotive, and will confine these units to the main lines. They are mainly used on the North Coast and Mount Isa lines. In early 2006, 2819 was rebuilt to standard gauge as a trial and operated on QR National standard-gauge trains. During 2010, it was transferred to WA, returned to narrow gauge and given the code PA. In 2012, 2815 was placed on standard gauge for coal traffic on the NSW North Coast line. Joined by two other units, they were renumbered 3209, 3215 and 3221 after extensive sound reduction work. Two units have since been stored.

GL 101 – GL 112

Type	CM30-7Mmi	**Wheel Arrangement**	Co'Co'
Engine	GE 7 FDL	**Length**	17.40 m
Cylinders	V-12	**Width**	2.96 m
Power	2380 kW	**Height**	4.24 m
Alternator	GE GTA 24	**Weight**	132 t
Motors	GE 752	**Axle Load**	216 kN
Builder	Goninan NSW	**Tractive Effort**	347 kN
Introduced	2002	**Maximum Speed**	115 km/h
Number Built	12	**Gauge**	1435 mm

These units are rebuilds of former NSW 442 class (DL-500G) locomotives, using refurbished power equipment removed from former Conrail C-30-7A units, which used 12-cylinder engines rather than the 16-cylinder engine used in most locomotives of that type. The rebuild was carried out at Goninan's Broadmeadow plant. These units are equivalent in power to the larger Clyde JT 26C units, and a considerable improvement over the DL-500G in its original form, also operated by CFCLA. Microprocessor control using the GE Brightstar system will reduce the parasitic load, allowing the relatively high net power rating. Cab air-conditioning has been installed. The original frame incorporates an integral fuel tank, similar to that of the later NR class, and this provides a fuel capacity of 7500 litres. The original MLW design bogies are used.

5057 – 5059

Type	C36-7	**Wheel Arrangement**	Co'Co'
Engine	GE 7FDL	**Length**	19.70 m
Cylinders	V-16	**Width**	3.13 m
Power	2685 kW	**Height**	4.6 m
Alternator	GE GTA 11	**Weight**	190.5 t
Motors	GE 752E5	**Axle Load**	310 kN
Builder	Goninan NSW	**Tractive Effort**	400 kN
Introduced	1978	**Maximum Speed**	112 km/h
Number Built	3	**Gauge**	1435 mm

These three locomotives were the first of the new generation of GE locomotives in Australia, and they were purchased, as were the later SD50S units, to break the Alco monopoly on the North West iron ore lines. They had some early problems, but have proved successful in the long term. While generally similar to the Alco, many details were quite different. One major difference is the arrangement of dynamic brakes, where the grids are located under the radiators, cooled by the same fan. While this is effective in preventing the radiators freezing in sub-zero conditions, in the usually hot Pilbara climate it required the addition of a separate radiator for use during dynamic braking. It is mounted in front of the engine above the traction motor blower, which provides cooling air. (The normal radiator is drained during dynamic brake operation.) The electrical control equipment was of the modular, card-mounted type, to simplify maintenance. These locomotives were used interchangeably with the Alco and GM locomotives on export iron ore traffic from Paraburdoo and Mount Tom Price to Dampier. After introduction of the Dash-9 locomotives, these locomotives were sold to NREC and placed in lease service in the USA.

5052 at Seven Mile Yard, August 2004. (Peter Clark)

5506 – 5513, later 5051 – 5052

Type	C36-7m	**Wheel Arrangement**	Co'Co'
Engine	GE 7FDL	**Length**	19.74 m
Cylinders	V-16	**Width**	3.10 m
Power	2800 kW	**Height**	4.68 m
Alternator	GE GTA 24A2	**Weight**	190 t
Motors	GE 752AF	**Axle Load**	325 kN
Builder	Goninan WA	**Tractive Effort**	431 kN
Introduced	1987	**Maximum Speed**	112 km/h
Number Built	8	**Gauge**	1435 mm

Although Hamersley Iron had rebuilt and modernised a number of Alco C-636 locomotives, and Mount Newman Mining had given many of its locomotives complete overhauls, this rebuilding of an Alco C-636 as a GE C36-7 was the first of its kind in the world. These were successful, but no more were performed since the type was superseded by the CM40-8, and all new locomotives and additional rebuilds were to the later design. In fact, many features of the Dash-8 series were included,

in particular the improved dynamic brakes and the new alternator design with internal series-parallel switching. This resulted in a power increase of 115 kW, and the locomotives were sometimes known as the Dash-7.5 type. They also used the HI-developed Pilbara cab although there were detail differences from the original arrangement. These units were originally used on the Mount Newman line to Mount Whaleback, and the former Goldsworthy Mining railway. With the arrival of the AC6000s, these locomotives were withdrawn and some units were sold to Goninan. Two of these were refurbished and repainted in Pilbara Rail colours for use at Dampier as shunting locomotives. These were:

5051, ex 5507, ex C636 5461
5052, ex 5508, ex C636 5466

5630 – 5633, 5646 – 5647

Type	CM39-8	**Wheel Arrangement**	Co'Co'
Engine	GE 7FDL	**Length**	20.19 m
Cylinders	V-16	**Width**	3.11 m
Power	2909 kW	**Height**	4.69 m
Alternator	GE GMG187	**Weight**	195 t
Motors	GE 752AG	**Axle Load**	325 kN
Builder	Goninan WA	**Tractive Effort**	485 kN
Introduced	1988	**Maximum Speed**	112 km/h
Number Built	6	**Gauge**	1435 mm

Satisfied with the performance of the rebuilt C36-7m locomotives, Mount Newman placed an order for four new locomotives with Goninan, and these were built in Welshpool. Apart from the Mount Newman version of the standard Pilbara cab, these were in all respects similar to contemporary US GE locomotives and had basically the same bogies as the Hamersley Iron C36–7s of a decade earlier. After some time in service, these units were adjusted to provide 4000 HP (2983 kW), effectively becoming CM40-8s like the following rebuilt units. The additional two units were ordered by the other component of BHP Iron Ore, Goldsworthy Mining, as part of a major upgrade of their system. These units were transferred to the Mount Newman line, being replaced on the Goldsworthy line by C36-7 rebuilds. These locomotives were originally all used on the former Mount Newman line from Mount Whaleback to Port Hedland, but since the withdrawal of the C36-7m locomotives, these locomotives are preferred for use on the former Goldsworthy line to the Yarri mine owing to their stiffer springing which gives a better ride on the lighter track.

9417 – 9420, 9424 – 9425

9424 was the only Dash-8 repainted in Pilbara Iron corporate colours following a derailment. It is seen at Seven Mile in July 2008. (Peter Clark)

Type	CM40-8m	**Wheel Arrangement**	Co'Co'
Engine	GE 7FDL	**Length**	19.74 m
Cylinders	V-16	**Width**	3.12 m
Power	2983 kW	**Height**	4.69 m
Alternator	GE GMG187	**Weight**	195 t
Motors	GE 752AF	**Axle Load**	325 kN
Builder	Goninan WA	**Tractive Effort**	485 kN
Introduced	1989	**Maximum Speed**	112 km/h
Number Built	6	**Gauge**	1435 mm

Following the successful rebuilding by Comeng WA of 9426 and 9427 from the underframes of former Conrail Alco C636 units, Robe River had a former Spokane, Portland and Seattle C636 rebuilt by Goninan in Western Australia as number 9417. This was the first of a series of conversions which later formed the majority of the Robe River fleet. Converted from Alco C-630m or C-636 types, they have Alco Hi-Ad bogies with external coil secondary suspension. Unit 9417 was not rebuilt from the Alco C630 unit that previously carried that number. These locomotives were all used on the line from Pannawonica to Cape Lambert. Since the Hamersley merger, these were mainly used for shunting at the ports and mines. A number have been sold to CFCLA.

9421 at Cape Lambert, September 2007. (Peter Clark)

9410, 9411, 9414, 9421 – 9423, CD 4301 – CD 4303, CD 4305

Type	CM40-8m	**Wheel Arrangement**	Co'Co'
Engine	GE 7FDL	**Length**	19.82 m
Cylinders	V-16	**Width**	3.12 m
Power	2983 kW	**Height**	4.69 m
Alternator	GE GMG187	**Weight**	195 t
Motors	GE 752AF	**Axle Load**	325 kN
Builder	Goninan WA	**Tractive Effort**	485 kN
Introduced	1989	**Maximum Speed**	112 km/h
Number Built	6	**Gauge**	1435 mm

These are externally very similar to the newly built BHPB GE locomotives but can be most easily distinguished by the type of bogie and fuel tank, which have been retained unchanged from the original Montreal locomotive. They have an MLW/Dofasco design bogie with rubber secondary suspension. They are slightly longer, 19.82 m over headstocks, than those converted from Alco Century design units. Unit 9410 was not rebuilt from the Goodwin/MLW unit that previously carried that number, but from a former BHP Iron Ore M636. These locomotives were all used on the main line from Pannawonica to Cape Lambert. Since the Hamersley merger, these were mainly used for shunting at the ports and mines. A number sold to CFCLA were rebuilt at Bassendean and renumbered as CD class for construction work on the Roy Hill line.

5638 at Boodarie, July 2006. (Peter Clark)

5634 – 5645, 5648 – 5669

Type	CM40-8m	**Wheel Arrangement**	Co'Co'
Engine	GE 7FDL	**Length**	19.74 m
Cylinders	V-16	**Width**	3.12 m
Power	2983 kW	**Height**	4.69 m
Alternator	GE GMG187	**Weight**	195 t
Motors	GE 752AF	**Axle Load**	325 kN
Builder	Goninan WA	**Tractive Effort**	485 kN
Introduced	1991	**Maximum Speed**	112 km/h
Number Built	34	**Gauge**	1435 mm

Following the success of the C36-7m and the new CM39-8, a program was commenced to rebuild all the remaining Alco C-636 and M-636 locomotives from the former Mount Newman mining fleet to the latest standard of GE locomotive. They are externally very similar to the newly built locomotives but can be most easily distinguished by the types of bogie and fuel tank, which have been retained unchanged from the original

Alco (or Montreal) locomotive. They all have Alco Hi-Ad bogies with external coil secondary suspension. The former M 636C units are slightly longer, 19.82 m over headstocks. As an experiment, units 5663 – 5665 were built without cabs for use as trailing units in multiple consists, but they were rebuilt with cabs to increase operating flexibility. The last four units, 5666 – 5669, were built with electronic fuel injection, rather than the mechanical fuel injection on the remainder of the class. Locomotives from 5648 onward are equipped with GE Integrated Function Control, rather than conventional instruments. Units 5650 – 5659 were equipped with Locotrol remote-control equipment. 5656, 5658 and 5659 could also act as remote receiver units. These locomotives are all generally used on the former Mount Newman line from Mount Whaleback to Port Hedland and branches.

9402 near Western Creek Junction, July 2006. (Peter Clark)

7043 – 7050, 7053 – 7098, 9401 – 9409, 9428 – 9436

Type	C44-9W	**Wheel Arrangement**	Co'Co'
Engine	GE 7FDL	**Length**	21.35 m
Cylinders	V-16	**Width**	3.03 m
Power	3270 kW	**Height**	4.69 m
Alternator	GE GMG-197	**Weight**	197 t
Motors	GE 752AJ	**Axle Load**	330 kN
Builder	GE Erie	**Tractive Effort**	526 kN
Introduced	1995	**Maximum Speed**	105 km/h
Number Built	78	**Gauge**	1435 mm

Hamersley must have been satisfied with the performance of the C36-7 locomotives, and the many GE rebuilds on the other Pilbara lines, when they ordered 29 of the then current standard GE locomotive and, for early delivery, specified construction in the United States. These also introduced the standard North American cab to Australia. Small modifications were made to the nose shape to improve visibility. Internally, the cab is equipped with Integrated Function Control using two multi function display screens instead of conventional instruments. The C44-9s replaced all the Alco 636 locomotives which had, in original or rebuilt form, dominated the lines since 1968. Following the merger with Robe River, similar locomotives were purchased and numbered in the Robe River series. These and later Hamersley units had a revised livery including red, black and yellow on silver, and were lettered 'Pilbara Rail' and later 'Pilbara Iron'. In order to get their operation under way quickly, Fortescue Metals Group ordered fifteen new locomotives numbered 001 to 015 based on the C44-9W type that had been delivered to Rio Tinto, in order to obtain a proven design quickly. These were the last of this design to come to Australia. These locomotives introduced Electronically Controlled Pneumatic braking to the Pilbara.

001 – 015

As a large number of these locomotives have been purchased in relatively small orders a complete list in order of the GE builders' numbers is presented below:

47744 – 47762	October 1994	7065 – 7083
47763 – 47772	November 1994	7084 – 7093
52841 – 52843	August 2000	7094 – 7096
53455 – 53457	October 2001	9401 – 9403 ex 9470 – 9472
54154 – 54159	April 2003	9404 – 9409
54160 – 54161	April 2003	7097 – 7098
54187 – 54189	August 2003	9428 – 9430
54241 – 54242	July 2003	9431 – 9432
54243 – 54244	August 2003	7063 – 7064
54766 – 54767	May 2004	9433 – 9434
54768	May 2004	7061
54769	June 2004	7062
55880 – 55885	April 2005	7055 – 7060
56154 – 56155	November 2005	7053 – 7054
57094 – 57101	August 2006	7043 – 7050
57102 – 57103	August 2006	9435 – 9436
58178 – 58172	August 2007	001 – 015

Above: NR 109 at Spencer Junction in July 2004. NR class are used to haul all of Great Southern Railway's passenger trains and a number of special colour schemes have been used. (Peter Clark)

Below: NR 84 in Southern Spirit colours at Dry Creek, 8 January 2010. (Peter Clark)

NR 1 – NR 120

Type	Cv40-9i	**Wheel Arrangement**	Co'Co'
Engine	GE 7FDL	**Length**	20.83 m
Cylinders	V-16	**Width**	2.94 m
Power	2126-3000 kW	**Height**	4.07 m
Alternator	GE GMG196	**Weight**	132 t
Motors	GE 793	**Axle Load**	216 kN
Builder	Goninan NSW	**Tractive Effort**	388 kN
Introduced	1996	**Maximum Speed**	115 km/h
Number Built	120	**Gauge**	1435 mm

NR55 at Moss Vale, 11 January 2014. This locomotive has been extensively rebuilt with a new engine and new cab electronics as part of a program to update the whole class. The most visible indication is the new dynamic brake outlet ducts, which can be compared with the originals on NR109. NR55 was one of a few units fitted with ECP brakes for stone traffic. (Peter Clark)

The first locomotives ordered by National Rail are most easily described as a locomotive of similar rated power to the FreightCorp 90 class, but lighter, so as to be suitable for operation on normal main line trackwork. Goninan were successful in obtaining the contracts, initially for 80, and later for an additional 40 locomotives. A letter added to the NR class model description is the 'v' following the C which indicates variable power with three distinct power settings. These settings are 2850 horsepower (2126 kW), 3560 horsepower (2655 kW) and 4020 horsepower (3000 kW). The bogie design uses rubber sandwich secondary suspension, the primary suspension using 'wing type' axleboxes, with the primary springs in clear view. To reduce their weight, the NR class bogies are of welded construction rather than the more usual castings. The more restrictive loading gauge and the lower overall height of the locomotive made the US radiator design impractical, and the radiator cores are contained within a flush-sided casing at the rear of the long hood. The air intakes are at the base of the hood and large muffler plates are attached to the walkway. The frame curves down between the bogies to form the fuel tanks and carry 12,500 litres of fuel. A program to update the whole class with new engines (to the same type) and new cab electronics commenced in 2012. These locomotives are used on all Pacific National intermodal and standard-gauge steel services. NR3 was renumbered NR 121 after a fatal accident. NR33 was destroyed in a level crossing collision in Victoria.

5001 – 5012

Type	C40aci	**Wheel Arrangement**	Co'Co'
Engine	GE 7FDL	**Length**	20.83 m
Cylinders	V-16	**Width**	2.94 m
Power	3000 kW	**Height**	4.25 m
Alternator	GE GMG192	**Weight**	176 t
Motors	GE GEB13	**Axle Load**	289 kN
Builder	Goninan NSW	**Tractive Effort**	586 kN
Introduced	2008	**Maximum Speed**	80 km/h
Number Built	12	**Gauge**	1435 mm

These locomotives look very similar to the NR class locomotives from the same builder, but they are substantially heavier and have a much higher tractive effort and a number of detail differences. The frame itself is very similar to that of the NR, although it is heavier, using thicker plate. The fuel capacity of the 5000 class is only 9900 litres compared to the 12,500 litres on the NR class. The bogies are standard GE cast steel bogies as used by US domestic AC4400CW locomotives. These have a longer wheelbase and are substantially heavier than the fabricated bogies used on the NR class. The AC traction motors are particularly suitable for continuous high power operation, and do not suffer the time related high power restrictions of DC traction motors. A feature of the locomotive is the Wabtech EPIC II electronically controlled pneumatic (ECP) brake. An additional cable for this system is located on the right side of the headstock, carrying 230 volts DC. The EPIC II system incorporates remote-control facilities, and will allow the control of remote locomotives through the brake control cable. The 5000 class, while meeting the standard clearance restrictions, is optimised for heavy coal haulage within the Hunter Valley.

9201 – 9215, AC 4301 – AC 4308, 6001 – 6012

Type	C44aci	**Wheel Arrangement**	Co'Co'
Engine	GE 7FDL	**Length**	20.83 m
Cylinders	V-16	**Width**	2.94 m
Power	3185 kW	**Height**	4.25 m
Alternator	GE GMG192	**Weight**	139 t
Motors	GE 5GEB30	**Axle Load**	230 kN
Builder	United Group NSW	**Tractive Effort**	453 kN
Introduced	2008	**Maximum Speed**	115 km/h
Number Built	35	**Gauge**	1435 mm

These locomotives look very similar to the NR class and 5000 class locomotives from the same builder, but there are a number of detail differences. The most obvious is the larger radiator which projects beyond the hood on each side, required by the higher engine power. The frame itself is very similar to that of the NR. The available fuel capacity varies with the allowable mass, 134t with 7300 litres, 136t with 10,000 litres, 139t with 13,500 litres compared to the 12,500 litres on the NR class. The bogies have a longer wheelbase than the NR but have fabricated frames as used on the NR class. The AC traction motors allow sustained high power operation in coal and iron ore traffic. The C44aci can operate with the NR on high speed intermodal traffic, and work with the 5000 class in heavy coal haulage within the Hunter Valley. The heavier GE engine, compared to the EMD 710 in the GT 46C ACe, puts the C44aci at a disadvantage regarding fuel capacity at normal ARTC network axle loadings. Locomotives 6002, 6005 and 6009 – 6012 are now class ACA for operation in WA.

Above: AC 4307 at Forrestfield, February 2010. (Peter Clark)

Below: ACA 6012 at Forrestfield, 15 November 2013. These units are used on Koolyanobbing to Esperance iron ore traffic. (Peter Clark)

CF 4401 at Port Waratah, January 2012. (Peter Clark)

XRN 001 – XRN 030, ACB 4401 – ACB 4406, CF 4401 – CF 4412, CEY 001 – CEY 007, GWU 001 – GWU 009, 9301 – 9317, 6021 – 6029, ACA 6030 – ACA 6032, MRL 001 - MRL 006, FIE 001 – FIE 003

Type	C44aci	**Wheel Arrangement**	Co'Co'
Engine	GE 7FDL	**Length**	20.83 m
Cylinders	V-16	**Width**	2.94 m
Power	3246 kW	**Height**	4.25 m
Alternator	GE GMG192	**Weight**	139 t
Motors	GE 5GEB30	**Axle Load**	230 kN
Builder	UGL NSW	**Tractive Effort**	453 kN
Introduced	2010	**Maximum Speed**	115 km/h
Number Built	102	**Gauge**	1435 mm

A small power increase from 3185 kW to 3248 kW was made starting with the XRN and ACB classes compared to the earlier C44aci units. The main engine air intake has been removed from the side panels just ahead of the radiator. While Pacific National and Aurizon have both obtained this type following their purchase of the earlier version, a number of new operators – Centennial Coal, Glencore, Mineral Resources and Fletcher International – have obtained this type as their only motive power.

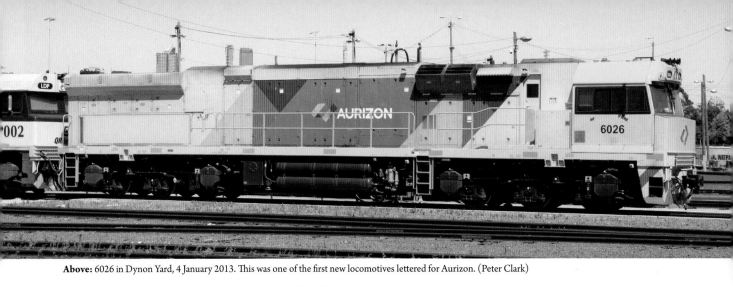

Above: 6026 in Dynon Yard, 4 January 2013. This was one of the first new locomotives lettered for Aurizon. (Peter Clark)

Below: MRL 001 in Forrestfield Yard on 9 November 2014 (Peter Clark)

5021 – 5039

Type	C44acHi	**Wheel Arrangement**	Co'Co'
Engine	GE 7FDL	**Length**	20.83 m
Cylinders	V-16	**Width**	2.94 m
Power	3248 kW	**Height**	4.25 m
Alternator	GE GMG192	**Weight**	180 t
Motors	GEB 13	**Axle Load**	294 kN
Builder	United Group Rail NSW	**Tractive Effort**	586 kN
Introduced	2010	**Maximum Speed**	80 km/h
Number Built	19	**Gauge**	1435 mm

The 19 units of the 5020 class represented more than a 150% increase in the QRN dedicated Hunter Valley coal traffic fleet. The 5020 class also introduced the post privatisation livery for QR National. The power increased from 3000 kW to 3248 kW with this class compared to the earlier C40aci units. This resulted in the larger radiator which projects beyond the hood on each side, the only significant external difference in appearance from the earlier type.

8100 – 8199

Type	ES44DCi	**Wheel Arrangement**	Co'Co'
Engine	GE V250	**Length**	21.99 m
Cylinders	V-12	**Width**	3.11 m
Power	3250 kW	**Height**	4.69 m
Alternator	GE 5GMG197	**Weight**	197 t
Motors	GE GE 752AJ	**Axle Load**	322 kN
Builder	GE Erie	**Tractive Effort**	526 kN
Introduced	2008	**Maximum Speed**	113 km/h
Number Built	97	**Gauge**	1435 mm

The Pilbara Iron Dash-9 was only slightly different from the USA domestic equivalent, but the ES44DCi is substantially different from the standard US ES44DC. The later GEVO 12-cylinder engine requires closer control of combustion temperatures to maintain the low emission figures and good fuel economy, and the Rio Tinto locomotives are to operate with ambient temperatures of 41°C. To meet this requirement larger radiators, as used on AC6000 units, have been fitted, requiring two radiator fans as well the separate air to air intercooler already fitted on domestic ES series units. These large radiators required a longer frame, and the ES44DCi uses the longer 22 metre underframe of the AC 6000 locomotive. Units 8197 to 8199 have the later cab design with rectangular front windows.

AN AUSTRALIAN LOCOMOTIVE GUIDE

RHA 1001 during testing in the USA. (General Electric)

9101 – 9114, RHA 1001 – RHA 1021

Type	ES44ACi	**Wheel Arrangement**	Co'Co'
Engine	GE V250	**Length**	21.99 m
Cylinders	V-12	**Width**	3.11 m
Power	3250 kW	**Height**	4.69 m
Alternator	GE 5GMG197	**Weight**	197 t
Motors	GE GEB13	**Axle Load**	322 kN
Builder	GE Erie	**Tractive Effort**	730 kN
Introduced	2013	**Maximum Speed**	113 km/h
Number Built	26	**Gauge**	1435 mm

While very similar in overall appearance to the preceding DC units, the ES44ACi has a few identifying features. Firstly and most obviously, the cab has been returned to the US standard with rectangular cab windows, rather than the so-called 'teardrop' windows. This change coincides with a strengthening of the cab structure, largely by increasing the plate thicknesses to 16 mm. Another change is an additional (third) dynamic brake unit in the raised hood area behind the cab, to cope with the greatly increased braking effort, 6500 HP compared to 5200 HP on the DC units. Rio Tinto have been slow in adopting the more powerful but more expensive AC traction units, but Roy Hill has obtained them as their first locomotives.

6073 on Finucane Island, July 2008. (Peter Clark)

6070 – 6077

Type	AC6000-CW	**Wheel Arrangement**	Co'Co'	
Engine	GE 7HDL	**Length**	21.99 m	
Cylinders	V-16	**Width**	3.11 m	
Power	4476 kW	**Height**	4.69 m	
Alternator	GE 5GMG192	**Weight**	197 t	
Motors	GE GEB13	**Axle Load**	322 kN	
Builder	GE Erie	**Tractive Effort**	kN	
Introduced	1998	**Maximum Speed**	km/h	
Number Built	8	**Gauge**	1435 mm	

These were the first locomotives ordered by an Australian railway to use alternating current traction motors, although diesel railcars have previously used this system. It was surprising to see an Australian iron ore railway select the relatively untried 6000 horsepower GE/Deutz HDL engine at a time when only two US domestic railroads were using these (and the EMD equivalent). This order did not replace many of the existing locomotives, but provided good experience into the economics of much more powerful locomotives. These locomotives used a different design of steering bogie than that used by CSX in the USA. By 2006, the original engines were replaced by the later GE design 16-cylinder GEVO/V250 of the same power. Locomotive 6070 was scrapped following a derailment in 2011. As new SD70ACe units arrived, the remaining units were stored and in 2014 were scrapped.

UGL 001 – 003

Type	PH37ACmai	Wheel Arrangement	Co'Co'
Engine	GE P616	Length	20.80 m
Cylinders	V-16	Width	2.85 m
Power	2600 kW	Height	3.87 m
Alternator	GE GTA 45	Weight	120 t
Motors	GE GEB24A	Axle Load	196 kN
Builder	UGL	Tractive Effort	460 kN
Introduced	2013	Maximum Speed	100 km/h
Number Built	3	Gauge	1067 mm

These locomotives are intended as demonstrators based on the Freightliner Class 70 Power Haul locomotives built for use in the UK. They are the first use of the Austrian designed P616 engine outside Europe and are intended for use in the extensive Queensland export coal traffic, currently dominated by the Downer GT 42CU AC on non-electrified lines. These are laid out generally like the larger standard-gauge C44aci units but have vee type radiators with cooling fans above them and dynamic brakes at the rear. GE has adopted the high-speed P616 engine to meet more demanding emission requirements, but it is both more compact and lighter than previous designs. Due to a downturn in the coal industry, these three locomotives have not yet been used.

DH 1 – DH 6

DH 6 shunting at Whyalla, 1978. (Peter Clark)

Type	CV-1	**Wheel Arrangement**	B'B'
Engine	Cummins NRTO	**Length**	9.96 m
Cylinders	2 x Inline 6	**Width**	2.74 m
Power	2 x 212 kW	**Height**	4.14 m
Transmission	Hydrodynamic	**Weight**	71 t
Model	Voith RS 17Y	**Axle Load**	175 kN
Builder	Walkers	**Tractive Effort**	204 kN
Introduced	1962	**Maximum Speed**	32 km/h
Number Built	6	**Gauge**	1435 mm

Unusual features of this type were the forward slope of the hood ends, projecting beyond the pilot beam, the extremely heavy construction of the bogie side frame, and the position of the headlights: twin sealed-beam units mounted vertically on the exhaust stacks. The remainder of the locomotive was of conventional appearance, not unlike an enlarged GE 44-ton shunter. After re-engining with Cummins V-903 V-8 engines and the fitting of new Niigata transmissions, the large stack casings were replaced by a pair of thin pipes, allowing the addition of a larger cab window. The locomotives were used on the standard- and narrow-gauge network around the Whyalla Steelworks. For light traffic, they could operate on one engine-transmission set. All were withdrawn, with one held in reserve until the ARG takeover of the Whyalla system.

DIESEL LOCOMOTIVES OF WALKERS DESIGN

1001 – 1004

Type	PV-1	**Wheel Arrangement**	B'B'	
Engine	Paxman YHXL	**Length**	10.36 m	
Cylinders	V-12	**Width**	2.85 m	
Power	520 kW	**Height**	3.58 m	
Transmission	Hydrodynamic	**Weight**	50.8 t	
Model	Voith L37zUb	**Axle Load**	125 kN	
Builder	Walkers	**Tractive Effort**	133 kN	
Introduced	1963	**Maximum Speed**	48 km/h	
Number Built	4	**Gauge**	1067 mm	

With the delivery of the 10 class, EBR completed their dieselisation program, started by the 12 RPHX-powered unit PVH-21. These conventional hood units are carried on outside equalised two axle bogies. Dual sealed-beam headlights are fitted at each end, above the builder's plates. These units are based on a North British design supplied to India for the metre gauge. The Paxman engines were replaced by the Caterpillar D-398 also fitted in the 11 class. No. 1004 was assembled by the Tasmanian Railways workshops in Launceston, partly from spares provided with the first three units. The 10 class operated in multiple with the 11 class on main line trains on the EBR. Following the takeover by Tasrail these locomotives were withdrawn and passed to preservation at Walhalla, Don River and Zig Zag.

The Aramac Walkers locomotive at Aramac, 1975. (Tony Bailey)

Aramac Walkers

Type	C-250	**Wheel Arrangement**	C	
Engine	Cat D333	**Length**	6.4 m	
Cylinders	6 inline	**Width**	2.74 m	
Power	174 kW	**Height**	3.8 m	
Transmission	Hydrodynamic	**Weight**	21.3 t	
Model	Voith RS15zSW1	**Axle Load**	70 kN	
Builder	Walkers	**Tractive Effort**	57 kN	
Introduced	1968	**Maximum Speed**	29 km/h	
Number Built	1	**Gauge**	1067 mm	

This unit was built for the Aramac Shire Council, as operators of the Aramac Tramway, which connected the town of Aramac to the QR Central line at Barcaldine. It was unusual as a railway size locomotive built by Walkers with a rigid frame. After the tramway closed, the locomotive was sold to Pioneer Mill, who use it on their 1067 mm gauge lines for their sugar collection trains.

DH 09 at Ipswich, 1993. (Peter Clark)

DH 1 – DH 73

Type	GH-500	**Wheel Arrangement**	B'B'
Engine	Cat D353E	**Length**	10.06 m
Cylinders	6 inline	**Width**	2.74 m
Power	350 kW	**Height**	3.8 m
Transmission	Hydrodynamic	**Weight**	36 t
Model	Voith L420rU2	**Axle Load**	90 kN
Builder	Walkers	**Tractive Effort**	80 kN
Introduced	1968	**Maximum Speed**	64 km/h
Number Built	73	**Gauge**	1067 mm

Walkers built the first GH-500, purely as a private venture. After prolonged evaluation trials in both shunting and line operation, the QR accepted W1 into service. After calling tenders QR placed a number of orders resulting in a further 72 units. These were equipped for multiple unit operation. Apart from the latter, the only modifications from prototype to production units were illuminated number indicators, projecting cab roofs and inter-unit communication step plates. The class retained the green and grey colour scheme, lined yellow, carried by the prototype W1. The DH class was used to replace steam shunting locomotives, and on branch lines where a standard 60-ton diesel-electric locomotive would have operated below capacity. These units have largely been withdrawn from QR service, but are now in widespread industrial use, and a number were transferred to Vietnam. Mount Isa Mines obtained one unit for use with their similar locomotive. A number have been modified for sugar cane tramway use.

1101 – 1107

Type	GH-1000	**Wheel Arrangement**	B'B'
Engine	Cat D398B	**Length**	10.96 m
Cylinders	V-12	**Width**	2.74 m
Power	520 kW	**Height**	3.82 m
Transmission	Hydrodynamic	**Weight**	54.8 t
Model	Voith L37zUb	**Axle Load**	135 kN
Builder	Walkers	**Tractive Effort**	156 kN
Introduced	1969	**Maximum Speed**	49 km/h
Number Built	7	**Gauge**	1067 mm

When an expansion of traffic was planned by Electrolytic Zinc, then in control of the EBR, orders were placed with Walkers for seven improved locomotives, incorporating lessons learned with the W1 prototype but retaining the transmission used in the 10 class. This group introduced the low nose for improved visibility, but retained the distinctive cab shape from the prototype. The colour scheme is deep and light blue, lined yellow. The 11 class were used in multiples of four and more on heavy concentrate trains to Burnie. They also operated in multiple with the earlier 10 class. Following the takeover by Tasrail these locomotives were withdrawn and passed to preservation by the Beaudesert railway and the Cairns Kuranda Steam Railway. One of the latter was leased to PN Queensland for shunting at Mackay.

AN AUSTRALIAN LOCOMOTIVE GUIDE

7301 – 7350

Type	GH-700V	**Wheel Arrangement**	B'B'
Engine	Cat D379B	**Length**	10.96 m
Cylinders	V-6	**Width**	2.82 m
Power	520 kW	**Height**	4.11 m
Transmission	Hydrodynamic	**Weight**	49.8 t
Model	Voith L4R4	**Axle Load**	123 kN
Builder	Walkers	**Tractive Effort**	109 kN
Introduced	1970	**Maximum Speed**	73 km/h
Number Built	50	**Gauge**	1435 mm

These were the first NSWR class to have been built in Queensland. The superstructure is of the conventional hood type, with the cab one-third from the front. The bogies are of the fabricated type without compensating beams. These were the first NSWR locomotives to have the reduced height front hood, giving better visibility for shunting purposes. They were introduced with the standard Indian red with chrome yellow lining and have carried most later schemes. The only significant variation in the class as built was the change to a single unit cab side window. The first units replaced steam shunters in Sydney Yard. They were used as shunters in most major yards throughout the state. Most are now withdrawn, with many preserved, and some in industrial service. Some units have been rebuilt for sugar cane tramway operation. 7301 remains as the only shunting locomotive in CountryLink colours, and 7334 gained a modified FreightCorp blue scheme.

M 1852 and MA 1862 at Forrestfield, 1975. (Peter Clark)

M 1851 – M 1852

Type	GH-700V	**Wheel Arrangement**	B'B'
Engine	VTA 1710L	**Length**	10.96 m
Cylinders	V-12	**Width**	2.74 m
Power	450 kW	**Height**	3.81 m
Transmission	Hydrodynamic	**Weight**	52.7 t
Model	Voith L4R4U2	**Axle Load**	123 kN
Builder	Walkers	**Tractive Effort**	109 kN
Introduced	1972	**Maximum Speed**	73 km/h
Number Built	2	**Gauge**	1067 mm

The WAGR purchased these locomotives for narrow-gauge hump shunting duties at Forrestfield yard, south-east of Perth. The M class were the first Walkers-built locomotive with a Cummins engine, specified for commonality with the B and T classes. They resembled the NSWR 73 class, of which the MA class were virtually a narrow-gauge version.

The standard WAGR larch green and red, lined yellow, colour scheme was initially carried by these locomotives, but versions of the Westrail orange and blue were later applied. After the closure of the hump, these locomotives saw little use.

MA 1862 at Claisebrook, April 1994.
(Peter Clark)

MA 1861 – MA 1863

Type	GH-700V	**Wheel Arrangement**	B'B'
Engine	Cat D379B	**Length**	10.96 m
Cylinders	V-8	**Width**	2.74 m
Power	520 kW	**Height**	3.81 m
Transmission	Hydrodynamic	**Weight**	44.6 t
Model	Voith L4R4U2	**Axle Load**	110 kN
Builder	Walkers	**Tractive Effort**	109 kN
Introduced	1973	**Maximum Speed**	73 km/h
Number Built	3	**Gauge**	1067 mm

While almost identical in appearance to the two M class hump shunters, the MA class had a Caterpillar engine, were lighter and were fitted for multiple unit operation. They were intended for general shunting duties, but spent most of their life in the Perth metropolitan area. They had the same colour schemes as the M class, but the survivor, MA 1862, is used at the Electric Multiple Unit depot at Claisebrook, and is finished in a TransPerth green and white colour scheme.

Mount Isa Mining No. 303
shunting in Mount Isa in July
1973. This one-off unit has an
end-mounted radiator, not visible in this view. (Peter Watts)

303

Type	GH-500V	**Wheel Arrangement**	B'B'
Engine	Cat D353E	**Length**	10.96 m
Cylinders	Inline 6	**Width**	2.74 m
Power	350 kW	**Height**	3.81 m
Transmission	Hydrodynamic	**Weight**	44.6 t
Model	Voith L4R4U2	**Axle Load**	110 kN
Builder	Walkers	**Tractive Effort**	80 kN
Introduced	1975	**Maximum Speed**	73 km/h
Number Built	1	**Gauge**	1067 mm

This was the final development of the series of Walkers diesel hydraulic locomotives, and consisted of the engine of the GH-500 in the body of the GH-700V. The GH-500 radiator is applied in the end of the long hood rather than the short hood as in the original design. The locomotive is painted yellow with black running gear and is used on the Mount Isa Mines industrial trackage.

DTD 5401 at Strathpine, December 2006. (Peter Clark)

5401 – 5404, 5405, 5406 – 5409

Type	DTD	**Wheel Arrangement**	B'B'
Engine	2 x MTU 12V396	**Length**	20.05 m
Cylinders	2 x V-12	**Width**	2.97 m
Power	2 x 1350 kW	**Height**	3.89 m
Transmission	Hydrodynamic	**Weight**	60t
Model	Voith	**Axle Load**	150 kN
Builder	EDI-Walkers	**Tractive Effort**	
Introduced	2003, 2012	**Maximum Speed**	160 km/h
Number Built	9	**Gauge**	1067 mm

These power cars created a new record in Australia for power to weight ratios, having a gross power of 2700 kW (about 3600 HP) with a weight of only 60 tonnes, compared to the 3200 HP and 108 tonnes of the 2800 class. This has been partly achieved by the use of high speed diesel engines in conjunction with a hydraulic transmission. Thus the designers chose a power and drive train combination also used in Spain for the 354 class Talgo train locomotives. In Spain, there is a line of development from the original German locomotives of the 1950s, with their complex Maybach-designed MTU 538 series engines, to the later 396 series, which were used to re-engine some older Talgo locomotives. The use of two power cars on a seven-car set ensures adequate power to keep the train at the maximum permissible line speed. The power cars are built from mild steel to a curved profile matching the tilting trailer cars. The nose moulding is similar, but not identical to, the nose of the electric tilt trains. 5405 was a replacement for a power car destroyed in a level crossing accident and cars 5406 to 5409 were built with strengthened cabs to allow the expansion of the service.

X 102 at Eveleigh Carriage Works, March 1975.
(John Beckhaus)

X101, renumbered X212, and the last rail tractor, X218 (renumbered X118) are seen at Port Kembla Locomotive Depot in January 1995. (John Beckhaus)

X 101 – X 102

Type		**Wheel Arrangement**	B
Engine	Bedford 300BIB	**Length**	5.79 m
Cylinders	Horizontal 6	**Width**	2.74 m
Power	69 kW	**Height**	3.37 m
Transmission	Hydrodynamic	**Weight**	17.8 t
Model	Allison Crt3331	**Axle Load**	88 kN
Builder	NSWR	**Tractive Effort**	17 kN
Introduced	1962	**Maximum Speed**	24 km/h
Number Built	2	**Gauge**	1435 mm

These are the earlier Rail Tractors originally classed as 80 when constructed in early 1962, but reclassified X100 as Rail Tractors before entering service as shunters at Wauchope and Coffs Harbour on the NSW North Coast. They were painted in the standard NSW colour scheme of Indian red with chrome yellow lining, but when built carried a non-standard red and cream colour scheme. X 101 in particular also carried the 1982 bright red scheme and the short lived Metropolitan verdant green livery. In 1994, this unit exchanged identities with the larger X212 and gained the Freight Rail blue scheme. Both it and X 102 are preserved.

OTHER DIESEL LOCOMOTIVES, GROUPED BY ENGINE

7004 at Delec Locomotive Depot. (RailCorp)

7001 – 7010

Type		**Wheel Arrangement**	C
Engine	Cat D397	**Length**	9.30 m
Cylinders	V-12	**Width**	2.74 m
Power	410 kW	**Height**	4.18 m
Transmission	Hydrodynamic	**Weight**	48.8 t
Model	Voith L37zUb	**Axle Load**	160 kN
Builder	Comeng NSW	**Tractive Effort**	113 kN
Introduced	1960	**Maximum Speed**	64 km/h
Number Built	10	**Gauge**	1435 mm

As with many other diesel-hydraulic locomotives, this class suffered from teething troubles. In this case both the transmission itself and the lightweight, high tensile coupling rods needed attention; the latter were soon replaced with much heavier 'I'

section rods. The original single large cab windows were modified to give one fixed and one movable panel. The class were fitted with radio transceivers. They also had very short oval buffers (in lieu of buffing plates). Multiple unit operation (within the class) was often used. The 70 class originally carried the standard NSWR Indian red colour scheme, with chrome yellow lining and black frame and wheels. The pilot was silver, and the buffer beam red. Later the 1979 yellow end and 1982 bright red liveries were applied. The class was allocated to Port Kembla, and carried out shunting and transfer duties on the former Public Works Department network until withdrawal.

4717 at Moss Vale. (Peter Clark)

4701 – 4720

Type	HFA-10C	**Wheel Arrangement**	Co'Co'
Engine	Cat D399	**Length**	14.02 m
Cylinders	V-16	**Width**	2.96 m
Power	746 kW	**Height**	4.20 m
Alternator	Hitachi	**Weight**	81.2 t
Motors	HS 366AN	**Axle Load**	135 kN
Builder	Goninan NSW	**Tractive Effort**	171 kN
Introduced	1972	**Maximum Speed**	113 km/h
Number Built	20	**Gauge**	1435 mm

These were the second NSWR class to be built by Goninan and were the first NSWR locomotives to have AC/DC transmission. They were of the conventional hood type, with a low leading hood to improve visibility for the driver. The Japanese designed bogies are equipped with underhung equalising beams. The cab entry is by side doors, unlike any other NSWR hood unit. The single chrome yellow waistband and Indian red bodywork gave the 47 class, as built, the simplest colour scheme on any NSWR hood unit. Many were later repainted in the 1982 bright red livery. They were to be used on coal traffic in the Newcastle area, but were allocated to the Western division, thus releasing 48 class for the coal traffic. They were eventually based at Broadmeadow until their early withdrawal. A number of units are preserved and one was rebuilt as a test vehicle.

TR02 is seen at Brighton Hub on 2 January 2015 (Phil Melling)

TR 1 – TR 17

Type	PR-22L	**Wheel Arrangement**	Co'Co'
Engine	Cat 3512C HD	**Length**	18.14 m
Cylinders	V-12	**Width**	2.90 m
Power	1490 kW	**Height**	3.84 m
Alternator	Kato	**Weight**	98t/111t
Motors	EMD D-43 BTR	**Axle Load**	160 kN/180 kN
Builder	Progress Rail USA	**Tractive Effort**	296 kN
Introduced	2013	**Maximum Speed**	100 km/h
Number Built	17	**Gauge**	1067 mm

These new Tasmanian locomotives are the first standard EMD export locomotives to be adapted to use a Caterpillar engine following Caterpillar's acquisition of EMD. The High Displacement version of the engine, with a 25mm longer stroke, was selected. The design is interesting since the single design is intended to operate at both main line and reduced axle loads. To reduce the weight for use on the Melba line, two traction motors must be removed, giving an A1A'A1A' wheel arrangement. In addition, ballast blocks are removed and the fuel tank only partly filled to reduce the all up weight to 98 tonnes.

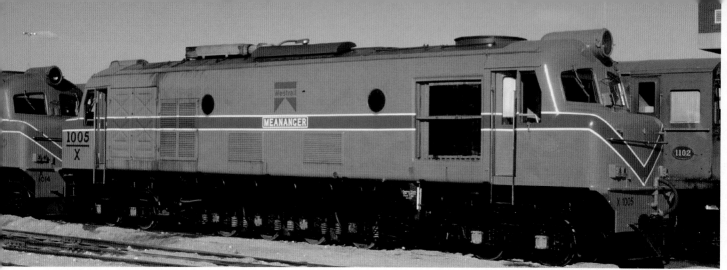

X 1005 at Forrestfield, 1978. (Peter Clark)

X 1001 – X 1032

Type	Crossley HST	Wheel Arrangement	2'Do2'
Engine	Crossley HST	Length	14.83 m
Cylinders	V-8	Width	2.74 m
Power	780 kW	Height	4.01 m
Generator	MV	Weight	79 t
Motors	MV 136	Axle Load	104 kN
Builder	M-V/B-P	Tractive Effort	54 kN
Introduced	1954	Maximum Speed	89 km/h
Number Built	32	Gauge	1067 mm

These locomotives were built by Metropolitan-Vickers/Beyer, Peacock Ltd of Stockton-on-Tees, UK. This group is the only example of the rigid-frame mainline unit in Australia. Although they greatly improved running times, both the rigid wheel arrangement and the prime mover proved troublesome.

However, subsequent modifications improved the position.

The type is easily recognised, with their boxy appearance and roof-mounted headlight, apart from the distinctive wheel arrangement. Nos 1004 and 1014 were fitted in 1965 with Pyle Gyralite oscillating headlights, to attract attention at level crossings.

The colour scheme was larch green with black running gear and later had red chevrons lined yellow at each end. The short-lived orange and yellow livery of 1975 and the Westrail orange and blue scheme were also applied.

These units operated over the Northern and Eastern lines, and worked passenger trains south to Bunbury and Albany.

XA 1401 – XA 1416

Type	Crossley HST	Wheel Arrangement	2'Do2'
Engine	Crossley HST	**Length**	14.83 m
Cylinders	V-8	**Width**	2.74 m
Power	780 kW	**Height**	4.01 m
Generator	MV	**Weight**	79 t
Motors	MV 136	**Axle Load**	104 kN
Builder	M-V/B-P	**Tractive Effort**	54 kN
Introduced	1954	**Maximum Speed**	89 km/h
Number Built	16	**Gauge**	1067 mm

The XA class were fitted for multiple unit operation when built. The XB class consist of X class locomotives fitted for multiple unit operation by the WAGR. The XA class may be distinguished by the end doors, gates and footplates for inter-unit communication. The use and colour schemes were the same as the X class.

Locomotive classes and names in next column:

1001 X	'Yalagonga'	1017 XB	'Ewenyoon'	1401 XA	'Pedong'
1002 X	'Bibbulmun'	1018 XB	'Inpirra'	1402 XA	'Targari'
1003 X	'Ditu-Wonga'	1019 X	'Ingarra'	1403 XA	'Wanbiri'
1004 XB	'Kadjerden'	1020 XB	'Jargurdi'	1404 XA	'Pardoo'
1005 X	'Meananger'	1021 X	'Jarroo'	1405 XA	'Warienga'
1006 XB	'Nangamada'	1022 XB	'Kardagur'	1406 XA	'Ungarinyin'
1007 X	'Natingaro'	1023 X	'Kariera'	1407 XA	'Wirngir'
1008 XB	'Warrangoo'	1024 XB	'Kogara'	1408 XA	'Wolmeri'
1009 X	'Arnga'	1025 X	'Loonga'	1409 XA	'Unambal'
1010 X	'Arawodi'	1026 X	'Mangala'	1410 XA	'Tenma'
1011 X	'Balgua'	1027 XB	'Marangal'	1411 XA	'Weedookarri'
1012 X	'Ballardong'	1028 X	'Meeraman'	1412 XA	'Noala'
1013 X	'Boonara'	1029 X	'Muliarra'	1413 XA	'Yabaroo'
1014 X	'Churoro'	1030 X	'Mooroon'	1414 XA	'Yindi'
1015 X	'Cheangwa'	1031 X	'Yauera'	1415 XA	'Wurara'
1016 X	'Djukin'	1032 XB	'Yeithi'	1416 XA	'Niligara'

X 203 at Yass Town Museum. (Peter Clark)

X 201 – X 206

Type		**Wheel Arrangement**	B
Engine	Cummins NHRS	**Length**	7.32 m
Cylinders	Inline 6	**Width**	2.75 m
Power	195 kW	**Height**	3.43 m
Transmission	Hydrodynamic	**Weight**	30 t
Model	Allison Crt5631	**Axle Load**	150 kN
Builder	NSWR	**Tractive Effort**	79 kN
Introduced	1963	**Maximum Speed**	39 km/h
Number Built	6	**Gauge**	1435 mm

This type of small shunting locomotive was classified by the NSWR as a Rail Tractor. Many surplus steam locomotive components, including axle sets from AD 60 class bogies, were used in construction, although coupling rod drive was incorporated. This first group had a superstructure similar to the Rolls-Royce Sentinel locomotives. The first six units originally had Hercules DFXHF horizontal six-cylinder engines, removed from railcars during the 1950s. They first carried the Indian red livery, lined yellow, but later many other schemes were used. They originally worked in the larger country yards. One survivor, with the train brake removed (to allow operation by traffic staff other than drivers), operates at Chullora workshops as X 106.

An SCT rail tractor, probably X 209, at Laverton North, March 2007. (Peter Clark)

X 207 – X 218

Type		**Wheel Arrangement**	B	
Engine	Cummins NHRS	**Length**	7.32 m	
Cylinders	Inline 6	**Width**	2.75 m	
Power	195 kW	**Height**	3.43 m	
Transmission	Hydrodynamic	**Weight**	30 t	
Model	Allison Crt5631	**Axle Load**	150 kN	
Builder	NSWR	**Tractive Effort**	79 kN	
Introduced	1965	**Maximum Speed**	39 km/h	
Number Built	12	**Gauge**	1435 mm	

These units were built to a much simpler design, owing something to the larger prototype, 7201. They were built with the Cummins engine. Their use was similar to the earlier group and the range of colour schemes was similar. Some are in use as X100 class, retaining their last two numbers. X 212 was last in use at Port Kembla renumbered as X 101.

A few are owned by private operators.

Worimi

Worimi at Carrington. (Leon Oberg)

Type	DH-45	**Wheel Arrangement**	C	
Engine	Cummins VT1710-L	**Length**	7.62 m	
Cylinders	V-12	**Width**		
Power	373 kW	**Height**		
Transmission	Hydrodynamic	**Weight**	45.7 t	
Model	Niigata DBSG115	**Axle Load**	150 kN	
Builder	E.M. Baldwin	**Tractive Effort**	157 kN	
Introduced	1973	**Maximum Speed**		
Number Built	1	**Gauge**	1435 mm	

This locomotive is unusual on two counts, being a standard-gauge product of a builder normally associated with narrow-gauge units for sugar cane tramway use, and being a rigid frame locomotive rather than a bogie design, also a trademark of E.M. Baldwin. It replaced a steam shunting locomotive in the Newcastle plant of Tubemakers, adjacent to the BHP Steelworks. With closer association with BHP, this loco was withdrawn from service and shunting was carried out by BHP locomotives. It is now used as a spare unit at the Carrington grain terminal. This unit was painted in a light green and yellow livery.

B 1601 – B 1610

1603, 1604 and 1608 at Forrestfield. Note the angled cab of the later units. (Peter Clark)

Type	JA	**Wheel Arrangement**	C
Engine	Cummins VT-12 B1	**Length**	7.78 m
Cylinders	V-12	**Width**	2.69 m
Power	352 kW	**Height**	3.81 m
Transmission	Hydrodynamic	**Weight**	38.9 t
Model	TD CF11500	**Axle Load**	130 kN
Builder	Comeng	**Tractive Effort**	80 kN
Introduced	1962	**Maximum Speed**	42 km/h
Number Built	10	**Gauge**	1067 mm

The first five units built in 1962 have a straight-sided off-centre cab, with mansard roof, but the cab side is canted inward from the waist on the remainder, built in 1965, in order to clear wharf cranes at Fremantle. The limited maximum speed confined these locomotives to shunting work, and they were allocated to Midland, West Perth and Fremantle goods yards.

A similar Mount Isa Mining locomotive differs only in coupling arrangements and in having a larger radiator to cope with the higher ambient temperature, the latter modification accounting for the increased length of 7.94 m. It has the same cab arrangements as the earlier WAGR locomotives, but with an arched roof.

T class original caption at right:

T 1801 – T 1805, TA 1806 – TA 1815

T 1814 at Forrestfield, 1994. (Peter Clark)

Type	S 1	**Wheel Arrangement**	C
Engine	Cummins VT-12 B1	**Length**	7.57 m
Cylinders	V-12	**Width**	2.57 m
Power	448 kW	**Height**	3.95 m
Generator	Brush TG 78/43	**Weight**	37 t
Motors	TM68/46	**Axle Load**	123 kN
Builder	Tulloch	**Tractive Effort**	69 kN
Introduced	1967	**Maximum Speed**	64 km/h
Number Built	10	**Gauge**	1067 mm

These were the first of a standard type of locomotive designed by Brush Electrical Engineering, UK. They had outside frames and balance weights.

The T class originally had cab sides canted inward above the waist, as did the later units of the B class. The original height of the T class was 3.82 m. Both T and TA classes had short hoods noticeably narrower than the engine hoods which have end-mounted radiators. The short hood incorporated the fuel tank. The TA class had the later VTA 1710L engine, of the same power. T class locomotives were allocated to North Fremantle and Avon Yard depots and shunted at Fremantle, Leighton and Avon Yards. All are now withdrawn. The last operating survivor is TA 1813, now owned by UGL at Bassendean.

7201

Type		**Wheel Arrangement**	B'B'
Engine	Cummins VT-12 B1	**Length**	12.80 m
Cylinders	V-12	**Width**	2.79 m
Power	485 kW	**Height**	3.84 m
Transmission	Hydrodynamic	**Weight**	55.9 t
Model	Clark CF16911	**Axle Load**	138 kN
Builder	NSWR	**Tractive Effort**	145 kN
Introduced	1965	**Maximum Speed**	72 km/h
Number Built	1	**Gauge**	1435 mm

This prototype heavy shunting locomotive utilised the underframe of a D-58 class tender. No. 7201 used the cast tender bogies, modified to take the final drives and bogie-mounted brake-cylinders. The plain-looking hoods ended with a projecting roof covering the headlight and number board assembly. Individual buffers were used in place of the usual buffing plates each end. The colour scheme was the standard Indian red, lined in chrome yellow with black below the running board except for the pilots, which were silver. The teething troubles experienced with this locomotive do not appear to have been overcome. It was used sporadically at Rozelle and later at ACDEP Eveleigh, but was eventually scrapped.

PB 1 – PB 7

PB 1 at Cringila, hauling hot metal ladle wagons on 27 July 2014. (Rocky Condello)

Type	2GS16-DE	**Wheel Arrangement**	Bo'Bo'
Engines	2x Cummins QSK19C	**Length**	15.44 m
Cylinders	Inline 6	**Width**	2.92 m
Power	2 x 522 kW	**Height**	4.20 m
Alternators	two Marathon	**Weight**	91 t
Motors	four EMD D-78	**Axle Load**	223 kN
Builder	NREC	**Tractive Effort**	217 kN
Introduced	2014	**Maximum Speed**	80km/h
Number Built	7	**Gauge**	1435 mm

The PB class is the second 'generator set' locomotive type in Australia, following the 1200 class from the same manufacturer, NREC. The locomotive itself looks generally similar to the Victorian Y class locomotives type G6B, although it is longer, heavier and more powerful. Each loco has two modular self-contained engine-generator units each with its own radiator and cooling fan, each producing more power than the 567C engine in the Y class, and has dynamic brakes not featured on the Y class. These locomotives are the first new locomotives purchased by PN specifically for use on the Port Kembla industrial network serving the Bluescope steelworks. These are the first new locomotives in Australia to use the EMD Blomberg B truck.

1201 and 1202 as delivered in Port Kembla in 2013. (NREC)

1201 – 1202

Type	3GS24C-DE	**Wheel Arrangement**	Co'Co'
Engine	Cummins QSK19C	**Length**	18.60 m
Cylinders	Inline 6	**Width**	2.90 m
Power	3 x 522 kW	**Height**	4.24 m
Alternator	Marathon	**Weight**	134 t
Motors	EMD D-78	**Axle Load**	218 kN
Builder	NREC	**Tractive Effort**	348 kN
Introduced	2013	**Maximum Speed**	115km/h
Number Built	5	**Gauge**	1435 mm

The 1200 class is the first 'generator set' locomotive type in Australia. The locomotive itself looks generally similar to the earlier NREC 1100 class locomotives, although it is about 700 mm shorter over couplers. The cab, frame, bogies and dynamic brakes are all similar to those on the 1100 although the height is lower. There are three modular self-contained engine-generator units each with its own radiator and cooling fan. These may be removed for major overhaul, and a replacement unit substituted. Only two units are in Australia and these have not seen regular service at the time of writing. Three further units are stored in the USA.

CBH 001 – 011, CBH 023 – 025

Type	MP27CN	**Wheel Arrangement**	Co'Co'
Engine	Cummins QSK60	**Length**	18.50 m
Cylinders	V-16	**Width**	2.85 m
Power	1700 kW	**Height**	4.01 m
Alternator	Kato 8P 6.5	**Weight**	98.5 t
Motors	GE 761	**Axle Load**	161 kN
Builder	Motive Power	**Tractive Effort**	285 kN
Introduced	2012	**Maximum Speed**	90 km/h
Number Built	14	**Gauge**	1067 mm

Motive Power Industries of Boise, Idaho, a subsidiary of Wabtech, are the designers and builders of these new locomotives. They have a long history of building new locomotives and rebuilding existing ones, but have been associated with EMD engines, and to a lesser extent Caterpillar engines in their locomotives. For this type, they have selected the Cummins range, in particular the K series engine. For the lighter narrow-gauge locomotive, type MP27CN weighing 96 tonnes, a 60 litre V-16 engine was selected, model QSK 60. These are operated by Watco, an American company, for CBH, a WA grain marketer.

AN AUSTRALIAN LOCOMOTIVE GUIDE

CM 3303 is seen on a ballast train near Yarra on 13 September 2014. (Peter Clark)

CBH 012 – 017, CBH 118 –122, CM 3301 – 3316

Type	MP33C	**Wheel Arrangement**	Co'Co'
Engine	Cummins QSK78	**Length**	18.50 m
Cylinders	V-18	**Width**	2.85 m
Power	2240 kW	**Height**	4.01 m
Alternator	Kato 8P 6.5	**Weight**	132 t
Motors	EMD D78	**Axle Load**	215 kN
Builder	Motive Power	**Tractive Effort**	345 kN
Introduced	2012	**Maximum Speed**	115 km/h
Number Built	74	**Gauge**	1435 mm

Although there are no visible external differences, six later units of the CBH order were fitted with a larger and more powerful Cummins QSK78 engine. This restricts the operation of the MP33CN narrow gauge locomotives to grain lines capable of taking the higher axle load of 196 kN, but does allow a larger fuel capacity. CBH also obtained five standard gauge versions, model MP33C which look very like the narrow gauge units, except for the standard gauge bogies. In theory, these locomotives can be transferred between gauges if the need arises. The standard gauge locomotives are heavier again and are fitted with EMD D78 traction motors rather than the GE design motors used on narrow gauge units. Standard-gauge CBH locomotives have numbers with a "1" prefix rather than '0'.

CFCLA also purchased sixteen standard-gauge locomotives of this type as their CM class, in two batches of ten and six. They have been used in grain and container traffic as well as operating track maintenance trains. These are based at Goulburn, NSW.

U1 – U6

U 3 at the Don River Railway, November 1998. (Peter Clark)

Type		**Wheel Arrangement**	B
Engine	Gardner 6LW	**Length**	4.50 m
Cylinders	Inline 6	**Width**	
Power	76 kW	**Height**	
Transmission	Mechanical	**Weight**	17.3 t
Model	Wilson Drewry	**Axle Load**	85 kN
Builder	Malcolm Moore	**Tractive Effort**	40 kN
Introduced	1958	**Maximum Speed**	21 km/h
Number Built	6	**Gauge**	1067 mm

These locomotives were originally in use in Victoria for tunnelling work by contractors, and were built to the 914 mm gauge. They were purchased by the TGR in 1958. An extensive rebuilding program at Launceston Workshops produced a regauged and re-engined locomotive, suitable for use in smaller yards. Two locomotives were similarly rebuilt, but to metre gauge, and were supplied to Thailand under the Colombo Plan.

Although these units were usually allocated to smaller yards such as Wynyard or Smithton, they have been used at Launceston. All are now withdrawn.

The older English locomotives looked quite different from the later Comeng locomotives, although they were technically similar. DL12 is seen at South Johnstone Mill as No. 10 in July 1999. (Peter Clark). DL 15 'Nerada' is illustrated by a Comeng builder's photo.

DL 12 - DL 20

Type	-	**Wheel Arrangement**	C
Engine	Gardner 8LW	**Length**	5.16 m
Cylinders	Inline 8	**Width**	2.08 m
Power	114 kW	**Height**	3.25 m
Transmission	Mechanical	**Weight**	15.0 t
Model	SCG R11A	**Axle Load**	49 kN
Builder	Baguley, Comeng	**Tractive Effort**	50 kN
Introduced	1954	**Maximum Speed**	25 km/h
Number Built	8	**Gauge**	610 mm

This rather varied class operated on the QR Innisfail tramway, which was the only state-owned 610 mm gauge cane tramway. It had always been publicly owned, originally by the local council. This tramway was closed by the QR and the locomotives were sold, DL 13 going to Moreton Central. DL 14 –DL 16 and DL 18 went to Mourilyan mill. DL 12, DL 17 and DL 20 went to South Johnstone mill. DL 19 started life on the 1067 mm gauge Aramac Tramway in Central Queensland, until 1974. Originally with inside frames, it was modified to outside frames on conversion to 610 mm gauge. It always looked very like the other Comeng units. The transmission behind the cab drives jackshafts with rod drive to the wheels. The original builder for units DL 12 and DL 13 was Baguley in the UK. Commonwealth Engineering built the remainder, which were shorter, 4.8 m, and lower, 2.97 m. DL 18 had the Gardner 6LX engine of 112 kW.

Z 1151 – Z 1153

Type		**Wheel Arrangement**	C
Engine	Gardner 8LW	**Length**	5.75 m
Cylinders	Inline 8	**Width**	2.00 m
Power	96 kW	**Height**	3.05 m
Transmission	Mechanical	**Weight**	15.1 t
Model	Wilson Drewry	**Axle Load**	51 kN
Builder	Stephenson	**Tractive Effort**	39 kN
Introduced	1953	**Maximum Speed**	16 km/h
Number Built	3	**Gauge**	1067 mm

Z 1151 was the first WAGR diesel locomotive, as distinct from railcars and power vans, both of which preceded it. These small, lightweight units, with off-centre cabs, disc driving wheels and jackshaft drive were designed for shunting on jetty tracks of very light construction. The builder was Robert Stephenson and Hawthorns, subcontracting to the Drewry Car Co. The Z class carried the standard larch green livery with black running gear. The hood ends were painted white for visibility. Westrail orange was later used. The Z class were allocated to yards at Albany and Bunbury, two being used at the latter. All are now withdrawn.

DL 1 at the Ipswich Museum, 2002. (Peter Clark)

DL 1 – DL 4

Type		Wheel Arrangement	1′C
Engine	Gardner 6L3	Length	6.25 m
Cylinders	Inline 6	Width	2.41 m
Power	114 kW	Height	3.34 m
Transmission	Mechanical	Weight	17.8 t
Model	Wilson Drewry	Axle Load	52 kN
Builder	QR Ipswich	Tractive Effort	34 kN
Introduced	1939	Maximum Speed	57 km/h
Number Built	4	Gauge	1067 mm

These units were built by the QR Workshops (DL 1), Robert Stephenson and Hawthorns (DL 2), and Walkers Limited (DL 3 and DL 4) The design was a standard Drewry unit, with a leading truck added after the construction of DL 1. The four locomotives of this class were built for the Etheridge railway to Forsayth in North Queensland. This extremely lightweight line was capable of carrying only this class of locomotives, having previously been operated with drawgear-equipped rail motors. DL 1 was the first government-owned diesel locomotive. The rear cab, with only canvas blinds and a waist-high door for side protection, was mounted above the driving jackshaft. Ahead of the cab was the engine hood with stovepipe stack, and in front of this a small end platform over the leading axle. The original colour scheme was red superstructure with black running gear.

The four locomotives could operate in multiple, and loads out of Forsayth were 50 tonnes (one DL) and 200 tonnes (four DLs). After 1968, 60-tonne diesel-electrics were permitted to take 350 tonnes singly, although the track strengthening for the larger units was minimal.

In 1971–72, two DL class were transferred to the South Western division. DL 1 received a new enclosed cab, with gas heating, and both DL class were repainted in the green, grey and yellow DH class colour scheme. They were then used as shunting locomotives. DL 4, in original condition, but with an Indian red and yellow scheme, is the relief unit for RM 93 on the *Gulflander* at Normanton.

V 5 at the Donnybrook shed, July 2004.
(Peter Clark)

V 1 – V 13

Type		**Wheel Arrangement**	C
Engine	Gardner 8L3	**Length**	6.85 m
Cylinders	Inline 8	**Width**	2.41 m
Power	152 kW	**Height**	3.62 m
Transmission	Mechanical	**Weight**	25.6 t
Model	Wilson Drewry	**Axle Load**	85 kN
Builder	Vulcan Foundry	**Tractive Effort**	64 kN
Introduced	1948	**Maximum Speed**	48 km/h
Number Built	13	**Gauge**	1067 mm

These were conventional end-cab hood units of English style. The engine hood was low compared to the cab roof, and power was transmitted to the wheels through outside coupling rods. The VA class resulted from the substitution of Gardner 6L3 engines, removed from railcars, for the original engines. The units concerned varied, depending upon engine changes during overhaul. The eight-cylinder engines removed from VA 1 and VA 8 were used in the later TGR-built locomotives. The colour scheme of the TGR locomotives was red bodywork with black frames and wheels. The TGR units were later repainted in the yellow and black livery. The TGR locomotives were used for shunting in the larger yards. V 2 was, however, on hire to the Emu Bay Railway from 1961 until the end of 1968, being used at Burnie. During 1969 EBR 22 was used on track reconstruction work operating out of Rosebery on trains of ballast, sleepers and rails. EBR 22 and TGR V 13 were similar locomotives originally owned by the Mount Lyell Mining and Railway Company and were purchased by their present owners when the Mount Lyell railway closed in 1963. These units are all now withdrawn but a number are preserved, in Victoria and Western Australia as well as in Tasmania. A similar locomotive, but fitted with a larger radiator, and thus with a taller engine hood, was obtained from the Drewry Car Company in 1953 by Mount Isa Mines, where it operated as No. 304.

AN AUSTRALIAN LOCOMOTIVE GUIDE

NB 30 following conversion at Port Augusta. (CR)

NB 30

Type		Wheel Arrangement	C
Engine	GM Detroit 6-71	**Length**	5.74 m
Cylinders	Inline 6	**Width**	2.13 m
Power	105 kW	**Height**	3.16 m
Transmission	Hydrodynamic	**Weight**	18.3 t
Model	Allison TC600	**Axle Load**	60 kN
Builder	CR	**Tractive Effort**	49 kN
Introduced	1957	**Maximum Speed**	32 km/h
Number Built	1	**Gauge**	1067 mm

This locomotive began life as an 0-6-0 saddle tank, built by Vulcan Ironworks, USA. It was purchased for construction work at the proposed Henderson Naval Base in WA. It was obtained by CR for shunting duties on the Central Australia Railway. In 1957 it was converted to a diesel-hydraulic hood unit, retaining the frame and wheels. This is the only example of such a conversion on a government system. The appearance is quite normal, features being a large overhang at the cab end; inside frames and cranks integral with wheel hubs; and a pointed radiator grille at the front. The normal CR maroon and silver livery was carried. NB 30 was last used as works shunter at Port Augusta. It is preserved at Quorn by the Pichi Richi Railway.

M 231 – M 232

M 232 at Newport Workshops, 1995. (Peter Clark)

Type		**Wheel Arrangement**	C	
Engine	GM Detroit 6-71	**Length**	6.71 m	
Cylinders	Inline 6	**Width**	2.89 m	
Power	112 kW	**Height**	3.41 m	
Transmission	Hydrodynamic	**Weight**	30.4 t	
Model	Allison TC500	**Axle Load**	100 kN	
Builder	VR	**Tractive Effort**	62 kN	
Introduced	1959	**Maximum Speed**	19 km/h	
Number Built	2	**Gauge**	1600 mm	

These small shunters were the first diesel locomotives to be built at Newport, although Fordson Rail Tractors had been constructed there in large numbers. They were easily recognised, with their semi-octagonal engine hood and mansard-roofed cab. The colour scheme was originally red superstructure with black below the footplate level but later the standard blue and yellow was carried. Brass number plates were carried front and rear.

The M class were used for shunting at the Newport Workshops. They are now preserved by Steamrail at the same location.

1 – 2

Type	60 Ton	**Wheel Arrangement**	B'B'	
Engine	GM Detroit 6/71	**Length**	7.85 m	
Cylinders	2 x Inline 6	**Width**		
Power	2 x 127 kW	**Height**		
Generator	Westinghouse	**Weight**	50.8 t	
Motors	WH 1443A	**Axle Load**	125 kN	
Builder	Whitcomb	**Tractive Effort**	kN	
Introduced	1949	**Maximum Speed**	km/h	
Number Built	2	**Gauge**	1600 mm	

This pair was amongst the first industrial diesel locomotives in Australia and replaced steam locomotives that had been obtained second hand from state railways. They were obtained for use at the Australian Paper Manufacturers plant in Maryvale, Victoria. They are typical of the early style of medium size US diesel shunting locomotives. They have only two traction motors, and the axles are coupled by rods. They were yellow in colour, with black striping. They were replaced , initially by an ex V/Line first series T class, which in turn was replaced by a Y class as that type became available.

NC 1 – NC 2

NC 2 shunting at Port Augusta, January 1970. (Peter Clark)

Type	DHI-110	**Wheel Arrangement**	C	
Engine	GM Detroit 6-110	**Length**	6.45 m	
Cylinders	Inline 6	**Width**	2.59 m	
Power	186 kW	**Height**	3.49 m	
Transmission	Hydrodynamic	**Weight**	28.4 t	
Model	Allison CRT5630	**Axle Load**	93 kN	
Builder	Clyde NSW	**Tractive Effort**	76 kN	
Introduced	1956	**Maximum Speed**	48 km/h	
Number Built	2	**Gauge**	1067 mm	

These small, centre-cab, rod-coupled locomotives served the Lakewood Firewood Company of Western Australia until their line closed. The Commonwealth Railways purchased both in 1966. In May 1966, NC 2 was placed in service at Port Augusta Workshops as the narrow-gauge shunter. NC 1 was overhauled at Port Augusta, had Westinghouse air brakes substituted for its vacuum brakes, and in November 1966 was transferred to the North Australia Railway for use as the shunter at Darwin. NC 1 was liveried in the standard CR maroon and silver lining but NC 2 retained the green and cream colour scheme of the Lakewood Company. In 1973, both locomotives were at Port Augusta Workshops, and remained there until sold for preservation.

DP 101 – DP 104

DP 104 in its final condition. (SRA)

Type		Wheel Arrangement	1A'A1'
Engine	GM Detroit 6-110	Length	19.05 m
Cylinders	4 x Inline 6	Width	2.87 m
Power	4 x 186 kW	Height	3.80 m
Transmission	Hydrodynamic	Weight	64 t
Model	Allison TCLA965	Axle Load	158 kN
Builder	NSWR	Tractive Effort	
Introduced	1937	Maximum Speed	113 km/h
Number Built	4	Gauge	1435 mm

These locomotives were used exclusively to haul lightweight air-conditioned trains, for which they supplied auxiliary power, from two GM 4/71 generating sets mounted transversely just behind the drivers' cabins. The propulsion machinery was arranged in facing pairs on the longitudinal centre line, with the inner engine slightly elevated. Each pair drove the inner axle of one of the bogies through a separate transmission. As built, these four power vans, as they were called, each carried two 330 HP Harland diesels, which left space for two baggage compartments. They were thus classified PH, the H indicating guard and baggage space. However, the original auxiliary power generators filled one such compartment, suggesting that air-conditioning was an afterthought. PH 105 was destroyed by fire, and only four were rebuilt to the DP class. After rebuild, one large sliding door remained in either side, providing access for the driver and to the six engines. End doors were also fitted. Both locomotive and matching passenger vehicles carried valances partially concealing the wheels. The DP class were based at Parkes and operated to Broken Hill, Dubbo and on Sundays to Lithgow. A number of cars are preserved.

DE 10

DE 10 on standard gauge at Whyalla, 1978. (Peter Clark)

Type	30 Ton	**Wheel Arrangement**	Bo'Bo'	
Engine	Mack EN 673	**Length**	6.43 m	
Cylinders	2 x Inline 6	**Width**		
Power	2 x 127 kW	**Height**	2.98 m	
Generator		**Weight**	28 t	
Motors		**Axle Load**	68 kN	
Builder	Davenport	**Tractive Effort**		
Introduced	1928	**Maximum Speed**	km/h	
Number Built	1	**Gauge**	1435 mm	

This was a very early internal combustion industrial locomotive, delivered in 1928 to BHP Whyalla as PE 1, indicating Petrol Electric. The builder's number was 2118 of 1928. It had two Continental Red Seal petrol engines of 78 kW each. It was not a great success and spent some time as a straight electric locomotive, becoming redundant when the electrification was removed from the Iron Knob open cut mine. It was thought to be of potential use in the steelworks. New diesel engines, as described, were installed in 1967. In 1968 it was converted to standard gauge using bogies from a Metropolitan Vickers electric locomotive. Its own bogies were not easily rebuilt to a larger gauge. The locomotive saw very little use. It was renumbered DE 10, and painted red with a yellow waistband. It was later preserved by the Pichi Richi Railway at Quorn, with its original bogies.

MDH 2 at Port Augusta, August 1969. (John Beckhaus)

MDH 1 – MDH 6

Type	HG-6R	**Wheel Arrangement**	C
Engine	Maybach MD 325	**Length**	8.68 m
Cylinders	Inline 6	**Width**	2.95 m
Power	405 kW	**Height**	4.22 m
Transmission	Hydrodynamic	**Weight**	45.6 t
Model	Mekhydro K 104U	**Axle Load**	150 kN
Builder	Clyde NSW	**Tractive Effort**	58 kN
Introduced	1958	**Maximum Speed**	81 km/h
Number Built	6	**Gauge**	1435 mm

A notable feature of this type was the outside frame, with inside coupling of axles: cardan shafts and final drives on each axle are unusual on rigid framed locomotives, but usual for bogie locomotives. The high, off-centre, mansard-roofed cab dominated rectangular hoods extending to the bare-looking pilot beams. Only the axle boxes beneath the deep running-plate valance revealed the asymmetrical wheel arrangement. The CR class leader was named, in the form of an enlarged signature on a brass plate, 'F.J. Shea'. The standard CR maroon and silver livery was carried. Although suitable for mainline work, with 81 km/h top speed, the MDH class were confined to shunting and transfer at CR's larger yards. The similar Electricity Trust of South Australia locomotive was allocated to the Curlew Point power station in Port Augusta. It carried the number 1, and was later joined by the former MDH 1, renumbered to 2. In 1973 only one of the Commonwealth locomotives remained in serviceable condition, the earlier GM class locomotives having replaced the MDHs as shunting locomotives. An MDH is preserved at Port Dock Museum.

Skitube Tulloch No. 1 at Bullock's Flat. (Skitube)

1

Type	DSL 120/15	**Wheel Arrangement**	B
Engine	Mercedes-Benz M204B	**Length**	5.41 m
Cylinders	Inline 4	**Width**	2.49 m
Power	90 kW	**Height**	3.31 m
Transmission	Mechanical	**Weight**	15.2 t
Model	Hydro-Cone	**Axle Load**	75 kN
Builder	Tulloch	**Tractive Effort**	
Introduced	1958	**Maximum Speed**	24 km/h
Number Built	1	**Gauge**	1435 mm

This small locomotive was originally used at the Rhodes plant of Tulloch Limited, and was later used by A.G. Sims at their Mascot scrap metal plant, in company with a larger BTH-Paxman locomotive. Automatic couplers were fitted at both ends. The locomotive was overhauled in mid-1973, being repainted from red to a leaf green shade with black frame and wheels and white buffer beam. It was later sold to Skitube, and is used in the yard at Bullocks Flat to shunt the rack multiple unit vehicles. It was extensively rebuilt in 1991, with a GM Detroit 4/53TA engine of 134 kW at 2200 rpm, and an Allison MT 643 Hydraulic transmission. The maximum speed is now 20 km/h, and BBC-Secheron couplers are fitted to mate with the electric cars. It now carries a blue, lined red colour scheme and a large yellow number one on each side.

AN AUSTRALIAN LOCOMOTIVE GUIDE

W 241 – W 267

W 241 at Creek Sidings, October 2004. (Peter Clark)

Type		**Wheel Arrangement**	C
Engine	Mercedes MB 820B	**Length**	8.18 m
Cylinders	V-12	**Width**	2.92 m
Power	485 kW	**Height**	4.27 m
Transmission	Hydrodynamic	**Weight**	48.8 t
Model	Krupp 2W1 D46	**Axle Load**	160 kN
Builder	Tulloch	**Tractive Effort**	130 kN
Introduced	1959	**Maximum Speed**	64 km/h
Number Built	27	**Gauge**	1600 mm

This class was one of the Victorian Railways' few variations from the EMD diesel-electric type. The cab is nearer the radiator end than the power unit end, and large shunters' steps at each end are linked by coupling rod protection boards. Only the first of a second order, W 267, was purchased along with a demonstrator, W 266, originally numbered 7101 on the NSWR register. The

latter was originally 1435 mm gauge and initially operated construction trains on the North Eastern standard-gauge line, and was later used as a coaching stock shunter at Spencer Street standard-gauge terminal. It was joined by W 267, after conversion from 1600 mm to 1435 mm gauge. W 266 was later converted to 1600 mm gauge, however. The class were allocated to South Dynon (Melbourne) and operated around the metropolitan area on shunting and transfer work, or shunted in larger provincial centres.

W 249 was the first of the class to be fitted with a GM Detroit Diesel 149 V-12 engine of similar power and running speed to the original Mercedes-Benz diesel. The conversion was performed in early 1973 and converted units could be identified by an extra exhaust stack near the front of the long hood.

CSR 001 – CSR 010, BK 001 – BK 002, QBX 001-QBX 006

Type	SDA1	**Wheel Arrangement**	Co'Co'
Engine	MTU 20V4000	**Length**	21.1 m
Cylinders	V-20	**Width**	2.90 m
Power	3000 kW	**Height**	4.24 m
Generator	Ziyang	**Weight**	134 t
Motors	Ziyang AC	**Axle Load**	219 kN
Builder	CSR	**Tractive Effort**	520 kN
Introduced	2012	**Maximum Speed**	115 km/h
Number Built	18	**Gauge**	1435 mm

This double cab locomotive uses the German built MTU 20V4000R53 engine. The engine has a gross rating of 3150 kW, giving an input to the alternator of about 3000 kW, similar to the power of the PN NR class. The new locomotives have a distinctive Australian appearance, like the GL class but longer, a full 22 m over coupling points. The cabs are isolated from the frame to reduce noise and vibration. The bogie is a Chinese design with a welded frame similar to the UGL C44aci design. The primary suspension has helical springs and location arms arranged alternately high and low each side of the axlebox, known as an Alsthom link. The internal equipment layout is generally like that of the UGL C44aci. CSR obtained six locomotives initially, but purchased another four lettered for 'Specialised Bulk Resources'. Bradford Kendall purchased two for lease operation, and QUBE obtained six for their heavier traffic.

8803 seen at the commissioning yard at Waitara on 22 June 2014. (Peter Clark)

8801 - 8805

Type	SDA-2	Wheel Arrangement	Co'Co'
Engine	MTU 20V4000R43	Length	22.0 m
Cylinders	V-20	Width	2.85 m
Power	2550kW	Height	3.87 m
Alternator	ABB	Weight	120 t
Motors	ABB	Axle Load	197 kN
Builder	CSR Qishuyuan	Tractive Effort	450 kN
Introduced	2014	Maximum Speed	100 km/h
Number Built	5	Gauge	1067 mm

The SDA-2 is a completely new design but is dimensionally similar to the Clyde GT42CU AC locomotive used by PN and Aurizon in Queensland coal traffic. It has the same overall layout with an end cab and narrow hood, and also uses radial bogies to reduce curve forces. The engine is the German MTU 20V4000R43, also used in the Kiwi Rail DL class built by CNR Dalien. The underframe has an integral fuel tank, much like that on the NR class, and there is an underframe mounted cab 'shield' as collision protection also similar to that on the NR. The bogies, described as type QSJZ18-Co, are welded fabrications and use wing type axleboxes with coil springs as the primary suspension. Rubber pads directly to the frame form the secondary suspension. There are no steering links to the body, with guidance being left to creep forces on the wheel treads. These locomotives are used in coal traffic.

Sims No. 19 shunting at Mascot. (Peter Clark)

19

Type		**Wheel Arrangement**	C	
Engine	Paxman 6RPHL	**Length**	7.26 m	
Cylinders	V-6	**Width**	2.82 m	
Power	170 kW	**Height**	3.74 m	
Generator	BTH RTB 7444	**Weight**		
Motors	BTH	**Axle Load**		
Builder	Yorkshire	**Tractive Effort**		
Introduced	1957	**Maximum Speed**	40 km/h	
Number Built	1	**Gauge**	1435 mm	

This locomotive was built at the Yorkshire Engine Co. Ltd Medlow Hall Works, UK, being their builder's number 2617. It is similar to a type of locomotive built in 1951 for the English Steel Corporation, which had, however, only two axles. SM No. 19 was used at the A.G. Sims Mascot scrap metal plant, in company with a smaller Mercedes-Benz locomotive. The locomotive was painted in leaf green, with a yellow buffer beam and black frame and wheels. Automatic couplers and buffers were fitted at both ends.

No. 21 shunting at Burnie, November 1998. (Peter Clark)

21

Type		**Wheel Arrangement**	D	
Engine	Paxman 12RPHX	**Length**	9.30 m	
Cylinders	V-12	**Width**	2.79 m	
Power	395 kW	**Height**	3.61 m	
Transmission	Hydrodynamic	**Weight**	43.6 t	
Model	Voith L-37V	**Axle Load**	54 kN	
Builder	North British	**Tractive Effort**		
Introduced	1954	**Maximum Speed**	40/56 km/h	
Number Built	1	**Gauge**	1067 mm	

This is an end-cab hood unit with rigid wheelbase, rounded ends on the upward tapering hood and inward canted cabsides above the waist. The drive is from a jackshaft under the cab through coupling rods to the eight driving wheels. Outside frames and exposed balance weights are features uncommon in Australia in such a large locomotive. The locomotive was re-engined by the EBR using a 410 kW Caterpillar D397 engine. PVH 21 was in use at Burnie as the EBR shunter until the merger with Tasrail. It has been preserved on the Derwent Valley Railway.

Y 1114 at North Fremantle, 1975. (Peter Clark)

Y 1101 – Y 1118

Type		Wheel Arrangement	Bo'Bo'
Engine	Paxman RPHL	Length	10.02 m
Cylinders	V-12	Width	2.51 m
Power	280 kW	Height	3.79 m
Generator	BTH RTB 8844	Weight	39.4 t
Motors	BTH 124PV	Axle Load	97 kN
Builder	Clayton	Tractive Effort	40 kN
Introduced	1953	Maximum Speed	72 km/h
Number Built	18	Gauge	1067 mm

These WAGR locomotives were characterised by their tall, narrow appearance and their closely set long wheelbase bogies, with no room for a fuel tank between them. The traction motor blower ducting was also prominent, beneath the footplate. The cab had side doors only. Large single headlights were fitted. The colour scheme was larch green, later with white ends; the lining was red, and the running gear was black. Later, Westrail orange and blue was applied.

The Y class were used for both shunting and branch line duties and were widely spread, having been allocated to Perth, Fremantle, Albany, Bunbury and Geraldton. Examples have been preserved.

4102 at Meek's Road. (Peter Clark)

4101 – 4110

Type		Wheel Arrangement	Bo'Bo'
Engine	Paxman RPHL	Length	13.11 m
Cylinders	2 x V-12	Width	2.90 m
Power	2 x 280 kW	Height	4.26 m
Generator	BTH RTB 10844	Weight	84.5 t
Motors	BTH 157AZ	Axle Load	205 kN
Builder	Metro-Cammell	Tractive Effort	102 kN
Introduced	1953	Maximum Speed	93 km/h
Number Built	10	Gauge	1435 mm

This NSW Railways class was not particularly successful, despite modifications which included extensions of the hood to the buffer beam, thus removing the original end platforms and various box-like projections on the hood roofs. These were generally attempting to improve engine cooling. The 41 class were fitted for multiple unit operation within the class, but were not so used because the position of the radiators mounted at the hood ends did not permit enough air circulation between two locomotives. It was also possible to shut down one engine and operate at a reduced load on the remaining one. These were centre cab, twin-engine locomotives with hood-roof-mounted headlights and paired exhaust stacks. There were two colour schemes, Indian red or verdant green, lined in buff, both with black undergear. All have been withdrawn from service and 4102 has been preserved.

XP 2000 – XP 2018

Type	XPT	**Wheel Arrangement**	Bo'Bo'
Engine	Paxman VP185	**Length**	17.33 m
Cylinders	V-12	**Width**	2.89 m
Power	1510 kW	**Height**	4.03 m
Generator	Brush BA1001B	**Weight**	76 t
Motors	TMH 68-46	**Axle Load**	190 kN
Builder	Comeng NSW	**Tractive Effort**	84 kN
Introduced	1981	**Maximum Speed**	160 km/h
Number Built	19	**Gauge**	1435 mm

These cars have a distinctive appearance based upon the British High Speed Train locomotives. Their dimensions are quite different, the XPs being taller, wider and shorter and with much larger radiators. They have only emergency couplings at the No. 1 end of the unit. They normally operate in pairs at each end of stainless steel car sets for which one power unit must provide all auxiliary power, reducing the power available for traction by 200 kW or more. Although all are basically to the same design, they were obtained in three groups, 10 in 1981–82, five in 1984 and four in 1993–94. The last group were built by ABB at Dandenong in Victoria. For the 140th anniversary of NSW railways, a dark blue and turquoise livery was applied to 2000 and 2009. These two were used on trials with a Swedish X 2000 tilt train car set during 1995, which required the addition of a new auxiliary generator set in each unit, removed at the conclusion of the trials. XP 2000 also carried a special blue scheme promoting the Sydney Olympic Games from 1998, and XP2001 carried a 'Centenary of Federation' scheme with orange as a major part of the scheme. The more modern and slightly more powerful Paxman VP185 engine replaced the same maker's RP200L Valenta engine from mid-2000. All XP power cars are still in service.

AN AUSTRALIAN LOCOMOTIVE GUIDE

E 30 in the museum at Bassendean, August 2004. (Peter Clark)

E 30

Type		**Wheel Arrangement**	C	
Engine	Rolls-Royce C6SFL	**Length**	5.59 m	
Cylinders	Inline 6	**Width**	2.29 m	
Power	185 kW	**Height**	3.23 m	
Transmission	Hydrodynamic	**Weight**	26.4 t	
Model	Twin Disc DF	**Axle Load**	100 kN	
Builder	Comeng WA	**Tractive Effort**		
Introduced	1957	**Maximum Speed**	40 km/h	
Number Built	1	**Gauge**	1067 mm	

This locomotive started the dieselisation program of the former Midland Railway of Western Australia by replacing two steam shunting locomotives at Midland Junction.

The E class had a conventional end-cab configuration, and had outside frames necessitating outside balance weights and coupling rods. The MRWA numbers and number plates were retained by E 30 but it was painted in WAGR standard larch green, lined red and yellow.

The E class was last used for shunting work at the WAGR Midland Workshops. It is now preserved by the ARHS.

Comeng Standard Shunter

Type	BB, BE, F	**Wheel Arrangement**	C
Engine	Rolls-Royce C6SFL	**Length**	6.98 m
Cylinders	Inline 6	**Width**	
Power	174 kW	**Height**	
Transmission	Hydrodynamic	**Weight**	30.5 t
Model	Twin Disc CO 10.052	**Axle Load**	100 kN
Builder	Comeng Qld	**Tractive Effort**	
Introduced	1957	**Maximum Speed**	40 km/h
Number Built	5	**Gauge**	1067 mm

These units are effectively Australian-built versions of the very successful Drewry design as used by the Tasmanian Railways as their V class. Two units were delivered in 1957 and 1958 to the Sugar Terminals at Mackay and

Townsville. They were used for shunting wagons received from the QR with export sugar with Comeng numbers F1018 and F1029, neither unit having a running number. Two locomotives very similar to these two, but with a Gardner 8L3 engine of 152 kW and SCG mechanical transmission, were used by the WA State Electricity Commission. These were Comeng BE 1117 and E 1020 also built in 1957. Mount Isa mines No. 305, also built in 1957, was Comeng BE 1016. A sixth locomotive, BB 1050, was built in 1961 for the Mount Isa line reconstruction but ended up at the sawmill in Pemberton in Western Australia where it is preserved.

A builder's photo of W 1. (Tulloch)

W 1 – W 2

Type		**Wheel Arrangement**	C
Engine	Rolls-Royce C8TFL	**Length**	7.01 m
Cylinders	Inline 8	**Width**	2.69 m
Power	250 kW	**Height**	3.84 m
Transmission	Hydrodynamic	**Weight**	28.4 t
Model	Krupp 2W1L115	**Axle Load**	98 kN
Builder	Tulloch	**Tractive Effort**	67 kN
Introduced	1959	**Maximum Speed**	48 km/h
Number Built	2	**Gauge**	1067 mm

These small Tasmanian Railways centre-cab hood units had distinctive inward canted upper cab sides. Although single engined, they were symmetrical in appearance. The two locomotives could operate in multiple, but were a little slow for mainline operation, and no pilots were fitted. The original colour scheme was red superstructure, black underframe and wheels and red buffer beams. The later yellow livery was also carried. These locomotives were allocated to Devonport and Launceston, and shared the shunting work with diesel-mechanical locomotives. Both are now withdrawn.

DR 1

Type	165 DM	**Wheel Arrangement**	B
Engine	Ruston 6VPHL	**Length**	7.80 m
Cylinders	Inline 6	**Width**	2.58 m
Power	112 kW	**Height**	3.61 m
Transmission	Mechanical	**Weight**	28.4 t
Model	SLM/Ruston	**Axle Load**	140 kN
Builder	Ruston	**Tractive Effort**	60 kN
Introduced	1953	**Maximum Speed**	32 km/h
Number Built	1	**Gauge**	1435 mm

DR 1 was obtained second-hand by Commonwealth Railways in 1964 from the Shell Company of Australia, which had used it at their terminal at Clyde, NSW. The power and transmission were similar to two shunting locomotives formerly in use by British Rail, and DR 1 was a typical British end-cab shunter. One unusual feature was the connecting rod from the jackshaft, which drove the more distant axle. DR 1 carried the standard CR livery of maroon body with a silver waistband and a black underframe. It was used as a standard-gauge shunter at Port Augusta workshops. A very similar 1600 mm gauge locomotive was used at Port Adelaide by Imperial Chemical Industries, within their plant. The only visible difference from DR 1 was the more conventional connecting rod driving to the nearer axle. A similar ICI locomotive carried no number, but was named 'W.L. Raws'. The colour scheme was cobalt blue, with a yellow ICI monogram on the cab backplate. Several other Ruston and Hornsby diesels, of this size or smaller, operated with various state authorities and private industries in NSW. A.G. Sims operated two units of this type in Sydney for some time. They were painted silver and shared the DR 1 connecting rod arrangement.

NSU 51 – NSU 64

NSU 59 and NSU 61 on a mixed train at Alice Springs, March 1969. (John Beckhaus)

Type		**Wheel Arrangement**	A1A'A1A'
Engine	Sulzer 6LDA28	**Length**	12.75 m
Cylinders	Inline 6	**Width**	2.85 m
Power	635 kW	**Height**	3.75 m
Generator	CP	**Weight**	63.5 t
Motors	CP C170	**Axle Load**	105 kN
Builder	Birmingham	**Tractive Effort**	68 kN
Introduced	1954	**Maximum Speed**	81 km/h
Number Built	14	**Gauge**	1067 mm

The NSU class were used to dieselise the Central Australia and North Australia Railways. They were of stubby appearance, with a broad flat nose, and with the headlight mounted on the central cab window pillar. The bogies were of the cast, inside equalised type. A spare set of standard-gauge bogies was delivered with the prototype. NSU 51 was named 'George McLeay'. The standard CR maroon and silver scheme was used. These were originally the only CR 3'6" gauge road locomotives and worked all traffic both singly and in multiple unit. They later shared the work with the NT class. After the conversion of the CAR to standard gauge, NSUs worked some former SAR 1067 mm gauge branches, to allow the 830 class to go to Tasmania. These were withdrawn when the lines closed. A number are preserved.

NT 65 – NT 77

Type		Wheel Arrangement	Co'Co'
Engine	Sulzer 6LDA28C	**Length**	14.20 m
Cylinders	Inline 6	**Width**	2.85 m
Power	970 kW	**Height**	3.73 m
Generator	AEI TG5302W	**Weight**	70 t
Motors	AEI 253AZ	**Axle Load**	126 kN
Builder	Tulloch	**Tractive Effort**	178 kN
Introduced	1968	**Maximum Speed**	81 km/h
Number Built	13	**Gauge**	1067 mm

The NT class introduced to Australia the flat-fronted cab, in wide use in Europe and the UK. The development in diesel engines is clearly shown when it is realised that an NT class developed 970 kW from the same unit, a Sulzer 6LDA28, as an NSU class which developed only 635 kW. The underslung-equaliser bogies on units NT 65 – NT 67 were initially connected by a control mechanism to reduce curve friction. The body side members carry the loads from equipment, traction and drawgear. Unusually, the main generator and the main control equipment are at the end remote from the cab, the latter being adjacent to the radiators. NT 65 – NT 67 were only 2.63 m wide, a feature of the original (double ended) design intended for use on overseas narrow-gauge railways. The NT class carried the standard CR colours of maroon with a silver waistband and roof. Some units received AN green and yellow. The NT class were used singly to haul *The Ghan* and were used triple headed on ore trains from Frances Creek to Darwin. All were used on the North Australia Railway after the introduction of the NJ class. Three units were used on the Eyre Peninsula to release 830 class for Tasmania. All are now withdrawn from service. NT 65 was named 'Gordon Freeth'.

A builder's photo of 1101. (VR)

1100 – 1101

Type		**Wheel Arrangement**	Bo'Bo'
Voltage	1500 V DC	**Length**	11.07 m
Power	420 kW	**Width**	
Equipment	General Electric	**Height**	4.31 m
Control	Camshaft type M	**Weight**	51 t
Motors	GE 237	**Axle Load**	125 kN
Builder	VR	**Tractive Effort**	63 kN
Introduced	1923	**Maximum Speed**	81 km/h
Number Built	2	**Gauge**	1600 mm

The initial plans for the Melbourne suburban electrification had been based on optimistic growth figures and a number of cars proposed for conversion to electric operation were not required. This left a number of sets of equipment unused, and these two electric locomotives were built using some of this excess. The bogies, pantograph motors and control gear were all of the same design as used in the suburban electric cars. Initially used as shunting locomotives at Flinders Street after electrification of suburban goods sidings, they worked goods trains within the Metropolitan area. They were withdrawn in 1955 as their underframes were not easily adaptable to automatic couplings. Both units were scrapped. They had no class letter, and were always painted black. They were easily recognised by the short sloping hoods at each end.

ELECTRIC LOCOMOTIVES

1102 – 1111

E 1105 and E 1103 at Spencer Street, 1980. (Peter Clark)

Type		**Wheel Arrangement**	Bo'Bo'
Voltage	1500 V DC	**Length**	11.79 m
Power	420 kW	**Width**	
Equipment	General Electric	**Height**	4.31 m
Control	Camshaft type M	**Weight**	56 t
Motors	GE 237	**Axle Load**	137 kN
Builder	VR	**Tractive Effort**	63 kN
Introduced	1928	**Maximum Speed**	81 km/h
Number Built	10	**Gauge**	1600 mm

Following on the success of the two prototype locomotives, seven modified locomotives were ordered, fitted with simplified box cab bodies. The order was extended by a further three, and by December 1929 all 10 were in service. This was no doubt assisted by all the electrical equipment, intended for suburban cars, being readily available. These units allowed the electrification of most suburban goods traffic. By 1963, the steam locomotives classed E were all off the register, although some continued working, and this class was given to these units, becoming E 1102 to E 1111. In 1968, they were transferred from the suburban car sheds at Jolimont to the South Dynon Locomotive Depot. From 1965, they had been painted in the blue and yellow colours of the VR diesel locomotives. They were withdrawn in the early 1980s by which time suburban goods (and parcel) traffic could be handled more economically by road.

7100 being transferred from Thirlmere to Broadmeadow for storage, August 2008. (Chris Walters)

4501 (7100)

Type		Wheel Arrangement	Co'Co'
Voltage	1500 V DC	Length	15.59 m
Power	2050 kW	Width	2.92 m
Equipment	Metropolitan Vickers	Height	4.41 m
Control	3 x Camshaft	Weight	110 t
Motors	MV 179	Axle Load	180 kN
Builder	Comeng/NSWR	Tractive Effort	125 kN
Introduced	1952	Maximum Speed	113 km/h
Number Built	1	Gauge	1435 mm

This locomotive was built to test design features proposed for a group of locomotives intended for use on the Blue Mountains line, where large increases in traffic were expected. The locomotive conformed in most respects to previous Metropolitan-Vickers designs, and had articulated bogies carrying the drawgear.

It was assembled by the NSWR at Chullora from major mechanical components supplied by Comeng and electrical equipment of M-V design. The control gear consisted of three sets of suburban electric equipment, effectively in multiple unit. The motors were manufactured by AGE at Auburn, to M-V design. Having proved the concept, 4501 was used as a bank engine on the Northern line, and for driver training. Being less powerful than the later 46 class, it was not used in regular traffic and spent most of its life as a shunter at Flemington. In 1961 it was renumbered as 7100. After the electrification to Glenlee, it was rebuilt with additional access doors, and was used on Glenlee coal trains. At this stage, it was repainted to Indian red from verdant green. Buff lining was used with both schemes. It was withdrawn and is preserved at the NSWRTM.

L 1150 – L 1174

L 1162 at Newport, January 2006. (Peter Clark)

Type		**Wheel Arrangement**	Co'Co'
Voltage	1500 V DC	**Length**	17.98 m
Power	1800 kW	**Width**	2.82 m
Equipment	English Electric	**Height**	4.21 m
Control	Camshaft	**Weight**	98.6 t
Motors	EE 519	**Axle Load**	161 kN
Builder	EE Dick Kerr	**Tractive Effort**	113 kN
Introduced	1952	**Maximum Speed**	120 km/h
Number Built	25	**Gauge**	1600 mm

These locomotives were ordered for the electrification of the Gippsland line, and were generally similar to other EE units of this general type. Many details suggest an influence from contemporary Baldwin/Werkspoor locomotives delivered to the Dutch State Railways. They were of a double cab design, and the paintwork and styling resembled the design prepared by General Motors for the B class diesels. They were used until the mid-1980s on the Gippsland line, on both freight and passenger trains. Soon after entering service, illuminated numbers were added at each end. One unit had the cabs modified and the noses lowered to improve visibility. In the early 1980s, maintenance problems were increasing, some of which were thought to be due to the pantographs bouncing off the contact wire at speed. This was countered by fitting a Brecknell Willis single-arm pantograph, which was intended to be used in both directions of travel. However, with reducing traffic, the electrification was no longer economic and the L class were withdrawn. Two units are preserved, including L 1150, named 'R.G. Wishart' after the commissioner at the time of their introduction. Apart from the blue and yellow scheme, they carried the VicRail orange and silver and the V/Line orange and grey. L 1150 carried the V/Line overall orange for a short time.

Restored 4632 at Delec Locomotive Depot. (Peter Clark)

4601 – 4640

Type	-	**Wheel Arrangement**	Co'Co'
Voltage	1500 V DC	**Length**	15.59 m
Power	2820 kW	**Width**	2.92 m
Equipment	Metropolitan Vickers	**Height**	4.42 m
Control	Camshaft	**Weight**	114 t
Motors	MV 272	**Axle Load**	187 kN
Builder	M-V/B-P	**Tractive Effort**	163 kN
Introduced	1956	**Maximum Speed**	113 km/h
Number Built	40	**Gauge**	1435 mm

These units were built by Metropolitan-Vickers/Beyer, Peacock Ltd of Stockton-on-Tees, UK. They were very similar to the prototype 4501, but had a more rounded body in the makers' current style and were more powerful. They were very soon in use on the Blue Mountains and were extensively used in both goods and passenger traffic until the multiple unit trains arrived. Because the planned coal traffic did not eventuate, the Northern line to Gosford was electrified and the 46 class took over most freight and longer distance passenger traffic on this line. The electrification to Glenlee on the South provided coal traffic, and with an extension of the electrification to Newcastle, the class were fully utilised. 4620 was involved in the derailment at Bold Street, Granville in 1977, and the articulated design was criticised for its lack of flexibility in curves. The original colour scheme was Indian red with salmon and buff lining. This was later modified to chrome yellow lining, with a few experimental schemes in these colours as well. The 1982 bright red livery and Freight Rail blue and yellow were also used. The class was finally withdrawn in 1996, when about half the class was still operating. 4638 has been retained and repainted in the original style.

8501 – 8510

Type	CL-627	**Wheel Arrangement**	Co'Co'
Voltage	1500 V DC	**Length**	17.73 m
Power	2880 kW	**Width**	2.96 m
Equipment	Mitsubishi	**Height**	4.33 m
Control	Camshaft	**Weight**	123 t
Motors	MB 485 AVR	**Axle Load**	200 kN
Builder	Comeng NSW	**Tractive Effort**	222 kN
Introduced	1979	**Maximum Speed**	130 km/h
Number Built	10	**Gauge**	1435 mm

With expansion of the electrification and the reducing availability of the 46 class due to increasing age, a new design of electric locomotive was ordered from Comeng. The design was a conventional locomotive similar structurally to contemporary diesel locomotives. In fact the 85 class was very similar in appearance to the 80 class, since common cab components had been requested for these two classes. The 85 class were much smother riding than the articulated 46 class and had a much greater speed capacity, 8501 having exceeded 160 km/h on trials. The 85 class were regarded as a success, and the following 86 class were basically similar, but minor control differences prevent multiple operation unless the 85 class leads. Four spare cabs were provided, but three of these were used following accidents. They remained in service, generally in export coal traffic until the sale of FreightCorp to Pacific National when they were all withdrawn from service.

AN AUSTRALIAN LOCOMOTIVE GUIDE

8602 at DELEC Locomotive Depot, 1992. (Peter Clark)

8601 – 8649

Type	CL-627A	**Wheel Arrangement**	Co'Co'
Voltage	1500 V DC	**Length**	18.73 m
Power	2880 kW	**Width**	2.95 m
Equipment	Mitsubishi	**Height**	4.40 m
Control	Camshaft	**Weight**	119 t
Motors	MB 485 BVR	**Axle Load**	194 kN
Builder	Comeng NSW	**Tractive Effort**	222 kN
Introduced	1983	**Maximum Speed**	130 km/h
Number Built	49	**Gauge**	1435 mm

These units were intended to operate the increasing export coal traffic and to take over any passenger traffic from the 46 class, which would then be confined to freight working. Until the advent of National Rail they worked much of the Northern interstate traffic, and are still used when diversion via the North Shore is required. Like the 85 class, they used Dofasco pattern bogies with rubber sandwich secondary suspension, and large 1250 mm driving wheels. They were delivered in the 1982 bright red livery, and several locomotives had stainless steel cut out numbers fixed to the sides. Two units were repainted in the NSW Bicentennial livery in 1988, but the whole class later carried FreightCorp blue. All remained in service until the sale of FreightCorp to Pacific National.

8650

Type	CL-627B	**Wheel Arrangement**	Bo'Bo'Bo'
Voltage	1500 V DC	**Length**	18.73 m
Power	2880 kW	**Width**	2.95 m
Equipment	Mitsubishi	**Height**	4.40 m
Control	Camshaft	**Weight**	119 t
Motors	MB 485 BVR	**Axle Load**	194 kN
Builder	Comeng NSW	**Tractive Effort**	222 kN
Introduced	1985	**Maximum Speed**	130 km/h
Number Built	1	**Gauge**	1435 mm

This unit was built to test the bogie design principles for the Queensland CL-629 locomotives, and to allow a comparison in service with the conventional 86 class locomotives. The central bogie is allowed greater lateral movement to permit operation in curves with low lateral force on the rails. The bogies support the body on Flexicoils, with traction forces being taken through articulated rods to the centre of each bogie. The electrical equipment is the same as other 86 class locomotives. 8650 was used interchangeably with other locomotives of the class until withdrawal.

3100 class and 3200 class

Type	CL-629	**Wheel Arrangement**	Bo'Bo'Bo'
Voltage	25 kV 50 hz	**Length**	19.38 m
Power	2900 kW	**Width**	2.72 m
Equipment	Hitachi	**Height**	3.90 m
Control	Thyristor	**Weight**	109.8 t
Motors	Hitachi	**Axle Load**	180 kN
Builder	Comeng Qld	**Tractive Effort**	260 kN
Introduced	1986	**Maximum Speed**	80 km/h
Number Built	84	**Gauge**	1067 mm

The 146 locomotive order for the Queensland coalfields electrification was split between two manufacturers, Comeng receiving the larger part of 76 units. These units are of Hitachi design, and are very box like in appearance, with simple welded steel bodies. These units initially were allocated to the Northern lines, working out of Jilalan depot. When the main line electrification went ahead, 10 more units were ordered, and some of these operated from Callemondah depot on the lines out of Gladstone. The second digit indicated whether the locomotive was equipped to lead a train with Locotrol remote control of mid-train locomotives. These units were painted light grey with orange and green trim. Some were repainted in the corporate maroon and yellow. 3101 was named 'Sir Joh Bjelke-Petersen' after the then premier. Units 3267 and 3281 were withdrawn and stored after the Black Mountain derailment of November 1994.

The command locomotives were: 3101 – 3104, 3108, 3112, 3116, 3120, 3124, 3128, 3132, 3136, 3140, 3144, 3148, 3152, 3156, 3160, 3164, and 3168.

Non-command locomotives were: 3205 – 3286 excepting those numbers above.

Sixty-three 3200 class locomotives were rebuilt using Siemens AC traction equipment as 3700 class, which rendered the remaining locomotives surplus to requirements.

3731 leading 3722 on a loaded coal train at Jilalan, September 2009. (Peter Clark)

3701 – 3763

Type	CL-640m	**Wheel Arrangement**	Bo'Bo'Bo'
Voltage	25 kV 50 hz	**Length**	19.38 m
Power	4000 kW	**Width**	2.72 m
Equipment	Siemens	**Height**	3.90 m
Control	IGBT Inverter	**Weight**	126 t
Motors	Siemens	**Axle Load**	210 kN
Rebuilder	United Goninan Qld	**Tractive Effort**	430 kN
Introduced	2005	**Maximum Speed**	80 km/h
Number Built	63	**Gauge**	1067 mm

Three Hitachi units were rebuilt as prototypes for conversion to AC traction using Siemens IGBT Inverter equipment. The basic locomotive shell and bogies were retained, although the bogies were modified and strengthened to take the higher output of the AC motors. Larger body side openings were provided to allow for the greater airflow required and the body end doors were removed. The rebuilt locomotives have only one cab, the other cab having had the windows and doors replaced by flush steel panelling. These units are equipped as lead units for remote-control operation. The continuous rated power has increased from 2970 kW to 4000 kW, giving a very high power to weight ratio. An order was placed for the conversion of 60 production locomotives, renumbered as 3704 to 3763. Siemens were the prime contractor for the rebuild program. The actual modification and installation task was subcontracted to United Rail Group's plants in Townsville and Broadmeadow. 3701 to 3703 were painted in the QR corporate livery of yellow with diagonal maroon bands, but the production units appeared in the yellow and black QR National 'Eagle' livery.

3524 on the loop at Barney Point, Gladstone, December 2006. (Peter Clark)

3500 class and 3600 class

Type	CF4B	**Wheel Arrangement**	Bo'Bo'Bo'
Voltage	25 kV 50 hz	**Length**	20.02 m
Power	2890 kW	**Width**	2.80 m
Equipment	ASEA	**Height**	3.89 m
Control	Thyristor	**Weight**	109.8 t
Motors	ASEA LJM 440-1	**Axle Load**	180 kN
Builder	Walkers	**Tractive Effort**	260 kN
Introduced	1986	**Maximum Speed**	80 km/h
Number Built	50	**Gauge**	1067 mm

The smaller part of the initial electrification order went to a consortium of firms called Clyde-ASEA-Walkers. ASEA provided the design, Walkers constructed the bodies and bogies and Clyde provided the motors, some electrical equipment and commissioned the locomotives into service. The ASEA design was easily recognised by the stainless steel side panels, and the complex double suspension of the central bogie. These units were introduced on the Gladstone lines and were initially based at Callemondah depot. When the main line electrification was approved, the original order for 70 units was reduced to 50, and the later group of 20 units was completed to the 39 class design. The numbering of the coal locomotives was separated between Locotrol and standard units, the former in the 35 series, and the latter in the 36 series. The original colour scheme was unpainted stainless steel, with orange ends and roof and green lining. 3501 was named 'D.F. Lane' after the then transport minister. These locomotives were progressively rebuilt and modernised, retaining the original traction equipment with the end doors removed and with all locomotives capable of command and receive distributed power operation. All locomotives were then numbered 3501 to 3550.

The command locomotives as built were: 3501 – 3504, 3508, 3512, 3516, 3520, 3524, 3528, 3532, 3536, 3540, 3544, 3546 – 3550.

Non-command locomotives were 3605 – 3645 excluding the above locomotives.

3901 – 3930, 3551 – 3569, 3573

Type	CF4B	**Wheel Arrangement**	Bo'Bo'Bo'
Voltage	25 kV 50 hz	**Length**	20.02 m
Power	2890 kW	**Width**	2.80 m
Equipment	ASEA	**Height**	3.89 m
Control	Thyristor	**Weight**	109.8 t
Motors	ASEA LJM 440-1	**Axle Load**	180 kN
Builder	Walkers	**Tractive Effort**	210 kN
Introduced	1988	**Maximum Speed**	100 km/h
Number Built	30	**Gauge**	1067 mm

The Clyde-ASEA-Walkers locomotives had a more sophisticated suspension, and the ASEA bogies allowed frame mounting of the motors which reduced vertical impact forces on the track at higher speeds. This modification of the design was chosen for the main line electrification between Brisbane and Gladstone. Ten additional locomotives were ordered and the final 20 of the similar coal locomotives were completed to the modified design, which was allowed to run at 100 km/h. The body design was slightly altered to allow operation through the old Brisbane city tunnels, but externally the 39 class could be recognised by the dark green and yellow trim that accompanied the stainless steel side panels. These locomotives were initially used for all freight and for the overnight passenger trains on the North Coast. However demand for coal traffic meant that all units were allocated to that traffic. Some units were fitted with coal locomotive bogies and were classified as 3900C with a 'C' suffix to the number. 3902 was withdrawn and stored after the Beerburrum accident in July 1994. From 2003, the remaining units from 3901 to 3919 and 3923 were rebuilt as coal locomotives equipped for distributed control numbered 3551 to 3569 and 3573. The other units numbered above 3920 retained their main line bogies and gear ratio but have mainly been held as reserve locomotives for coal traffic. The rebuilding of the 3551 series restored the number (less the one withdrawn) of coal traffic units originally ordered.

3301 – 3304, 3316 – 3318, 3405 – 3415 and 3419 – 3422

Type	JAE 30B3	**Wheel Arrangement**	Bo'Bo'Bo'	
Voltage	25 kV 50 hz	**Length**	(19.38) m	
Power	2900 kW	**Width**	2.72 m	
Equipment	Hitachi	**Height**	3.90 m	
Control	Thyristor	**Weight**	109.8 t	
Motors	Hitachi	**Axle Load**	180 kN	
Builder	Clyde NSW/Vic	**Tractive Effort**	260 kN	
Introduced	1995	**Maximum Speed**	80 km/h	
Number Built	22	**Gauge**	1067 mm	

After the Comeng organisation was absorbed into ABB, later Adtranz, QR placed an order for 15 further locomotives to meet expanding coal traffic. Clyde, no longer associated with ABB, offered a Hitachi design similar to the previous 31 and 32 classes, but with improved bogies and altered traction motor blowers. These were to be assembled at the Kelso plant, but problems arose with the design that resulted in long delays, and some work was transferred to Campbellfield. These units were introduced in the corporate maroon and yellow livery, but are otherwise very similar in appearance to the Comeng units. The bogies may be distinguished by triple flexicoils rather than the twin springs on the Comeng locomotives, and the heavier traction rods of different design. These units were used interchangeably with the earlier locomotives. They were mainly confined to operating as trailing units and were not popular with crews.

3801 – 3845, 7101 – 7142,
BMACC 001 – BMACC 013

Type	EG40-V1	**Wheel Arrangement**	Bo'Bo'Bo'
Voltage	25 kV 50 hz	**Length**	19.5 m
Power	4000 kW	**Width**	2.89 m
Equipment	Siemens	**Height**	3.89 m
Control	IGBT Inverter	**Weight**	132 t
Motors	Siemens	**Axle Load**	216 kN
Builder	Krauss-Maffei	**Tractive Effort**	450 kN
Introduced	2007	**Maximum Speed**	80 km/h
Number Built	100	**Gauge**	1067 mm

QR National (now Aurizon) ordered 45 locomotives, 3801 to 3845, and Pacific National obtained 42 units numbered 7101 to 7142. Both operators initially used these units on the Goonyella system although they are also used by Aurizon on the Blackwater lines. The Aurizon locomotives operate interchangeably with the 3700 series. BHP Billiton Misubishi Alliance purchased 13 locomotives which are operated by Pacific National on the Goonyella system.

These are new locomotives fitted with the same AC traction equipment as the rebuilt 3700 class locomotives. They were built in the Krauss-Maffei factory in Munich, Germany. They were very similar in appearance to the rebuilt 3700 type, but are heavier with a slightly higher tractive effort. The frame is deeper which shows up as the deeper yellow stripe along the lower body. The rear end of the German units is flat unlike the shaped end of the 3700.

Above: 7128 stops to change crew on an empty train at Nebo, 22 June 2014. (Peter Clark)

Below: BMACC 013 leads a loaded train through Jilalan Yard on 22 June 2014. (Peter Clark)

Glossary

Alternator: a machine which produces alternating current when driven.

Compensating beam: A form of interconnection between axle-boxes to minimise unloading of individual axles on uneven track.

Engine: A prime mover providing a locomotive with its source of power.

Epicyclic gearbox: A speed reducing gearbox, involving planetary and internally toothed gears.

Equalising beam: See compensating beam.

Final drive: The bevel gear drive from shafting to the axle.

Flexicoil: A pattern of bogie frame using helical springs for suspension.

Fluid coupling: A fluid drive turbine and rotor unit without torque multiplication properties, often used instead of a clutch.

Generator: A machine which produces direct current when driven.

Hi-Ad: A form of bogie layout, intended to minimise transfer of weight at starting. Motors are mounted inboard of the axles.

Hostler controls: Limited controls, intended only for movement of locomotives without trains.

Intercooler: A device for cooling air before its entry to cylinders. The temperature reduction reduces air volume and contributes in increased potential power.

Mansard: An architectural term, often applied to rail vehicles with three-plane roof panels in a semi-hexagonal arrangement.

Mechanical staff exchanger: A device for exchanging safeworking tablets, operated by hand or compressed air.

Motor: An electric motor, driving one or more axles.

Multiple unit: A method of direct control of more than one locomotive by a single driver.

Naturally aspirated: A term indicating that no compression of air occurs before intake to the cylinders.

Roots blower: A device for compressing air before intake to the cylinders, consisting of lobed rotors, driven from the engine crankshaft.

SCOA-P: A patent pattern of spoked wheel with 'U' section spokes. The letters refer to the patenting company (Steel Company of Australia) and the initial letter of the designer's name.

Torque converter: A turbine and rotor unit, with a fixed set of blades, with torque multiplication properties.

Turbocharger: A device for compressing air before intake to the cylinders, consisting of a centrifugal compressor driven by an exhaust gas turbine.

Index of Locomotives by Original Operators

Commonwealth Railways

CL class	191
DE class	257
DR class	340
GM 1 class	167
GM12 class	170
MDH class	327
NB class	321
NC class	324
NJ class	149
NJAB 1	31
NM class	69
NSU class	341
NT class	342

Electricity Trust of South Australia

MDH	327

Emu Bay Railway Company

No. 8	67
10 class	291
11 class	294
PVH	333
V	320

Fletcher International

FIE class	243

Fortescue Metals

Dash-9-44CW	276
SD90MAC	220
SD70ACe	214

Freight Victoria / Freight Australia

V class	213
XR class	203

Freightlink

FQ class	213

Genesee and Wyoming

GWA class	215
GWN class	164
GWU class	283

Greentrains

RL class	209
U class	262

Hamersley Iron

4079	59
C415	93
C628	109
C636	111
M636	113
S2	92
C636R	117
M636R	118
C44-9W	276

John Lysaght (Australia)

45 ton	258
70 ton	259

Midland Railway of Western Australia

E class	337
F class	228
G class	237

Mineral Resources

MRL	283

Mount Goldsworthy Mining

1	232
3	244

Mount Isa Mining

302	309
303	298
304	320
305	338

Mount Lyell Railway

Nos 1 to 5	33

Mount Newman Mining

C636	112
F7	169
M636C	114
M636	116
C36-7	271
C39-8	272

National Rail

NR class	279

Index of Locomotives by Current Operator

AN AUSTRALIAN LOCOMOTIVE GUIDE